# blest atheist

*elizabeth mahlou*

For information, contact:

MSI Press
1760-F Airline Highway, 203
Hollister, CA 95023
Orders@MSIPress.com
Telephone/Fax: 831-886-2486

Library of Congress Control Number 2008943744

ISBN 9781933455112

Cover design by CDL Services

Cover photograph © 2008 CDL Services

# Table of Contents

# Foreword

Joseph Campbell says, quoting Meister Eckhart, that the ultimate adventure is "to get rid of the life that you have planned in order to have the life that's waiting to be yours." To a great extent, this holds true for "Elizabeth Mahlou" because despite her long-ingrained resistance to the idea of God, she ultimately took the risk of opening herself to the Transcendent, and it changed her life. Although Beth describes her former self as an atheist, she was open-minded and did not scorn the possibility of other levels of existence, of reincarnation, of angels, of psi or other paranormal phenomena. She had what Robertson Davies calls "the Shakespearean cast of thought" – "a fine credulity about everything kept in check by a lively skepticism about everything."

Beth's central resistance was to the idea of God. As you will see when you read this book, her formative years were in some ways brutal and in other ways ordinary; the one thing that Beth could not tolerate was hypocrisy: putting on one face for one's neighbors and another (scary one) for one's children. It was this central experience of hypocrisy and the church's collaboration with that pious fraud that pierced deep into Beth's psyche to the degree where, betrayed and outraged, she shut the door on God and locked it.

But God kept knocking on the door. From time to time, Beth would experience what seemed like a miracle, a divine intervention, or a supernatural experience, but, apprehensive about attributing such interventions to a benevolent deity, she chalked it up to those two irrepressible but unexplainable forces, coincidence and luck. Then finally Beth experienced what Mircea Eliade calls a "hierophany," a breakthrough of the sacred into the mundane and profane everyday world, a stark manifestation of the power of the Holy.

I have known Beth over 25 years and always admired and trusted her because of her supreme lack of pretense in a world filled with self-important and pretentious people and because of the strength of her personal integrity. In a way, she embodied Christian virtues far more strongly than most clergy that I know, and those virtues radiate from her at all times. It was hard for me to understand that she denied the existence of God when she so strongly and passionately carried out His will through her deeply humane caring for those less fortunate than she.

Read this book. Beth's narrative will sweep you from continent to continent, from past time to present time, from laughter to tears. Her spiritual journey takes some dark and dangerous turns, but ultimately brings her, and you, the reader, into the light.

*Karin Ryding, PhD*

# Acknowledgments

I could not have written this book without a number of very special people. Some of them have for years encouraged me to write about one or another facet of my life, including my abusive childhood, my experiences as a parent of exceptional children, my international work, and/or my conversion from long-time atheist to believer, all of which are crucial to the tale I have been led to share with readers, a tale that examines the question, where is God in the midst of trauma? Other people acknowledged here have been especially critical to my spiritual journey; without them, I would never have asked the questions that are the essence of my tale. Still others were essential to my successful survival of a tormented childhood. If the motto of the Boys and Girls Clubs, that it takes just one adult to give a child self-confidence, is true, then I have indeed been blessed for I cannot begin to name here all the adults in my life who helped me understand as a child that in spite of a wide variety of daily abuse at home, I was a worthy being.

I would like to begin by thanking the adults from my youth who were instrumental in the development of my sense of self-worth that was critical to a successful life: teachers, librarians, coaches, and youth-group leaders. Among them was the elderly rich lady, who passed away many years ago. A long-standing member of the Grange, she noticed that one of the officers of the Junior Grange did not have a life like most of the children she knew, and for two summers in a row she paid for me to attend a prestigious summer camp. I wonder if she knew that the best part of those summers was two whole months of bliss where no one hurt me.

From that same time frame, there was another group that was very important to my psychological well being: peers who supported me. Many have stayed in touch to this day: Bobby, Butchie, Esther, Gail, Tommy, Vicky. In grade school, they also prevented, in some cases knowingly and in other cases unknowingly, more serious abuse from Ma.

Julie Trudell (Virginia) has long thought the story of how my siblings and I survived an extremely abusive childhood might help others in similar circumstances, given that there are probably more people who have grown up in difficult conditions than those who have known carefree childhoods. Julie herself played an important role in one of the greatest series of modern-day miracles I have ever witnessed: the story of Shura, which is recounted in Part I of this book. Over time, she and I have become sisters as American guardians of Shura, serving in a parenting triumvirate with Shura's Siberian mother, Lara. Over time, too, Julie has continued to press me to tell "my story." I could not do so earlier for it is not my story. It is God's story, and I could not have told it until I recognized that.

I want to thank, as well, Martina Helberger (Austria) for pointing out some of the pitfalls the publication of any story about my abusive childhood might bring, especially in the reaction of those described in the book who might not like how they appear to others. I thank her for giving me some suggestions for handling them.

A special acknowledgement goes to my dear friend, Dr. Omar Imady, a Muslim humanist and devout Sufi from Damascus, who spent many Amman (Jordan) evenings with me over dinner, trying to understand my atheism and why when I came into contact with people, their faith increased, not decreased. He eventually attributed this oddity to my head not knowing that my heart has always belonged to God, a fact that he thought facilitated my being used for good things without my awareness of it. Over time, I have come to think that Dr. Omar was probably right. Together, Dr. Omar and I explored questions of spirituality, he from the point of view of his own brand of Islam and I from the point of view of a happy atheist with intellectual curiosity about belief systems of all sorts. My curiosity should not have been surprising since I was also teaching an undergraduate course in social philosophy (morality and ethics) at the time. In what turned out to be one of my most interesting assignments, as an American atheist, I managed to teach an objective (I think/hope) history of morality to a Middle Eastern, principally Sunni Muslim, class without causing them to compromise their faith. When I left Jordan and Dr. Omar, I felt ripped away from more than a good friend and colleague. I felt like I had lost my beloved *sputnik* (the Soviet term for a "fellow traveler"). I know he felt the same.

Dr. Omar set me out on a path that would ultimately lead me via a Californian Christian, whose identity I have chosen not to reveal for reasons I also choose not to share, to Old Mission San Ignatio in the sacred little town of San Ignatio with which I have fallen in love. San Ignatio is the only town I know where the statues commemorate only religious figures. A recent visitor of Russian Orthodox heritage described this town as *namolein* (soaked in prayer). My subsequent research into local and theological history has led me to an intense admiration of Saint Francis, the founder of the order that established the San Ignatio mission in 1792. My intersection with the order of St. Francis was a matter of divine provenance. The spirituality exemplified by St. Francis fits with my lifelong-held values of the right of all to respect and equal opportunity, love of nature, comfort with mysticism, and dedication to a simple life—although on the surface my life probably looks anything but simple.

People who are willing to read pre-publication manuscripts are real blessings. They help fine-tune a book before, rather than after, it sees the light of day, thus saving the author from potential embarrassment and readers from all sorts of misunderstandings. Nonetheless, my experience in publishing a dozen other books reveals that no book makes it to press without some undetected errors. For such errors, I take full responsibility and apologize to the reader in advance.

For reading and providing feedback on various versions and portions of the pre-publication manuscript and especially for pushing me to think more introspectively about my experiences, I would like to thank the following friends: Diane Bolduc (New Hampshire), Marie Cosgrove (California), Theresa El-Jallad (Jordan), Lucille Gordon (Montana), Fatema Hashem (Bahrain), Dr. Geri Henderson (Lithuania), Dr. Omar Imady and wife Inas Sarraj (Syria), Natalia Lord (Virginia), Dr. Rebecca Oxford (Maryland), Sylvia Rodriguez (California), Dr. Karin Ryding (Virginia), Boris Shekhtman (Maryland), Melva Simmons (California), Julie Trudell (Virginia), Rocio Txabarriaga (Massachusetts), and Ken Wilcox (New York).

I want to thank my sisters, Katrina, Danielle, Sharon, and Victoria, brother Willie, and sister-in-law Erica for reading the manuscript, sharing memories, and correcting details from my sometimes partially suppressed memories and some-times simply old memories. Their contributions helped make some of the events described in this book more compelling and more multifaceted. I especially thank all my siblings for sharing their "things that scared the wits out of me." Unfortunately, describing some of the events that have occurred in my life means describing some unhappy events in the lives of those who have shared my life with me. Reluctantly, I have done so, not wanting to hurt anyone but at the same time needing to present an accurate picture. In this, I would like to thank my sister-in-law Erica for her staunch support for the need and the right to tell the truth. Of course, I thank all my siblings for a lifetime of support.

Father Barry Brunsman, the first priest I came to know as a believer, was the first person I told about the manuscript and the first person to read it. I do not believe it an accident that I ended up at Old Mission San Ignatio where he was filling in as parish priest at the time that I was first coming to faith. His homilies fill one with an understanding that God is joy and love, not fire and brimstone, and this helped me feel comfortable with a close relationship with God once it became clear that no matter what God's back was never going to be turned on me nor was it going to be acceptable any longer for me to turn my back on God.

I would be remiss not to mention as well those who have subsequently con-tributed to my spiritual growth: Marie Cosgrove, Sr. Maria del Rey, Fr. Edward Fitz-Henry, Dr. Geri Henderson, Juan Rodriguez, and Dr. Karin Ryding top the list. Special among this group is Padre (Father) Julio César Guarín Sosa, a young priest from Colombia to whom I ended up teaching English. In the process, I met other members of his family as they came to visit, learned about his impoverished but God-enriched childhood, and joined him in his efforts to bring education and work opportunities, alternatives to violence and insurgency, to the children of his home area of Palomar through an organization he founded, Por Amor a Los Niños de Colombia (www.poramoralosninosdecolombia.org). Through Por Amor, the English lessons in which we used the Bible and homilies as textbook and texts, and Padre Julio's standing beside me (literally) during my daughter's brain surgery at Stanford University Hospital, I learned much more about God's love, Biblical interpretation, and spirituality than any seminar could ever have offered me. More important, I gained a very special "brother."

Two direct contributions were made to the book in the form of poems. Much gratitude goes to Dr. Omar for his poem about me and to my brother-in-law, William Smith, for his descriptive poem of the environment, in which my siblings and I grew up. I thank them both for allowing me to reproduce them in this book.

I thank Fr./Dr. Victor Oliver for important assistance during the concluding stage of turning the draft manuscript into a book. I will be forever grateful that he pushed me into discussing the contents of the book prior to publication with my siblings and their spouses, whom I found to be supportive. He was wise in that suggestion, and wisdom has been very much needed in the writing of this book.

As for the book itself, there are several things that the reader should know. Mostly they deal with anonymity—when and why I have chosen it for specific episodes described in the book. While all the events are true, given the nature of the events, anyone who might be embarrassed by a piece of ancient history has undergone a name change in these pages as have the places associated with them. In spite of the requirement for anonymity, the story needs to be told for such things have happened to many people who sometimes think that they are unique (and even perhaps to blame for that which they cannot be expected to control) or without help (or even unworthy of help) and therefore without hope. They need to know that they are not to blame, not unique, and indeed worthy of help. They need to know that there is, for certain, hope. Teachers, neighbors, doctors, and community leaders should be aware of how children can suffer under their very noses while they praise the perpetrators for good parenting or are even unwitting perpetrators themselves. Finally, perhaps some of those who are still wounded will receive solace knowing that the eight of us made it out of our "burning house" alive. Those, I think, are justifiable enough reasons for putting my experiences into the public domain.

In truth, it does not matter who I am. The glory is God's. It could have been any atheist who was protected and blessed in the way I have been, and many atheists have also likely felt God's blessing without recognizing it. As Thomas Merton said in his introduction to the Japanese version of his autobiographical book, *The Seven Storey Mountain,* "I seek to speak to you, in some way, as your own self. Who can tell what this may mean? I myself do not know, but if you listen, things will be said that are perhaps not written in this book. And this will be due not to me but to the One who lives and speaks in both." I do not have the insight, wisdom, or theological depth of Merton. However, this book is only superficially about me. It is more about you, about each reader who has ever wondered where God was in a moment of desperation, unhappiness, abandonment, or torment, who has ever questioned and doubted, or who has ever pocketed reaction-to-hurt resentment that he or she has pulled out to reexamine from time to time only to place it back in his or her pocket. My sister, Danielle, whose own tormented childhood is chronicled in these pages, commented, "If this book helps only a dozen people, it will have been worth the writing."

And now, given the encouragement of all these people, with God's help and a prayer per page, here goes!

*elizabeth mahlou*

## Opening Words to the Reader

When one fortuitous coincidence after another occurs in one's life, sometimes on a daily basis, other times on a weekly basis, and at the very least on a monthly basis, what does one call that? For far too many years, I called it serendipity. When people pointed out the unusual number of remarkable blessings that seemed to come my way, I was always quick to point out any apparent randomness as "proving" that these blessings were not blessings at all but simply a matter of chance.

Indeed, remarkable blessings might not be an expression that anyone else would use to describe a childhood saturated with physical, emotional, and sexual abuse. Much of this abuse was coldly prepared and served burning hot by my now-widowed mother although such treats were not exclusively her domain.

Nor might this be an expression that anyone else would use about my adult life. Those years have been no less challenging. Take two children with multiple birth defects, including a severely retarded son with 18 birth defects. Add to that two gifted children, one of whom skipped two school grades and another of whom skipped four grades and ultimately had to be home schooled. Increase that by three children whom my husband and I took in: one physically handicapped artist from Siberia, one gifted dyslexic from a Latino barrio, and one future singer from Moscow currently working the Hollywood scene. Given this array of barriers to a mainstream lifestyle, I can see the point of those who may think that my days upon this earth have been truly difficult.

They are wrong. My life has been filled with blessings and miracles in spite of having been a staunch atheist for more than five decades. Moreover, most of my life I have been chronically happy. Perhaps that was why I was an atheist. Happy people rarely set out in search of God or hear God's voice calling to them. Unless one has been raised in faith—and accepted it—in childhood, it is generally unhappy people who feel a need for divine support, perhaps because the circumstances that make people despair are the same circumstances that promote the humility necessary to accept the forgiveness and assistance of God.

Perhaps, for that reason, my friend Sylvia, whom I met in my later adult years, cannot connect my chronically happy manner to my tormented past. At the same time, my siblings, for the most part, feel that I have understated the fear and danger in which we lived for nearly 20 years. Some of them feel that I have offered undeserved justifications for our parents' unacceptable behavior and have forgiven them too easily. "No," I would tell my siblings, "forgiveness was not easy." And "yes," I would tell Sylvia, "I was both abused and happy." Whether or not there is some level of self-deception going on, I cannot say. I only know that my past does not trouble my present, and I am indeed a happy person today. As soon as I left home, I cast aside my bitter childhood and embarked on a happy adulthood for as Jim Palmer (*Divine Nobodies*) has written, "A bitter adulthood is no consolation for a stolen childhood."

Not being unhappy nor particularly humble, I did not see the blessings and miracles for what they were until much later although it is likely that their very existence is what contributed most to my happiness. Instead, I credited my own willpower with my surviving a highly abusive childhood with intact self-esteem and only one minor lasting physical injury. My ability to excel at academics I attributed to genetics, being the daughter of a man with a genius-level IQ who spent his life as a farmer and shoe-cutter, his inability to reach his intellectual potential haunting him until his death. As for my boundless (in the opinion of others) energy, incurable optimism, and unrelenting curiosity that drew me to a career of travel, adventure, and learning, well, I just accepted those traits as natural and did not really understand why everyone did not exhibit them.

As I progressed from child to university student, high school teacher, Army officer, university professor, author and editor, international consultant, mentor, and educational administrator, my atheism congealed at the same time that my confidence in life and openness to Serendipity's gifts, taskings, and opportunities increased. These odd parallel paths—my conscious marriage to atheism and my unconscious acceptance of divine direction—never seemed contradictory to me, perhaps because I recognized only the conscious emotions.

Adult life, as I experienced it, did have some challenging moments even for a chronically happy person. I frequently had to fight for my children with the very people to whom society entrusted their survival, future success, and ability to enjoy life. My husband, Donnie, stood by in support of "Beth the Bitch," as I came to be known in educational and medical circles. Were I to live my life again, I would engage in the same campaigns to knock down the same barriers, but this time I would do it not thinking that I was alone but rather with the full awareness of God's help. What a difference that knowledge would have made had I had it years earlier!

Not that our family ever was without divine intervention. I just thought we were. In reality, God was always there, making the miracles that I could not see or that I would not admit were miracles. An infinitely patient and probably infinitely sad, if not frustrated, God put people, specialists, and thoughts into our lives so that our children might live, in some cases against all odds, and so that they might have better lives. Just when it seemed that we were about to fall into one deep chasm or another, there was God pulling us back from the abyss. Sometimes it was money from unexpected sources at the last minute. Other times it was unexpected survival of a dangerous surgery. We often commented in those days that it seemed like every time we fell off a cliff a parachute we did not know we possessed opened to ensure a soft landing.

It was not just our family that God reached out and touched. It was also people with whom we came into contact or who appeared suddenly in our lives, needing assistance. From somewhere came my capability either to provide them assistance or to round up others who could provide the assistance. With them, too, often money or other needed resources came out of nowhere or multiplied like the fishes and loaves in the story of Jesus feeding an entire crowd from barely enough food for a handful of people.

I cannot remember all the miracles that God did for me and through me, try as I might. The ones I remember are vividly remarkable. A child lived when others died. Three children were wrested from death's grasping hand. Hundreds of ill children (some of them mortally ill) escaped a poisonous environment. Families received a new start. Warmth crept into the lives of people dwelling in cold. Even God's small creatures (cats, among them) found a better life.

I attributed the goodness to chance and to the basic kindness of people, devoid of any influence by God. Yet, now, when I look back upon those events, the image of a loving God, unseen earlier, shines out from behind every one of them. Perhaps my sharing with you God's unseen presence in my life will help you draw parallels to the same Presence, maybe unrecognized until now, in your own life and experience the greater joy of knowing from where comes the help given to all of us. If we see it, if we know the Source, if we are in communication with the Source, how much more precious is the help!

That many don't see the help God gives is not exclusively a contemporary phenomenon. The prophet Hosea relays God's commentary on this situation in the following way: "I took them in my arms, yet they have not understood that I was the one looking after them" (Hosea 11:3).

This book hopes to convey an understanding and trust that we are not alone, that we are in God's arms even when we don't admit the existence of a deity. We may not see God carrying us over the nearly insurmountable hurdles we are sometimes required to leap, but God is there. We may not notice God shepherding us along the convoluted obstacle course that we encounter in our journey through life, but there, nonetheless, is the divine Shepherd. Moreover, when we are lost, that Shepherd does leave the ninety-nine to rescue the one as promised. I know because for many years I was the one, happily cavorting in the brambles. We may not think that God gives messages to people anymore, but the Master of the sotto voice does if we listen.

Many things have happened to me that others might consider impossible to survive. I survived and thrived, and so did my children and my siblings. So have friends in similar circumstances. God did not cause the horrible things that happened to us. God did not cause the childhood beatings I suffered. God did not cause the birth defects of our children that limited their ability to ambulate or even, in one case, to breathe normally. The free will of other people did that, and the free selection of nature's gene pool did that, too. What God did was help us survive—with peace and joy. In many cases, our personal disasters were divinely commuted into widespread good for a great number of people.

The good that only God can create from disaster is so unbelievable that one becomes reluctant to relate it. How could anyone except those friends, colleagues, and relatives who have shared my days and have lived through one or another of these experiences with me believe the amount of trauma, drama, and miraculous triumph that has filled and continues to fill so many of my breathing moments? These are the stories of which fables are made. They are also the story of my life and of the lives of people like me, through whom God, for whatever reason, chooses to bring help to others. The greatest and most unexplainable miracle of all, in my opinion, has been God's choice to carry out divine work through an atheist.

God's presence in my life, even when I did not know that God was there, has enriched it beyond belief. For that reason, I can tell only part of my story in this book. It is however the best part for it is the part about God's role in it. An early reviewer of this book called me a "flawed heroine." I believe he is correct. I also believe that only a flawed heroine could tell this story for we are all flawed, each in our own way. If I were without flaws, then this story would be about me, but it cannot and should not be about me for I could have been anyone. This story is, in fact, about God.

# I

*elizabeth mahlou*

# Siberia on Easter Morning

"*Khristos voskres*" (Christ is risen). One person after another greeted me with these words as I climbed the stairs of the little, wooden church in Akademgorodok, a tiny town at the end of the man-made Ob Sea, bejeweling the Siberian steppe 45 minutes south of the city of Novosibirsk. The intertwining snow-covered birch and *kedr* (Siberian pine) trees created an illusion of a land of fantasy, made more so in the late evenings by the moon reflecting off the naked silver-white birch bark onto the dark red-brown trunks and evergreen branches of the pines. This was not yet the inhospitable *taiga*; it was somewhat south for that, but nonetheless the birch and *kedr* trees stood closely side-by-side like brothers-in-arms against a hostile white and cold universe.

"*V istinu voskres*" (truly, He is risen). If my words of response rang hollow, there was a reason. They came from the lips of a *bona fide* atheist, convinced that religious congregations were delusional. Certainly, they contained well-meaning folks, ones often filled with great compassion, but nonetheless, in my opinion at that time, delusional. Raised in a so-called Christian home and an attendee at, but not engaged participant in, Methodist and Baptist churches in my early years, I found no sense in the sermons of the ministers who were often more interested in large donations than in holy deeds, no examples set by the deacons who were often bedding the wives of their friends, and no love of God in the forsythia switches wielded by my parents that demanded their few ounces of blood every Sunday morning before we marched into church as a model family. God, to me, was a fantasy, created by evil-doers to make themselves feel better.

When given a chance at the age of 16 to preach the Youth Sunday sermon, the topic of which was "The Christian Home," I pointed out all of these things, to the great discomfort of the congregation. "If this is the way you intend to live your lives," I challenged the adults sitting in front of me, "at least do so without the self-deception of ostentatious holiness."

Ignoring their looks of disbelief that slowly turned to anger, I continued with a freeing sense of abandon. "Why do you feel the need to carry on this charade each week?" I asked. "Is it to feel worthy of something you do not deserve? To justify the unjustifiable?"

I pointed out books and articles written by children of religious leaders who described how their parents emotionally traumatized them. Their expectations for their children to be paragons of perfection, to be models of a concept of holy purity that they themselves concocted was unachievable, according to these self-reports, and led to feelings of inadequacy that haunted some of them long into their adult lives.

I concluded that sermon with the suggestion that considerable thought be given to the advantages of raising a child without hypocrisy, i.e. in an atheistic environment. "Accept a world without divinity," I urged them. "Raise your children honestly, in an atheistic home."

Whence came the audacity of a child to make such statements from a pulpit? I don't really know. Perhaps I envied the lives of my peers who were not abused each and every day and in resentment needed to point out something wrong with their lives, too. Perhaps I had expected the church community to rescue my siblings and me from our physical and sexual tormentors and blamed the people in the congregation when no one stepped forward. In any event, that sermon had ended my churchgoing days. My family had been asked to leave the church, and I had not been punished by them in any way. I suspect that my parents had feared that after such a sermon, were they to have hurt me as a result, I would have flounced into church with that announcement as well, completely destroying their reputations. Or perhaps their sense of the awfulness of what I had done paralyzed them into inaction. In any event, there being no other church within reasonable travel distance, I spent the rest of my growing-up and adult years in the atheistic environment I had exalted.

My parents never lost their faith as a result of their expulsion from the church, but they never again talked much about it in front of me. We no longer were forced to listen to grace at meals. Bibles disappeared from our bedsides onto the crowded bookshelves in our library. Although they never mentioned anything to me, looking back, I imagine that my parents felt that something became very broken in their lives that Sunday morning. At the core of their lives festered a desperate need to be respected by the community, perhaps fostered by childhoods in which neither had experienced much respect. Dad's unusually high level of intelligence brought him only a sense of disappointment and failure when, in keeping with the social norms of the time and my grandfather's thinking that eight grades of school were more than enough education, he found himself forced out of school in the eighth grade and turning over to his father his weekly pittance from work as a shoe cutter, a trade he plied, along with farming, his entire life. Ma had always been the little doll of her family, if my great-aunt's assessment is accurate, but had found herself rejected and ridiculed by classmates while her brother, who was in the same grade, served as class president. As adults, my parents became community leaders, Dad serving on the school board and Ma becoming actively involved in one social cause after another, looking for approbation from peers long ago grown up. We children suffered their anger when we failed to make up for their dissatisfaction with their own lives and their sense of underachievement, Dad intellectually and Ma socially. Their church activities provided them the lifeline with which they had clung to the community respect that they so desperately desired. I had cut that lifeline with one sermon.

As for me, I felt that something got fixed in my life that morning. No more hypocrisy. No more pretending to be a pew-filling, perfect family. No more Sunday morning races when I would refuse to get dressed for church, Dad would want to beat me into compliance, and I would run. As young as the age of eight, I could out-run Dad. I could also run far. Neighbors enroute to church pretended not to see the two of us running—around the front yard, across the street, through the tall grass of an abandoned field, and into the nearby woods, my long hair flying straight back into the wind and Dad brandishing a switch, usually broken off from a forsythia bush, large but supple, perfect for leaving welts just long enough to remember the pain and occasionally sharp enough to rip flesh but in such a way that the marks could be passed off as having tumbled into the bushes. I could feel the wind brushing past my face, the adrenalin coursing through my veins from fear of the whip, and nerve endings on fire with the thrill of the race, my legs fueled by competing thoughts: the stubbornness to do what I wanted, the fear of a dire outcome should I slow down or stumble long enough to be caught, and exhilaration at the thought that just perhaps I could run away from all of it, from the switchings, from the demeaning name calling, from the hypocrisy of pretending that we were the picture-perfect family, and especially from pretending to love and obey a God who for me did not exist and whom my parents used as a threat.

Teachers who wondered why the shortest kid in the class (me) would win the school races every year had only to ask our neighbors who watched my every-Sunday-morning running practice. That running practice later stood me in good stead when I had to keep pace with male Army officers a foot-and-a-half taller than I and even today when a late-arriving aircraft dumps me a ten-minute flat-out race from the departure gate of my connecting flight.

Only when Dad lost the switch and was too spent to care anymore about hitting me would I run home. Running back into the "burning house," as my future brother-in-law would later call it, was the only option that ever entered my head for any neighbor in northern New England of those days would have brought me back to my parents. Having run home, I always ended up in church. There, sitting in a pew, watching Dad and Ma acting devout and being viewed by the church community as ideal parents, my anger toward them would reach a quiet but full zenith. After the church service concluded, my parents would accept the sympathetic comments of my friends' parents, especially those who happened to catch a glimpse of our Sunday morning marathons. These people would knowingly smile, nod, and assent as to how difficult I must be to raise—and my seething frustration at the unfairness of it all made me want to run again—far away from my parents, the church, and the complacent people in the church pews. I resented being abused, and I trapped the church and its people in the web of angry emotions that encompassed my teenage years. I never asked how others in my family felt about being alienated from the church. I did not care. I had been freed.

Until now. Now I was about to address another church congregation. It was the first time in 30 years I would speak to such a gathering.

Uttering the expected words of greeting as I mounted the steps to the vestibule of the church was not uncomfortable. They were, after all, meaningless to me. While I would have preferred another form of greeting, I had somehow managed to end up at this humble Russian Orthodox Church on Easter morning. So, the greetings were to be anticipated.

When I reached the top of the stairs, a priest extended his hand. As I had been taught in advance to do, I kissed it. The priest smiled and said, "There is no need to follow our customs. I have been told that you are an atheist. I'm Father Boris, and I am very happy to meet you at long last. I do need, though, to find some way to introduce you to the congregation. I have given this some thought and wonder if I may introduce you as a Good Samaritan?"

I knew the parable. Is there anyone who does not?

> On one occasion an expert in the law stood up to test Jesus. "Teacher," he asked, "what must I do to inherit eternal life?"
>
> "What is written in the Law?" he replied. "How do you read it?"
>
> He answered: "Love the Lord your God with all your heart and with all your soul and with all your strength and with all your mind," and "love your neighbor as yourself."
>
> "You have answered correctly," Jesus replied. "Do this and you will live."
>
> But he wanted to justify himself, so he asked Jesus, "And who is my neighbor?"
>
> In reply, Jesus said: "A man was going down from Jerusalem to Jericho when he fell into the hands of robbers. They stripped him of his clothes, beat him, and went away, leaving him half dead.
>
> A priest happened to be going down the same road, and when he saw the man, he passed by on the other side.
>
> So too, a Levite, when he came to the place and saw him, passed by on the other side.
>
> But a Samaritan, as he traveled, came where the man was; and when he saw him, he took pity on him.

*He went to him and bandaged his wounds, pouring on oil and wine. Then he put the man on his own donkey, took him to an inn and took care of him.*

*The next day he took out two silver coins and gave them to the innkeeper. 'Look after him,' he said, 'and when I return, I will reimburse you for any extra expense you may have.'*

*"Which of these three do you think was a neighbor to the man who fell into the hands of robbers?"*

*The expert in the law replied, "The one who had mercy on him."*

*Jesus told him, "Go and do likewise." (Luke 10: 25-37)*

I agreed with Father Boris that my introduction as a Good Samaritan would be appropriate. Apparently, others had passed through this remote village in Siberia, had even met young Aleksandr Ivanovich, affectionately referred to as Shura, a teenage artist dying from complications of spina bifida (a congenital malformation in which the spine does not fully close during the first six weeks of gestation). These passers-through had expressed a desire to help him, but, like the beaten man's countrymen, ultimately passed him by. Perhaps they thought they could not help. Most were from Russia, and Russia in the early 1990s, just emerging from 70 years of a failed experiment in communism, was an impoverished nation—except, of course, for the nouveau-riche oligarchy and the emerging mafia (often an intermixed group) that held the purse strings and the real power in the new "democracy." Others were from foreign countries, and perhaps the complicated immigration laws gave them pause. I, on the other hand, found myself unable not to stop. And so here I was at Shura's church with him to share his recently restored life with his neighbors on the day known as the Resurrection.

On wobbling prostheses, which he had not yet learned to control completely, and clinging to the railing, Shura, the pride of this tiny community, had triumphantly led me up the stairs of the wooden church, his church. There he had been raised in a faith that carried him through the torments of a physically handicapped childhood, during which he had spent nearly 75% of his life hospitalized, the agony of waxing and waning hope that he would be able to come to the United States for treatment as he lay again in a hospital with waxing and waning life, and the difficult decision to amputate both gangrenous legs at the University of Virginia Hospital and replace them with prostheses. It had been the kind of life that could challenge the faith of a saint. Yet, he was but a teenage boy, one with resilient faith that God would find someone to help him.

And now we both stood in front of a hushed congregation of Russian Orthodox believers, all of them wrapped in the swaddling fur coats commonly worn during Siberian winters, thick head and neck scarves for the women and fur hats with ear flaps for the men, and the warm felt boots worn by all from childhood through old age. The unheated, dimly lit vestibule, where the lack of pews made the room look empty in spite of a crowd that filled it to overflowing, exuded a different kind of warmth and a different kind of light, that which comes from inside, not outside, from natural sources, not artificial ones.

Father Boris introduced me as the Good Samaritan who had rescued their Shura, the young man they loved and for whom they had despaired and now hoped. The crowd looked at me in eager anticipation. What was an atheist to say to this expectant gathering of believers?

# Mercy

The Samaritan stopped because he was filled with mercy. He also had clearly been blessed with the resources to help. I stopped by habit. Very early I internalized the concept that helping even one person toward a better life is a way to justify one's own existence. That may well have given a positive balance to the daily abuse I experienced throughout my childhood. Knowing that someone was better off because of something I had done—whether it was teaching a kindergarten class when I was in first grade, working as the teachers' helper in conducting an extra reading group for the struggling readers in my elementary school classroom, or serving as an evening telephone resource to the eighth-grade members of my advanced mathematics class whose teacher kept confusing us with high school juniors—established a sense of self-worth that logically should never have appeared, given all the abuse I experienced at home.

Development of self-worth was not a natural part of what passed for nurturing in our home. As the oldest and most defiant of the eight children born in rural New England to my parents in the 1950s and 1960s, I received perhaps the greatest number of beatings, but I did not receive the worst of them. That was reserved for Rollie, my younger brother, who was a happy-go-lucky, live-for-today fellow with sandy hair, supple body, and a smile for all occasions. When accosted, though, he had my spirit of defiance. Rollie, as a teenager, could easily have dropped Ma to the floor but had sufficient residual respect for her role as a mother not to use his physical size to return the hurts she delivered to him. He mainly used words, but no words admitting being hurt ever slipped past his lips. Not even when he was stabbed twice, once by Ma and once by Dad. In both cases, he remained defiant.

Ma's stabbing of Rollie was not undertaken for any reasonable motive. Reasonable people don't stab their children. In a moment of rage, Ma stabbed 11-year-old Rollie in the buttocks for putting the hamburger planned for supper that evening in the roadside mailbox where no one could find it, something he did for spite for Ma's beating him about something else. (Rollie, like me, could be spiteful; "don't get mad, just get even" tended to be a *modus operandi* for both of us.) Realizing that she had drawn blood, Ma became even angrier, not at herself as one might think, but at Rollie.

"Look what you made me do to you! You bastard!" A master at self-justification, Ma was a good example of modern-day cognitive dissonance theory, side-stepping all responsibility for the abuse she rained on us. "Don't you dare cry, or I'll do it again. And don't you dare tell, or I'll do it again. This is all your fault. If you would behave, you would have no problems."

None of us ever knew what "behave" meant. Ma's expectations differed from moment to moment, depending on her mood. Her flash-floods of rage, thunderstorms of criticism that were punctuated by lightning strikes of negative pronouncements of our worthlessness, faked heart attacks that rarely earned her the sympathy she hoped they would, and spitting fests seemed unconnected to any particular events. Neither of our parents drank, used drugs (unknown in that part of the world in those days), had affairs, or otherwise lived anything but what appeared to a life straight from the *Decalogue*. (How we wished that there was an eleventh commandment: Thou shalt not abuse thy children. Instead, there was only a frightening aside about punishing children for the iniquity of their parents.) In any case, beatings were always our fault.

"Go wash your hair, bitch," Rollie retorted in defiance, referring to the fact that when Ma's hair was dirty she was at her meanest. I often said the same to her, including using the word *bitch* or other equally pejorative label. Through example, she taught us a rich vocabulary of colorful epithets at a very early age. We never used them at school or in the community, but we had much practice listening to and using them at home in spite of Ma's threats to wash our mouths out with soap.

"Don't you tell me what to do," she threw back at him. "I'll show you who needs a hair washing!" She grabbed him by the hair and pulled him to his knees. "Now, say you're sorry. Beg me not to hurt you more!"

"Hell, no, bitch," he said. "You beg me to forgive you!" I understood Rollie. I would never beg for mercy, either. Fighting back was what kept our self-esteem intact.

Rollie twisted away, wrenching himself free from the hand that was holding him by the hair. "Hey, bitch," he taunted her in defiance, "You want to try for the other side? I have two cheeks. You only got me in one!"

Of course, he did not wait for an answer. He took off running. She would not be able to catch him, and by the time he would return, she would have washed her hair and mellowed or have found a different child to beat. This particular event, this stabbing, would be over. It was a completed disciplinary action.

Years later, Ma would not deny the stabbing but would try to justify it. "I did not stab him," she told me in a phone conversation in 1998, "I hit him. I just forgot I had a knife in my hand." As if hitting were all right!

Dad, too, had a moment of rage that left a permanent scar on Rollie's body and an emotional one on his spirit. It was the end of the summer a couple of years earlier, and we had just finished haying the lower field. Hardly anyone in rural New England of those days had the modern automatic haying equipment that bundles and ties hay into cubes or rolls. We had to do everything by hand.

Dad had been driving the tractor. Ma and we three older girls, Katrina (18 months younger than I), Danielle (three years younger), and I (fourteen at the time), had been pitching the made hay into the wagon. ("Made hay" is mowed hay dried in the sun; hence, the expression, *to make hay while the sun shines*). The three younger boys, Willie, Rollie, and Keith (the two younger girls, Sharon and Victoria, not having been born yet), had been treading the hay, walking on it with bare feet as we tossed it into the wagon so that the later forkfuls would intersect with and weigh down the earlier ones and the hay would not fall out of the wagon as it was driven back to the barn.

We did not have a large hayfork that could be lowered from the upper story of the barn and mechanically sweep the hay through the upper story window into the hayloft. Instead, we had to drive the tractor into the barn and toss the hay up into the loft with pitchforks. It was extensive hard physical labor. At the time, only our parents and we older girls were strong enough to pitch hay that far.

The boys were told to climb into the hayloft, and we began pitching the hay up to them. The boys were supposed to weave the sailing and falling hay together into mounds much like the way it is tread while being thrown into the hay wagon.

Rollie could not keep up with the amount of hay coming in his direction. Not being tread into the mix fast enough, hay kept falling back into the hay wagon by the forkful. Dad was clearly at the end of his physical and emotional endurance. An exasperated and provocative word from Ma, "Bartholomew, he's horsing around again!" drew a sudden burst of anger from Dad. He heaved his pitchfork into the hayloft.

Dad's rages were more frightening than Ma's. Ma's were routine events in our lives, stronger on certain days of the month than others but always roaming the skies like burgeoning cumulus clouds waiting for the final drop before bursting. Dad rarely raged alone but was easily kindled into flame by Ma. More important, Dad really did love kids, especially young ones. He would spend hours after work playing train engine, choo-chooing a chain of us through the 13 rooms in our old farmhouse. Even when exhausted from a long day at the factory, he would always find enough time and energy to change a diaper, dandle a baby on his knee, show us how to play the violin, listen to us practice the piano, or rehearse me for the spelling bee championship. So, when he raged, the loss of his love—the only safety parachute I had—put me into an emotional free-fall.

Regardless of what prompted Dad to throw the pitchfork, he did it. It went sailing through the air and, still with a good deal of force behind it, sliced through Rollie's lower leg and nailed him to the floor of the hayloft. Nine-year-old Rollie stood still, speechless, for a stunned moment, realizing that he was pierced and pinned.

We were all shocked, so much so that I don't remember if Rollie said a word, if anyone said a word. Wordlessly, Dad climbed the built-in ladder to the hayloft and worked to free Rollie from the pitchfork. I don't remember if Rollie screamed. I do remember Dad sending the freed Rollie with eleven-year-old Danielle for bandaging. Danielle applied bag balm, a wondrous salve that we used on the cattle when they had cuts and abrasions, and wrapped Rollie's leg. I suppose it should have been no surprise to anyone that she grew up to be a nurse. Her extensive childhood practice helped her to become a very good one.

No doctor ever saw what happened to Rollie. It must only have been by the grace of God that his leg healed with no more damage than a scar as a reminder. None of us, though, needs a reminder. Both stabbings of Rollie are among our most vivid childhood memories.

I began fighting Ma at a young age. When I was small, Ma was like a god, a strong, mean, and angry one. She loomed large, powerful, and seemingly omniscient. As I grew older, however, I learned that I could fight this god and retain my dignity, and as I grew even older I found that I could fight this god and win. Perhaps my growing ability to vanquish the earthly god in my life colored my own disposition toward God the Almighty.

Small, with "dark eyes that could sparkle with delight or flash with fire," according to relatives who remember those days, I apparently exhibited from birth a profound orneriness. The pediatrician could not calm me at my six-week checkup and strapped me to a table, waiting for me to stop screaming. For two hours, my screams pierced the doctor's closed window, causing passersby in the city square below to stop and wonder what was happening. The doctor sent Ma to take a walk. I often wonder if that episode and other displays of my strong will frightened her into wanting to control me with every trick she had, including violence. Finally, I fell asleep. That incident was telling. I would go through childhood screaming, as I defiantly thrust my lance at the paddles of the immutable windmill known as Ma.

Perhaps this defiance made Ma even more brutal. Having felt like a loser at school in her growing-up years (something I learned through a variety of sources in later life), she was now unacceptably finding herself a loser when pitted against her oldest, and for a very short while, only child.

My first memory of windmill-tilting defiance is a conversation that took place between Ma and me, a kindergartener at the time. It was a conversation engendered by an unfortunate decision. Possessing a great imagination and surprisingly, given our abusive home, being an inveterate risk taker, I had set up a play barbershop one afternoon and had had the audacity to take real scissors to Danielle's tidily braided hair. I snipped off one of her two pigtails. Danielle instantly became afraid of repercussions from Ma, but I reassured her.

"Don't tell Ma," I said. "She is too dumb to notice."

That advice worked for a couple of hours. Then suddenly Ma looked at Danielle strangely and commented, "Danielle, what happened to your hair?"

Danielle melted in fear and wailed, "Bethie said you were too dumb to notice!"

Whether Ma was angrier about the hair cutting or about the comment that I thought she would be too dumb to notice did not much matter. After cutting off the other pigtail and then hitting and kicking Danielle until she could barely crawl to bed, Ma turned on me.

"You go get me a switch right now! You are really in for it!" She nearly spat at me, and rage shook her entire body as if rage itself were the living being and Ma an obedient symbiant.

A "switch" was a forsythia branch from the bush in the yard. Danielle, who to this day thinks that Ma grew that bush for the sole purpose of having handy switches, and Katrina used to scurry off after their own switches in frightened obedience to Ma's demand that we all bring our own switches to her, but I was too defiant to do that. If she were going to beat me, I certainly was not going to make it easy for her!

My youngest son, Doah, whose name was derived from Shenandoah, a valley near which we lived for nearly six years, must have inherited that sense of defiance. Actually, I know for a fact that he did, but had I needed proof, a multi-month visit by Ma to our house when Doah was eight years old would have been adequate proof. One day, when I arrived home from work, Ma asked me if I had moved the wooden spoons because she could not find any. I looked. They had, indeed, mysteriously disappeared. Weeks later, as my husband Donnie left for the airport with Ma firmly strapped into the passenger seat, Doah appeared beside me.

"Gramma all gone?" he asked, in the mentally challenged language that is the best communication he can manage to this day.

"Yes," I told him. "She is going back to New England now."

"No come back?"

"No, sweetheart, she is not coming back. At least, not for a long time because New England is very far away."

"Good," he pronounced and walked over to our never-used sofa bed. Opening it, he reached below the mattress, pulled out all my wooden spoons, and took them into the kitchen, putting them into the drawer where they belonged.

"Doah," I asked him, "why were the wooden spoons under the sofa bed?"

"Gramma say she hit me with wooden spoon," he replied. "No wooden spoon! No hit!" He grinned. Indeed, mentally challenged or not, he is my child!

Back on the pigtail day in 1956, I would not cry out for mercy. I was stubborn about those kinds of things. Left without a switch, Ma grabbed the nearest instrument available, a wooden hairbrush. Since I refused to get switches, the chosen weapons of torture used with me were more unique than the ones typically used with my siblings: paddle ball handles, brooms, hairbrushes, shoes, belts—whatever solid object was handiest at the moment. Ma held me tightly by the hair with her left hand and with her right hand thumped me forcefully again and again with the hairbrush until the handle snapped off. Exploding with anger over the broken hairbrush (probably wondering where she was going to get money for a replacement) and blaming me for the breakage, she pummeled me with her fists and stomped me with her feet, screaming over and over "I'll teach you to break my hairbrush," "Have you learned not to break my hairbrush yet?" "Tell me when you've learned not to break my hairbrush."

At these moments, I would let my body go limp, mentally "step aside" from the pain, and analyze what was going on with my body, rather than feeling it. While it may not have been the best approach to stop the beatings, it did serve as a way to manage a situation in which I was the weaker. Stepping outside my body to manage intense pain—mind over matter—is a technique I learned as a toddler. This survival technique, like many others I developed in childhood, turned out to be good preparation for an allergic-to-painkiller adult life in which I have had to use the mind-over-matter approach with doctors doing grin-and-bear-it biopsies and dentists doing root canals without anesthesia.

Grin-and-bear-it was an attitude enforced from a young age. One of my most painful experiences was not deliberately inflicted—a wonder in and of itself. It was, however, home treated, and painfully so. I was running across the yard—I was always running, either away from anticipated abuse or just using those well developed leg muscles for play—and tripped on wood that had been torn off the chicken coop and piled for later disposal. I sprawled across a board, and a rusty nail pushed itself through my right lower leg like a skewer forced through a ham shank for roasting on a spit. When I stood up, the board was tightly attached to my leg. I called to Dad—I would never have called to Ma for fear that she would blame me for causing some kind of damage to the way the boards were stacked or otherwise find a reason to beat me for what had happened. Dad came, saw the situation, and said that he had to pull the nail out of my leg. He told me to stay still until he came back. He returned with a clean cotton rag and that wonder drug, mercurochrome. My lip must have trembled when he pulled the board away from my leg, sliding the nail back out, for he ordered me, "Don't be spleeny!"

Being spleeny was a bad thing. Being spleeny meant that you had no backbone, that you cried when there was no need to cry. Every cry, even in the midst of being beaten, was considered unnecessary. Punch! "Don't be spleeny!" Kick! "Don't be spleeny!" Bite! "Don't be spleeny!" Splinters, burns, cuts, scrapes? "Don't be spleeny!" No, sir, no one would ever call me spleeny. Being spleeny was just something I was not, even from my very earliest days. Tolerate the pain of removing a rusty nail from half-way through the leg? Piece of cake!

Actually, though, that day I really wanted to be spleeny as the nail emerged from my leg with a long hot flash of pain that continued to hurt for days. I wanted to be able to cry, but I dared not. I wanted to have a loving parent who would hold my hand and soothe me. Hah! That only happened in books. Hugs? I saw other parents do that so I knew what a hug was, but I never knew what a parental hug felt like. Even Dad, who loved babies, stopped hugging us as soon as we started walking. So, that day I bit my lip and put my mind in that other place that just observes what happens to my body and ceases to feel it. Since the mercurochrome was applied while I was in an altered state, I felt the sting only as vicarious pain. In the same way, I experienced the wrapping of the wound. I was definitely *not* spleeny.

I don't remember how long the wound took to heal. I don't remember being taken to a doctor—I do not believe I was. The leg did heal, and all I have left is a small scar as a reminder, making the nail injury a permanent reminder never to cry about pain, no matter how bad.

Spleeny went beyond hiding pain. It expanded to include hiding all emotions. To this day, my family and friends are much more likely to know how I think than how I feel. When someone asks me how I feel about something, I can rarely answer.

The ability to tolerate pain was honed through the daily beatings. I did not cry out at those, either, other than to hurl ever increasingly obscene epithets. I would not give my parents the satisfaction of knowing that they had succeeded in hurting me. I just "managed" the pain. First, I saw no alternative. I knew that mercy would not be forthcoming although the pleas of my siblings in such situations sometimes brought the beatings to an earlier conclusion. Second, I knew that Ma would eventually run out of steam. Third, somewhere deep down I knew that I could not let whatever happened get the best of me, or my identity, which was very important to me, would be lost. So, instead of pleading, I argued. When I got older, I fought back physically, replying to scream with scream, slap with slap, punch with punch, kick with kick, bite with bite, hair pulling with hair pulling, spit with spit, and insult with insult.

In this early memory of snipping off Danielle's pigtail, I was only five, so the only way I could fight back was to bite, kick, and try to escape. I was, however, clearly physically the weaker, and Ma's beating became heavier and heavier until I could do nothing but close my eyes in the hope that when I woke up, the immediate pain would be gone even though there might be some leftover pain from the bruises. Bruises I could manage. I was used to feeling that kind of pain most of the time, and I hid the physical marks under sweaters and the long pants that I wore under my skirts. (Girls in rural New England in the 1950s were not allowed to wear pants to school unless they wore skirts over them).

Whenever I realized that I had lost the physical battle and that there was nothing to do but wait for the rain of blows to stop, I would further distract myself from the pain with thoughts of revenge. Revenge was something that I learned to accomplish to perfection although once I left home I quickly realized that thinking up avenues of revenge is a very ineffective way to manage anger. Perhaps that is because I no longer had a need to deal with daily abuse, and that sense of relief turned me nearly instantly into a chronically happy person, like the bubbles of carbonation rushing into the air with the opening of a bottle of Perrier water.

In this childhood memory, I planned the ultimate revenge, at least, in the mind of a five-year-old. My parents were well-respected members of the community, hiding the abuse of their children behind political involvement and a show of their children being well-taken care of. Of course, we were raised to fear telling anyone although sometimes we did tell and were not believed, so strong was the image of the perfect family that our parents had successfully produced. Ma would do anything to keep alive the false image of this ideal family.

My revenge, then, was to do something that would embarrass my parents and in this instance as a five-year-old unversed in matters of embarrassment to self was well-planned. While I was severely beaten for it afterward, I savored every second of relating it to Ma. Arriving home from kindergarten, I announced in a proud and contemptuous tone, "You beat me yesterday. Well, I got you! Today I wore no underpants to school, and I showed all the boys. I told them you won't buy me any."

Ma raised my skirt, and sure enough, I was telling the truth. Truth-telling caused me to receive more beatings than most of my siblings although infliction of physical pain followed the routine of daily vitamin pills for all. For each one of us children, the physical, sexual, and emotional abuse was differently apportioned, but we all were treated to at least a little of each kind and a major helping of the physical variety. The irony is that we went to school looking well cared for: scrupulously bathed, immaculately clothed, hair combed (and, for the girls, braided). The wounds were in the heart, in the mind, and on the covered parts of our bodies.

## Defiance

Physical abuse quickly became routine for us. We just expected to arrive home to a daily rain of blows, kicks, bites, deliberately inflicted sprains, or airplane rides.

We all feared Ma's airplane rides. She would grab one arm and one leg and rotate in the middle of the room like a dervish, swinging us around and around in circles, allowing the free arm and leg to hit pieces of furniture one after another after another until she was out of breath and let us go. When she let go and we flew into the wall or the furniture, the impact was stunning, and often we lost consciousness from it. Not only were the airplane rides painful, but also they left us feeling dizzy and disoriented whether or not we lost consciousness.

As we got bigger, airplane rides became less manageable for Ma, and these were replaced with sled rides (being pulled down a flight of stairs by our hair). I did not accept that type of punishment meekly. My defiant nature rising to the fore, I would cling desperately to the slim, round rails supporting the banister and marvel at the strength of human hair. Sometimes Ma would end up with a handful in her hands. Sometimes the angle was such that I could not hang on and would end up being yanked down the rest of the stairs. But sometimes, just sometimes, the hair would hold fast, and one of the rails would loosen. The damage to the railing, of course, made Ma even angrier and the sled ride down the stairs, with rail in hand, inevitable, but that loose rail for me symbolized another successful form of revenge. I would laugh and laugh. That laugh increased the severity of the pelting I got at the bottom of the stairs, but it was, indeed, a heartfelt laugh.

It was a laugh of defiance, and that defiance always got me into trouble—and still does. It is not that I forget about the trouble it has caused. I have a constant reminder of that from a frequently aching finger, thanks to another interlude with Ma, in which she grabbed my hand, trying to force me to my knees in front of her by bending back one of my fingers.

"Say uncle," Ma insisted. "Tell me you're sorry."

I no longer remember what it was I was supposed to be sorry for, but I do remember that it was something for which I was definitely *not* sorry. There was no way, no matter what, that I would lie and say that I was.

"Say you're sorry," Ma repeated, as she continued to bend backward the middle finger on my right hand. She had caught me off guard and now had me in her complete physical control. I was nine or ten at the time and still too small to take her on once she had me in her full grasp, but I was determined, whether or not I could get away, that she would not win because no matter what, I would not say I was sorry for something that I thought was the right thing to do.

"I will keep bending this finger until you say you're sorry," she said. And she did.

"I am not sorry," I repeated. She bent the finger farther backward.

"I am not sorry," I repeated again. She bent the finger even farther backward.

"I'm sorry you're such a bitch," I snarled, as the pain went off the Richter scale.

The finger went limp. It could not be bent any farther because Ma had apparently broken it. She pushed me away. "Don't you ever call me a bitch, and don't you complain about that finger. It was all your fault." With those words, she stormed off, ostensibly in search of one of my siblings.

Breaking fingers, hitting, biting—the trademarks of a playground bully—served as Ma's childrearing techniques. In essence, we children were being raised by a child. Ma had never developed the emotional maturity to guide and support us. In fact, the thought of having to support us in the fuller meaning of that word terrified her. We found that out one evening when I was about eight years old. Dad had left the house around midnight for a reason we never learned. Ma pulled all of us out of our beds and sat us on the staircase. I was near the bottom, and the others, two to a stair, were lined up above me. Ma had a box of rat poison in her hands,

Shaking—at the time I thought it was with anger but now realize that it was probably with fear—she scolded us, "Your father is gone, and I will not bring you up alone. I can't deal with all of you. So, if he is not back by 5:30, I am going to feed you this rat poison. When he finds you dead, he will be sorry."

I did not think Ma would really kill us. My unshaking vision of a future over which I would eventually have control propelled me past Ma's histrionic moments, allowing me to ignore her faked heart attacks and threats of many sorts. Able to sleep nearly anywhere, I dozed off. My siblings, though, were terrified.

The minutes tiptoed past, and Ma grew increasingly agitated. I opened my eyes to find that a couple of hours had passed, Dad had not returned, and somehow while I had been dozing, Ma had fetched a can of kerosene and matches.

"Forget the rat poison," she said. "It will be quicker to douse you with kerosene and set you on fire. If he is not back here by 5:30, I will show him." (She was always going to "show" someone.)

And so we sat for another couple of hours. I was annoyed at this attempt at drama and wanted to sleep in my bed. My siblings' faces, however, registered fear. To this day, they tell me that they are convinced that Ma fully intended to carry out her threat and that my blasé sleepiness was naive. Fortunately, Dad came back at

5:00, and Ma quickly shooed us all back to bed with a threat that if we told him, she would get us good.

Wanting to eliminate us, whether by fire or poison or some other means, was nothing new. Ma was always demanding that Dad get rid of one or another of us, I being the one that she most often wanted to get rid of. During one rage, Ma insisted that Dad get rid of me or she would leave. In one of his more supportive acts, Dad refused, saying, "I will not choose between my wife and my child." In response, Ma grabbed a pillow and blanket and flounced off to the woods, where she spent the night.

My childhood contained two compartments: home and not-home. Not-home was a special place that I kept carefully separated to prevent the excesses of home from tainting it. Not-home was the place where I received validation, especially from teachers who encouraged me in many ways. Several of my elementary school teachers used me as a reading group teacher. Others encouraged my propensity for writing poetry and mysteries. Still others brought me whole libraries of books from their homes which I would inhale the way I had inhaled all the books in our small school library. My French teacher in high school encouraged me to write French poetry for our bilingual school journal. As even more validation, I won awards for public speaking, drama competitions, spelling bees, and other competitions that my teachers encouraged me to try.

I also won the city's history-writing award. Years earlier, someone had left a fund for a monetary award to be given annually to the eighth grade student who wrote the best essay on the history of the city. The Hannah Dustin Award was named after a New England heroine, a colonist and mother of thirteen, living in Haverhill, Massachusetts, Dad's birthplace. When her twelfth child was six days old, Hannah was captured by Abenaki Indians who killed the baby by slamming it against a tree. Rather than seeking a means to slip away undetected, when the opportunity came, Hannah Dustin defiantly took on the Indians with the help of other captives and won, freeing all the captives. About her captivity, a genealogic work, *The Dustin/ Duston Family*, cites her as saying, "I Desire to be thankful that I was born in a Land of Light & Baptized when I was young and had a good education by my Father, tho' I took but little notice of it in the time of it—I am Thankful for my Captivity, 'twas the Comfortablest time that ever I had. In my Affliction God made his Word Comfortable to me." That part of Hannah I could not then understand. About Hannah and the escape on Contocook Island, John Greenleaf Whittier wrote: "Taken hostage, she fought back with deadly force." That part of Hannah I could always understand.

For the competition, I wrote an essay on the evolution of the city's library. That essay was nearly disqualified. When the jury read my essay, they claimed it had been plagiarized because "no eighth-grader writes like this."

No eighth-grader wrote like that because no eighth-grader read like I did. Reading "promiscuously" had become my downfall. Even at that age, my writing was influenced by the likes of Joyce, Faulkner, Thoreau, and Dickens. These authors and many others gave me a psychologically-stabilizing broader picture of the human condition. Promiscuous reading I inherited from Dad, who, in spite of his poverty-level income, always found a way to bring books into our house. In fact, he built a library for us and stocked it with most of the great works of literature. Dad, the eighth-grade dropout, was an intellectual at heart, and he raised an intellectual: me. Our home library, the public library, the school library, and the philosophical discussions with Dad in the car on our 26-mile roundtrip to and from high school developed my intellectual interests. Those were the good times with Dad: when Ma was out of the picture, when he and I were alone. These were "not-home" times for me, as well, and resulted in a more trusting relationship with Dad than would have developed had these times not occurred and which never did occur for my younger siblings. They rode the bus to elementary school. If my parents wanted me to attend high school (many of my classmates did not), they had to provide the transportation to a city or town that had one. So, my eighth grade year (which was the first year of high school in our farming community), I spent many hours in exciting, one-on-one, intellectual discussion with Dad, hours in which I would feel validated by him, just as I felt validated by my teachers, especially when involved in intellectual endeavors. Dad would sometimes take positions with which he did not agree and require me to do the same to make me develop my debating skills. Obviously, then, I did not think like an eighth grader, either.

Mr. Corwin, my eighth-grade social studies teacher, thankfully leapt to my defense. He brought the jury samples of my writing on essay questions on his social studies tests. I received the award. To this day, I remember how I learned about the award. As I was walking through the hall on the day the winner was announced, I felt a tug on my ponytail. I turned around to see that it was Mr. Corwin trying to get my attention. He told me what had happened and then gave me some words of advice that have stood me in good stead over time: "Young lady, always remember to 'dumb down' your writing for grown-ups."

I do not remember when I first became an independent thinker, but somehow even as a young child, I knew I had to be, that this was the route to survival. Over time, the books showed me how. I remember moments of independence dating back to very young years.

One such instance revolved around a gift of seven dollars that Gram had given me for my seventh birthday. I wanted a bank account, and my parents had helped me put this money into savings. I wanted some day to add to the savings. Perhaps with a little money, when I grew up—or even before then—I would be able to leave the burning house. However, my hopes and plans were dashed several months later when my parents decided that I needed a new pair of shoes. The ones they wanted for me cost exactly seven dollars. Holding up my bank book, they told me to get in the car so that we could go to the bank and take out my money for the shoes. I resisted. I would rather have continued to wear the shoes I had a while longer than use all of the only money I had to buy new ones. My expression of this preference infuriated my parents, and both of them began hitting me. I fled the wrong way. With no way out, I crawled as far under the dining room table as I could and curled into a ball. Dad kicked my stomach hard over and over, trying to wedge me out. When he had budged me a little, my head came within striking distance of Ma's high heels. She danced around my head, lashing out with her heels, her eyes flashing almost gleefully with excitement and rage. I instinctively covered my eyes, and Katrina and Danielle began screaming, "You're going to make her blind," to which Ma replied, "It's her choice—seven dollars or her eyesight; I don't care if I kill the little bitch."

Ultimately, I lost consciousness, and my parents pulled me out from under the table. When I came to, I was in the firm grasp of both. They marched me into the car and then into the bank. So much for the hopes built on seven dollars.

Since it was clear that I could not save dollars, I saved candy. I did not like the taste of it, but it was among the countable things I owned. It became my treasure. I kept it in a bag under the eave on the roof outside my window. I would sneak out at night to check on the candy and count it. How easily I could have fallen on the New England-style sloping roof! Somehow, though, I felt protected as I darted with abandon along its slopes that circled the third story of our house. For four years, I successfully saved Easter and Christmas candy, the only times that we got candy. In that time, the bag grew big enough to attract Ma's attention from the ground. One day, she crawled out, retrieved the bag, and ate all the stale candy. All of it. Ma was a big woman, but even so it was astonishing to be confronted with the bag, void of its treasures.

"Beth, what were you thinking of, putting candy under the eaves and crawling out there all the time," Ma demanded to know. "You could have slipped off the roof and been killed." I could not even imagine slipping and falling. When I was on the roof, I always felt safe from the exploding wrath that filled the inside of the house.

I looked at the forlorn bag, held up in remonstrance in Ma's hand, and then at Ma's big belly. "My treasures are gone," I thought.

And so, from the age of 11, neither money nor material things any longer attracted me. I began to prefer the less evanescent realm of books, thoughts, and people.

Even independent thinkers and bookworms, though, need supporters, a source of comfort, someone who thinks you are always right. I found that support in the boy next door. Since we were toddlers, Bobby and I were pals. We played together nearly from the moment we could walk. At age two, I gave him a piece of my candy bar, and when he would not give me a lick of his ice cream cone, I knocked him flat on the ground even though he was considerably bigger than I was. He forgave me for that. We sneaked into Gram's house and ate her doughnuts when we were three. When he was four, he swallowed a balloon at my birthday party—the concern from that I remember to this day. As he grew older, I think he knew a lot more about what went on in the burning house than he ever said because he was very protective of me all the way through school. In elementary school, he was one of the people who would walk me home when I was sure that a severe licking awaited me for something I had done or failed to do or be. In high school, Bobby sat behind me in English class. He would ask me questions about how to handle his dates. When he encountered difficulties with schoolwork, I would give him answers. In return, I knew that there would always be someone who would emotionally support me if I got into trouble at home that I could not handle.

By my high school years, fortunately, I needed far less external support. Physically, I was giving tit for tat in the home wars.

Verbally, I was also giving tit for tat. "You will never amount to a hill of beans." How often Ma told me that! What she did not understand was something that Eleanor Roosevelt once said: "No one can make you feel inferior except you yourself."

My response was always intentionally disrespectful. "I don't want to be a hill of beans," I would spit out at her. "I want to leave this bean farm, and when I do, I will make sure that the life of my children will be better than what you have shown me."

I vowed that my children would never experience the torment of my childhood, and I kept that vow. All of us in the 8-pack, the name that Rollie gave to Ma's eight children, made similar vows, and we all kept them. While we had to learn our parenting skills from peers, doctors, books, and conscious attempts at inverting our childhood experiences, which meant that we would, of course, make mistakes—I know I did upon occasion—none of us stabbed our children, abandoned them to the wilderness, allowed them to be repeatedly used to feed the sexual hunger of male relatives, or emotionally eviscerated them.

# Rage

Rage was a constant during my childhood. Even when Ma was calm, we knew a rage attack could be as close as 30 seconds away. When we were very young, Ma's rage attacks most commonly resulted in airplane rides. No matter how frequently we experienced them, we dreaded each one anew. They were painful. They caused bruises. And we often passed out from them.

It took no effort at all to get a ticket for an airplane ride. For example, one day Danielle went off to clean up her room, but in the process, she became distracted by her dolls. Unlike Ma, Danielle, the future nurse, had a nurturing nature. As a little five-year-old that day, she was playing with her dolls—gently and kindly. Who had ever taught her that? This was not the first instance in which one or another of the 8-pack would display attributes that lend credence to the nature-over-nurture explanation of cognitive and affective development—or perhaps to an unfelt and unseen but nonetheless protective divine hand.

Bang! Danielle's attention was ripped away from her dolls and toward the approaching storm cloud as the door blew opn.

"What in hell are you doing?" screamed Ma, her fists clenched and face contorted with growingly venomous irritation that quickly eliminated any hope for self-control. "I told you to clean your room!"

"I'll clean it, Ma, I will. Right now I will." Small, pixie-like Danielle quickly put her dolls away and started to pick up some toys from the floor.

"You bet you will!" Ma screamed even louder. Now the storm had taken over the person. "You will because if you don't, you're gonna get an airplane ride."

"Get a wiggle on," Ma continued. "I said *now*. I don't have all day." She started throwing Danielle's toys into the toy chest, and with each toss, she flipped her hand in Danielle's direction, whipping her across the face. It became a rhythmic motion— toss, backhand, toss, backhand.... Slap! Slap! Slap!

Tears started flowing down Danielle's face, but she knew better than to cry aloud. It would only fuel the storm.

But the storm that day needed no more fuel than the touch of flesh on flesh and the energy awoken from the physical labor of tossing toys. It happened like a flash of lightning. One moment the dolls were being flung through the air; the next it was Danielle. She would not be able to avoid the airplane ride this time—or the next.

"That's it! You are dawdling. I will show you how to work!" Ma grabbed one of Danielle's arms in her right hand and the leg on the same side of the body with her left hand and quickly stood up. Then she started twirling around in the center of the room, faster and faster, angrier and angrier.

"I will teach you, so help me, I will teach you! You will do what you are told. Do you understand? You will listen to me. Do you hear? Now! Now! Now!" Each turn was accompanied by a string of venomous words. The strings got shorter as the twirls became faster. With each twirl, Danielle's free arm and free leg hit furniture as her body passed by it—Danielle's bed post, the toy box (only the leg got banged on that one), Danielle's bureau, Katrina's s bed, Katrina's bureau, Danielle's' bed post again, and around and around until Danielle did not know which piece of furniture her appendages were slamming into. And then in mid-twirl, Ma let go. Danielle's hair streamed straight behind her, like that of a Barbie doll, tossed through the air.

The landing never hurt as much as the airplane ride itself because we were already dizzy and no longer really feeling much of anything except generalized excruciating pain and numbness. Danielle flew into the wall and then slid to the floor. She lay crumpled in a heap. If Danielle had cried, that might have satisfied Ma, who would have left with a kick to her stomach or head and the words, "Next time, do as you are told, and this won't happen to you. It's all your fault for making me mad."

This time, though, Danielle had lost consciousness. Ma's parting words would not be heard, and something about that infuriated Ma. She sprang to where Danielle lay, still crumpled beside the wall, and began stomping Danielle with her feet, kick-kick-kick-kick-kick-kick, over and over and over. Beating us pumped Ma up.

"Wake up, damn you, wake up and listen to me!" Danielle finally opened her eyes, only to close them again, curl up in a ball, and try to protect her head with her arms. With that, Ma seemed to run out of steam, and with her customary final kick to the abdomen, she left the room, warning Danielle never to make her mad again.

We usually had lots of bruises after the airplane rides, but as with all our bruises, neighbors, relatives, and teachers dismissed them as results of klutziness, did not look under the clothing that covered them, or perhaps did not want to know what really happened. And they might not have been really sure where our bruises were coming from because Ma presented such a good image of an involved mother. Moreover, we were not confident enough in our ultimate safety to confide in any of them. In those days, suspected child abuse did not have to be reported as it is today, and Katrina, the only one among us who gave a moment of consideration to calling the police, worried that the 8-pack would be separated and as a result the supportive webbing that connected us lost. If we knew anything, we knew we needed each other. We did not dare lose the connective webbing. So we were left in a tough situation because while there was a door through which we might escape, it seemed to be permanently locked.

Why is Grandma so mean?" Danielle's daughter asked years ago, and Danielle had no answer. Recently, Lizzie, my oldest daughter, in completing her Ph.D. in psychology, has found a plausible, albeit partial, physiological explanation for Ma's worst rages: Pre-Menstrual Dysphoric Disorder (PMDD). If that were the whole answer, then we would have had to worry only a few days a month, not every day. PMDD, if indeed Ma suffered from that, was enhanced by lack of maturity, stress from caring for as many kids as the old woman in the shoe (she, too, would "give [us] some broth without any bread, whip [us] all soundly and put [us] to bed"), and a deep misunderstanding of what "spare the rod, spoil the child" meant together with an incurable need to appear perfect to the community (without knowledge of effective child-rearing techniques, she would use the rod liberally in the attempt to control her children and create the appearance of perfection). PMDD then was not likely an isolated disorder but one of several disorders from which Ma suffered for reasons that her progeny may never be able to elucidate.

PMDD is an inherited disorder, in which anger, which might not be a natural part of someone's personality, emerges as a response to even small irritations right before the menstrual period or during it, and for Ma it seemed to occupy all of those days. As children we knew that although we could not have articulated the problem. What we knew is that if we saw blood on Ma's clothing, it would not be long before our own blood would be spilled.

That gene slid down the matriarchal path into the oldest female in each generation: Ma, me, Lizzie. Lizzie keeps her PMDD under control through medication that was not available in my mother's time. Without knowing about the gene, I nonetheless kept mine more or less under control through my great desire not to be like Ma.

There were failures from time to time, of course. I not only raged against Ma in my childhood, but also in my adulthood I remember a few occasions of overwhelming anger overcoming my strong but fallible willpower. Once was together with Ma when she was visiting and became annoyed at the failure of my younger daughter, Noelle, to learn her homework. Ma's rage, of course, only made the learning more difficult for Noelle and the rage increasingly stronger within Ma. I could feel it building and seeping into me. The rage compelled full attention and obedience. Fortunately, that time Lizzie intervened, as she did so often with her grandmother. Finally, I understood the inability of Dad, whose temperament and interests I inherited, to stand up for us against Ma's rages and why he got sucked into them.

Generally, I was able to divert my rage toward inanimate objects. The older kids remember the day that I threw knives at the ceiling and they stuck there. "Better the ceiling than the kids," I reasoned, to the extent that I was capable of reasoning with raging hormones coursing through my veins.

My husband, Donnie, did not fare as well. On a few occasions, he came face to face with my compelling gene. The first time I felt helpless against it was in Montana when Lizzie was little and Rollie was living with us. I had spent a half-hour over a hot stove on a hot day after long hot hours at the day care center we owned, preparing a seemingly simple meal that even I, as a contender for the title of World's Worst Cook, could not destroy: macaroni and cheese. However, I did apparently destroy it. The macaroni was lumpy, and the cheese was clumpy. Donnie refused to eat it. Instantly, unpredictably, rage took over, and without thinking a second thought, I growled at Donnie, "Fine. If you don't want to eat it, wear it!" With those words, I dumped the entire pot of macaroni and cheese over his head. It was not one of my finer moments.

Another incident, one that Lizzie and her friend Carmen will probably always remember, centers on a cereal box. I do not remember what engaged the rage, but I do remember sending a cereal box sailing in Donnie's direction. He ducked. Carmen, who was stopping by to pick up Lizzie for their daily walk to school, opened the door at precisely that moment, and the cereal box sailed over her head, through the crack in the door, and into the snow beyond. Meet rage personified!

As with the knife-throwing tantrum, generally when my willpower weakened, I was able to direct the rage into the ether, grabbing the hostile environment that I so often found wrapped around me and shaking it. Crusading medical-school doctors, obtuse bureaucrats, and wrong-headed social workers all met the rage gene. Martha Beck, a life coach and former Mormon famous now for her journey away from organized religion into faith (described in her book, *Leaving the Saints*), tells her clients that "anger is the immune system of the psyche, necessary despite its dangerous, volatile energy because it is the only healthy response to injustice."

"You can do it; I know you can do it." The encouraging words came from former Green Beret staff sergeant, Bob (last name unremembered), my closest friend during our military intelligence officer basic course at Fort Huachuca, Arizona. We were running up one of the barren and steep hills that formed the mountain chain separating the United States from Mexico. At the top of the mountain, helicopters waited to lift us off to another training polygon.

The U. S. Army, where I spent two years as a soldier and two years as an officer on active duty, followed by four years in the reserve forces, was a great antidote to the rage gene. First, this being the latter days of the conflict in Vietnam, there was a real political enemy to fight against, or at least to prepare to fight against. Second, there was a perceived philosophical enemy to fight against: inequality of the sexes—I was one of only six women in my hundred-person-strong officer basic course and later one of only two women in the entire Army in the specialty of combat intelligence. Many of the male officers (but thankfully not all since I worked nearly exclusively with men throughout my military career) refused to believe that a woman could understand the principles of combat intelligence. Third, really tired people don't have the strength to give in to the rage gene; they give in to sleep when and if they can get it—and that was daily life in the Army: never enough sleep.

As Bob and I ran up the Huachuca mountains, my whole, 3-month-pregnant body ached with exhaustion. Fortunately, only Bob knew about the pregnancy. Donnie and I had kept it quiet. We had to because pregnancy was an automatic wash-out from military training in the 1970s. Fortunately, since everything military, including the clothes, were too big for my diminutive size, hiding the baby in cloth folds and gear piles was indeed possible. How Bob found out, I do not remember, but he not only kept the matter quiet, he also became a one-person cheering squad to help me continue to try when what I really wanted to do was give up.

I made it to the top of the hill, bent low, and scrambled into the helicopter as the blades whirled over my head. We sat side by side, six of us on each side of the helicopter, belts around our waists, and rifle straps over our shoulders. As the helicopter lifted off, it banked. Facing down toward the earth was quite an interesting experience, especially when I realized that my belt was too big for me and was not holding me in the aircraft. I quickly wrapped the belt several times around my hand, taking up the slack. With my right hand at my waist, keeping me from slipping out the door of the helicopter, and my left hand holding onto my too-large pot helmet which threatened to dive off my head and dash to the ground below, while my rifle dangled from my right shoulder, I must have looked an interesting sight, not exactly how one imagines an officer approaching a battle objective.

Actually, nothing fit me in the Army. My pot helmet nearly reached my nose, my protective mask dangled below my knee, and my butt pack kept slapping me in the back of the thighs. During bounding overlay exercises in the mountains of Arizona, in which several of us would run ahead of the others and then lie down and set up a line of protective fire, followed by those remaining behind then doing the same (an effective tactic for quickly and relatively safely securing an objective), I would always have a little trouble getting up and running ahead again. Once on the ground, my downward-sliding center of gravity from the low-hanging gear would throw me off-balance when I tried to stand up, and my flailing much resembled a turtle on its back. When I was the keeper of the machine gun, matters became worse, especially when I fired the thing. I tried very hard to hold the gun barrel steady with the weight of my body, but unfortunately all I had available at the time was 95 pounds so the firing of the gun generally picked me up a few inches off the ground and the recoil "whumped" me down again, multiple times a minute as the barrel shot off its collection of rounds: whumpity-whump, whumpity-whump, whumpity-whump.

For the most part, though, I managed to keep up with the bigger officers in my training unit. Aside from the small problem of day-long morning sickness, alleviated by occasionally sneaking away from my unit into nearby grasses (not much in the way of woods exists in Arizona), I succeeded at the training. I easily learned to fire all the weapons, and on the weapons test got a perfect score. Leadership problems were my forte, and while I had to fight to take charge in situations in which I was the only woman, my solutions were usually the ones that the training leaders were looking for. After two months, I had completed all the training requirements with a top score and now faced the final portion of the Physical Training test: 40 sit-ups. As luck would have it, Bob ended up being my spotter for the sit-ups. As he held my ankles and counted, I approached the number of sit-ups required for a maximum score. "Thirty-seven, thirty-eight, thirty-nine," he counted, then called out triumphantly, "Forty!"

Bob looked up at the training officer who was marking down the test scores. "Forty," he reported. "Not bad for a pregnant lady, huh?"

"Bob!" I remonstrated him nervously.

"What's the problem?" he asked. "You have just completed the last test and passed the course; they cannot drop you out now. I think they should know the extent of your achievement."

It was from friends like Bob that I not only learned to test my body to its last ounce of strength but also developed a willingness to rely on friends for support. The kinds of learning I had to do in the Army differed significantly from the academic tasks of high school and college. Although leadership skills and combat intelligence require the kinds of out-of-the-box thinking associated with the critical thinking that academic study develops, in general, my tit-for-tats with Ma and the Sunday runs-away-from-Dad prepared me much better for the Army than did any classroom. Clearly, of course, the need to keep on going through all kinds of physical pain in childhood, not to be spleeny, prepared me well for the physical tests of military training. Once again, I could trace the appearance of good to an earlier experience of something bad.

During my Army days, I learned that physical action curbed the rage gene, which rarely appeared in those days. This knowledge about how to tame the rage gene was useful information that helped me forever after. (Of course, I did not even know at the time that there was a name or reason for the massive feelings of anger that periodically cropped up. Nor did I see any pattern to when they cropped up— but Donnie did. His comment on that, though, was often *not* helpful.) It is odd that practice combat would countervail the feelings of rage, but it did, perhaps by giving a meaningful direction and focus to its expression. Or, perhaps it was because the

Army taught me patience, one of the antidotes to rage. "Hurry up and wait" is a military motto, and I found myself in endless lines involving open-ended waiting—at clinics, at the personnel office, on the firing range, for in-processing, and other nearly daily routines.

And then there were the friends. There is nothing deeper or more enduring than a military friendship. Knowing that should we go to war our lives would be in each others' hands creates a camaraderie unlike any other, one in which ten years can now pass as we move along different paths and through unrelated life activities and yet then come together and pick up the conversation where it left off ten years earlier, an experience I recently had in Austin, Texas. Equally important, friends who shared a sense of mission provided a sense of stability that I never found in childhood. They became a great calming influence.

By the time I left the military, I was raged out. Well, almost.

Knowing about the rage gene lets us change our behaviors. As with alcoholics, overeaters, and people who suffer from dozens of other addicting behaviors, addictions, whether they stem from allergies, chemical imbalances, or hormonal disturbances can be controlled. Today many can be controlled with medicine. Back then, they could also be controlled by a commitment not to be taken over by an autonomous or subconscious motivation, a commitment to staying in charge of oneself and being responsible for all of one's actions, for deciding not to rage this one time.

Knowing about the rage gene also lets us forgive the bad things that were done to us while under the influence of that bad gene. Knowing about the presence of a bad gene helps me better understand how Ma could be both very bad and yet very good, for, in spite of her moments of rage against us, Ma had strong inclinations of kindness toward others, helping many children in the community through her work in 4-H, Junior Grange, and petitions carried door to door for school improvements. And, for certain, we were always clean and kempt, as was our house—not an easy task, given a large farmhouse, eight children, and the demands of the fields for daily hoeing, plowing, sowing, or harvesting.

The rage gene, though, did not explain everything because the rage gene hits women only on a few bad days each month. Ma hurt us every day of the month. Her "special days" were the worst, but every day brought a little torment into each of our lives. Finding an explanation for those other days is a topic of discussion any time the 8-pack gathers for our lives were formed in the fires of rage. Understanding it helps us understand ourselves and move on to more tempered experiences.

# On the Wings of Serendipity

Standing nervously in front of the expectant gathering at the little wooden church in Akademgorodok on that Easter morning after Shura's first surgeries, wondering how an atheist would or could address a congregation of believers, my long-standing connection to Russia rescued me. As Christians and therefore members of a community that I had turned my back on as a child, the people standing before me may have been a bit alien to me, but as Russians, they were no strangers to me. By the time Shura entered my life, my peripatetic peddling of pedagogy had navigated me around all of European Russia, including to Moscow and Leningrad, where, in 1982, I was one of only 19 Americans allowed behind the Iron Curtain.

My working travels even, and especially, took me to Siberia on many occasions. Each time I returned, my friends and colleagues would tell me, "We knew you would come back because you left your heart here in Siberia." They were, of course, right. My love affair with Siberia began in the winter of 1984-1985 when I was the first American to conduct research at the Philology Institute of the Siberian Branch of the Academy of Sciences of the Soviet Union in Akademgorodok, and that love affair, the *tyaga* (deep emotional drawing) toward Siberia, has never ended.

Ultimately, I traveled to all but one of the former Soviet republics, where I provided consultation to their ministries of education and conducted seminars for K-16 teachers, professors, and administrators. Each one left a unique impression on me, remarkable in its own right and marked by its own culture.

Of all these locales, Siberia was the place I most loved in the entire world. These folks standing before me in the Akademgorodok Orthodox Church, then, were people I knew. Perhaps not personally—although I did know some of them personally. Rather, they were Siberians, and Siberians share predictable traits: hospitality, interpersonal warmth, a man-against-wilderness willingness to help each other, and an impoverishment of goods together with a richness of spirit. These were among the few people who understood what I meant when, using their own local idiom, I told them that I had chosen Siberian dialects of Russian as my doctoral research topic and had kept returning to Siberia on various pretexts over the intervening 15 years because *norka na menya svistit* (the mink whistles at me), in other words, for unknown emotional reactions and not intellectual reasoning.

For my part, I understood the significance of this gathering, a significance that extended beyond one Good Samaritan and one young man needing help. Russia had just emerged from communism through *glasnost'* to *perestroika*. Less than five years earlier, anyone caught celebrating an Orthodox service would have been arrested and mostly likely jailed. No one in Soviet times carried a Bible or any other religious book openly but rather wrapped in newspaper, hiding it from even an accidental glance of the eyes of a *stukach* (KGB stool-pigeon) coincidentally standing nearby or sharing a metro seat.

Religion, though, had never left Russia. Anyone who knows Russia knows that. The communist extolling of atheism merely drove religious faith underground. A popular political joke during the Cold War times has Brezhnev leaving the USSR for a week on a visit to another country and telling his assistant that while there were few problems in the Soviet Union, if he wanted to occupy himself with something worthwhile during his time as "acting" president, he might look into the "religious problem." When Brezhnev returns, he visits a wooden church in the countryside outside Moscow, not unlike the one I was now standing in, to reassure himself that his assistant could no better handle the "religious issue," especially among the older generation, than could he. To his surprise, he sees a little old lady shuffle up to the church, open the door, spit inside, and leave. Astonished, he hurries back to his assistant and asks what he did. "Oh, once I gave it some thought," the assistant replies, "it was pretty easy. I took down the icons and put up your portrait." Soviet political humor surpassed that of most other countries in its wittiness and ability to zero in on the core of political issues. Yes, indeed, religion (Orthodoxy, that is) had never left Russia.

More than knowing all this, I felt it. I have from time to time been forced to agree with one or another Russian who has solemnly pronounced that I have "*polurusskaya dusha*" (a half-Russian soul). I could feel comfortable with these people even in this church setting in spite of my being an atheist and they believers.

Moreover, I should clearly not have worried about what to say to the Orthodox congregation I found myself in front of that Easter morning. The minute I began to speak, an awed "*ona govorit po-russki*" ("she speaks Russian") ran through the crowd. My ability to use the language effortlessly, along with my rescue of Shura, predisposed all standing there to like me, regardless of whether or not I shared their faith. I shared their language and their love—of things Russian, of this young man, of Siberia—and that was enough.

So, I told them the story of Shura in America. To me, it was a great story of serendipity. To them, it was a story of a great miracle. Over time, I have come to realize that it is both.

Shura represented a significant challenge to anyone who chose to stop. Already a teenager, he had been hospitalized again and again at the local hospital in Akademgorodok. Well-educated by his mother, he had never been able to attend school, but he did play with the neighborhood children, many of whom taunted him for his inability to walk, to combat which he would resort to fisticuffs, developing a strong sense of self-determination and a tinge of pugilism. The sac that contained the end of his spine had never been repaired, and his legs constantly threatened his life with gangrene. At the same time, he was a talented artist. At the age of 12, he had already had his first exhibit at *Dom uchenykh*, (the famous, government-supported House of Scientists that was part of the Academy of Sciences). By the age of 15, he had published both his art and his poetry, had had yet another exhibit at the House of Scientists, and had appeared in a television documentary about his unique talent and life. Also by the age of 15, it was obvious that he would not survive without better medical assistance.

The question as to why I was the one who should help him is fairly clear. By the time that I met Shura, I had borne four children, two of them with multiple birth defects, including Noelle, who, like Shura, was born with spina bifida. I spoke Russian and had also worked for six years in the US State Department. Who better to assist than a mother of another spina bifida child, who knew how to care for such children at home and also knew doctors who could help? Who better to pry a visa out of the U. S. Embassy in Moscow than a former State Department language program supervisor who had trained many of the diplomats working at the embassy? Who better to provide assistance to a speaker of Russian than someone who spoke Russian? Who better to help a child of the cold Siberian winter assimilate into California sunshine than a grown child of the cold New England winters living in California? Who better to help a child from the wooded steppe than an American researcher who had lived and worked in the same steppe, loved the steppe and its people, and knew its literature and its culture? The number of coincidences between what was needed and what I had learned or experienced in my life up until that point was truly amazing. Or was it so amazing?

Looking back, I cannot dispute the contention that my life has been filled with what I called amazing coincidences and what others called miracles. Some even say that coincidences are those times that God chooses to remain anonymous. That God was willing to use an atheist to help create miracles is a miracle in itself. Why God would so bless an atheist only the Almighty knows. How it was done was on the wings of serendipity—the ride of a lifetime.

## Full Measure

I stopped in Siberia to help Shura not from an understanding of mercy for such a concept had not been nurtured within me but from habit. Someone needed help, and it had become my habit to provide help. As with other habits, some force that I could neither define nor escape pushed me in this direction whenever the opportunity arose.

Like my Russian counterparts who did not stop, I did not have the financial resources needed for Shura. In fact, at the time I first stopped, we were raising five children and living on a poverty-level income made even more limited by the overwhelming daily expenses associated with raising two physically handicapped children. That did not matter. Creativity in the face of lack of resources was a lesson I had learned in childhood from a science teacher.

In seventh grade, my science teacher, Paul La Croix, wanted me to enter the science fair, but I declined. Living on a truck farm where my parents were able to feed but do little else for eight children, I knew that there would be no money to buy the supplies for science experiments. Mr. La Croix insisted, however, telling me that science is all around us; it does not cost money. So, together with a friend in similar circumstances, I selected the topic of optics and took on the challenge of creating a science fair project out of nothing. Mary Ann and I made prisms by using pieces of broken window glass and gluing black paper to the flat sides of the glass in order to force the light through the prism in a cohesive ray. We also built a light enclosure out of kindling wood and wool scraps for showcasing a glass of water to illustrate the refraction of light on dust particles, imitating the effect of the atmosphere on the rays of the sun as they passed through it. Yes, Mr. La Croix was correct: one could create a nearly free science project. Our pleasure with our home-made devices turned to embarrassment, however, when we arrived at the science fair and saw the fancy equipment our classmates had purchased. We wanted to leave, but Mr. La Croix would not let us. He caught us sneaking out the door with our cardboard box of prisms and display parts and marched us back into the auditorium. Ashamedly, we laid out what we had brought, eying all the time the fancy blood circulation demonstration in the booth next to ours; the parents of our classmate had clearly laid out a pretty penny to buy the machinery for his demonstration. As the evening wore on, though, we stopped comparing our awkward-looking homemade apparati with the sleek kits of our classmates because we became too busy answering the insightful questions of the judges who clearly enjoyed the topic of optics as much as we did. They came back several times to ask follow-up questions. When those judges awarded us first place, we were astonished. Mr. La Croix was not. He knew that by having to design a no-cost project, we would learn much more about science than we ever could from a commercial science kit. I learned something else that day, too: it is not what you have that counts but what you do with it.

So, I never questioned whether I had sufficient money to help Shura because I had internalized Mr. La Croix's science fair lesson. I had a different kind of resource: talents and skills of various sorts, creativity, a growing network of friends and ac-quaintances with financial means and good connections, and an irrepressible trust in the general goodness of people. There is an apt Russian proverb: "*Ne imei sto ru-blei, a imei sto druzej*" (Don't have 100 rubles, have 100 friends). One hundred rubles I certainly did not have. One hundred friends I did.

I find new friends wherever I go. Rather than buy expensive souvenirs with money I don't have, I bring home only that which I stumble across: abandoned snail shells from the Borjomi mountain springs in Soviet Georgia, a rock from the Yam-bash River near Turkmenistan's border with Iran, a turquoise tile from a 14th century mosque being repaired in Samarkand, Uzbekistan. More important to me—the real keepers among my memories of any country—are the people I stumble across. With many of them I have developed long-term friendships. That is how I have built the networks that have leaped into action on behalf of those who need help.

The significance of my proclivity for focusing on people, not things, became very clear while traveling with a colleague to Samarkand. He had come with me to Tashkent, the capital of Uzbekistan, to co-teach a two-week, school-to-work semi-nar for school principals from across the country. To thank the two of us, the semi-nar sponsor treated us to a trip to Samarkand, a city dating from 2000 B.C.

My colleague was delighted at the prospect of visiting this beautiful, historic city, a place that has changed names and nationalities on many occasions over the intervening four millennia. It came to look something like its present-day self when Amir Temur (known in the West as Tamerlane) successfully forced Genghis Khan out of the region, established the first schools (Muslim *madressaat*), mosques, and a library. Three centuries later these early establishments served as the beginnings of modern Uzbekistan. Today, these buildings, in their maintained 14th century form, together with the cavernous observatory and immense telescope built by Amir Temur's grandson Ulugbek, comprise the core of a unique tourist attraction.

I had been to Samarkand before. At one time, I had done much faculty devel-opment for local school teachers and the professors at Samarkand University. Very much liking Samarkand and its people, I was always ready to visit again.

My colleague, a typical American, said that he would like to be housed in a "nice" hotel. I, on the other hand, chose to stay with a family, any family. So, the sponsor picked out a family for me. When our tour guides took me to the family, my colleague was with us. Out came Bella, the mother in the family where I would be staying. Upon seeing me, she exclaimed, "Beth, they did not tell me that it was you who would be staying with us!"

Bella knew me from my days of providing consultation to the administrators at the University of Samarkand where her husband works. He had helped me in copying materials I needed for a lecture, and I had ended up at dinner with Bella and him.

I replied, "And I thought I was going to be staying with strangers. What fun that they found someone I know! This is a wonderful surprise!"

To my words, my American colleague responded, "It's not a surprise." He looked at Bella and explained, "Some people collect stamps. Beth collects people."

With Shura, I would need my people collection. Indeed, hundreds of friends— old and new—and strangers-turned-friends would join in the endeavor to help him. The networks I had built sprang into action, but they would not have been enough. To them were added many other, new acquaintances, who, upon hearing about Shura from one source or another, queued to help. Could so many people lining up to help Shura really have been an accidental collection?

Perhaps even my involvement was not accidental. At the outset, I thought I stopped because I have always chosen to stop and help. What I ascertained about myself much later, however, is that my heart apparently knew what my mind neither knew nor would have believed at the time: I probably chose to stop because God expected me to stop. I was used to God's taskings and to God's help even while I was oblivious to both. Most of us are oblivious to "whatever privileges life has handed us," according to Carol Tavris and Elliot Aronson, authors of *Mistakes Were Made— But Not By Me: Why We Justify Foolish Beliefs, Bad Decisions, and Hurtful Acts*, for "privilege is our blind spot."

God not only tasked me but also gave back to me in more than full measure. Listening to the latest episode in my life, my Damascene friend, Dr. Omar Imady, when dining with me at my house or his house or at some restaurant in Amman, Jordan where we lived and worked together over a two-year period, would solemnly tell me, "God spoils you."

Dr. Omar, to use the appropriate Arabic form of address, was right, but I never admitted it in those days. In fact, I was unaware of Luke 6:38: "Give, and it will be given to you. A good measure, pressed down, shaken together and running over, will be poured into your lap. For with the measure you use, it will be measured to you."

From divine taskings, I developed a sense of self-worth, self-confidence, and the dogged determination that came from "knowing" that everything in life will turn out well if you just keep working at it. These were unrecognized blessings as well as developed character traits that I would need to traverse the five decades of rocky terrain known as my life. Good measure I did receive, again unrecognized, in the networks of friends who have rushed to my rescue whenever I have stumbled, animals that have followed me around as if I were the pied piper, and employees who have always happily given an extra effort. Perhaps these rewards came precisely because my heart was listening to God even while I was rejecting God intellectually.

One of the most remarkably rewarding experiences of my life took place over a period of several years in Belarus and mostly through the hands of another Good Samaritan, Pyotr Volkovich. In 1986, the nuclear reactor in Chernobyl, Ukraine melted down, releasing a cloud of radiation into the atmosphere. That cloud traveled over the Ukraine, where it contaminated the rivers and reservoirs and made Ukrainians sick for years with throat cancer and other radiation-induced diseases. The cloud then passed from Gomel, the twin city of Chernobyl, located on the Belarus side of the Ukrainain-Belarus border in what was then the Soviet Union, over all of tiny Belarus to Finland. From there, the changing air currents pushed it south, back over Belarus to Gomel. On Gomel it dropped its highest load of radioactivity.

When I came to visit Minsk, Belarus in 1989 with a group of school children from Portland, Oregon, whom I had been asked to accompany as interpreter and guide, I met Pyotr, who was then the vice president of the Belarus Peace Committee. (Government-sponsored Peace Committees that involved individuals, even children, in promoting the ideas of peace in opposition to a West perceived as warmongering could be found in nearly every Soviet city of any size in those days. One of the most poignant pleas for peace came from a young child in a drawing contest sponsored by one of the peace committees. He drew the earth against a clear blue background and then etched the frame of a house around it. Across the top, in a child's awkward hand, appeared the words, *u nas net drugovo doma*—we have no other home.)

Pyotr could have been an adult version of this child in his fervor, dedication to peace, and love of his Belarusan home. Belarus needed him for when I came to visit Minsk in 1989 25% of the children in Gomel were already ill with poisoning from direct exposure to radiation that descended from the Chernobyl cloud and indirect exposure that came from eating produce grown in irradiated soil.

Ill also was Sasha, the ebullient husband of Zinaida, director of School #54, who came to be a friend of long duration. Sasha was a chemical engineer of portly proportions who had been sent poorly clad to the Chernobyl reactor station to measure the output of radiation post-accident. As a scientist, he was aware of the exposure he was getting but could not convince the government to take more protective measures. In 1989, he predicted his imminent demise from his earlier extensive exposure to radiation although at that time he looked healthy.

Pyotr, in contrast to bear-like Sasha, was a mouse: barely five feet tall, thin, and well past seventy. However, when he spoke of the needs of Belarus and how to save its people, especially the children, his eyes sparkled mightily and he radiated energy from an inextinguishable source that made him seem twice as tall and half as young. Pyotr gave me a list of medical supplies and equipment desperately needed by doctors and hospitals to cope with the growing number of cancers from radiation. I published that list in an international newsletter that I edited and thought no more of it until I met Pyotr a year later in Portland, Oregon.

Pyotr had brought the Minsk Superintendent of Schools (whose name I have now forgotten), Zinaida, and some children from School #54 to Portland on an exchange visit. The school administration in Portland was unable to communicate with Pyotr, Zinaid, and the superintendent of schools. So, the Board of Education asked me to come and assist as interpreter as well as to finalize the binational and bilingual exchange agreement that I had drafted and negotiated with the Belarus Ministry of Education the year before.

Pyotr himself was in Portland to be the keynote speaker at the 1990 International Rotary Foundation Convention. I remember parts of Pyotr's speech word for word, first because he asked me to interpret his speech, about which I had not been forewarned, and second because of what he said. He talked about a loss of 25% of the population in Belarus during World War II and how now, in the 1990s, Belarus was about to lose another 25% of its population, mostly children, because of the aftermath of Chernobyl. He ended the speech by presenting the Rotary Foundation with the serial plate from the last surface-to-surface missile disassembled under the SALT treaty. The room thundered with applause. Pyotr stood there, waiting for the applause to die down.

Then he began to speak again. "All around the world there are bells," he said. I translated the word *kolyakolya* as *bells* nervously because talking about bells made no sense to me. I wondered if perhaps there was another meaning for that word.

Pyotr eased my worry, though, as he continued. "They are large bells, warning of impending nuclear disaster. I did not bring you a big bell, though."

With these words, he pulled out a very small bell and rang it. "I brought you a small bell. To hear the sound of this bell, you need the silence of peace."

Needless to say, Pyotr's speech brought tears to the eyes of this group that was still struggling with a re-envisioned Soviet Union during the last days of *glasnost* and *perestroika* and barely a year before the *putsch* that would put Yeltsin in power. It was, indeed, a *smutnoe vremya* (time of troubles) in the Soviet Union, a term that the Russians use in alluding to a parallel time in history, when from 1584 to 1613 Russia experienced a period of unrest, rapid turn-over of leadership, no legitimate heir to the czar's throne, and a short period of Polish domination. During the contemporary *smutnoe vremya*, the Soviet Union was trying to find itself and re-define the nature of its governance. As we now know, the Soviet Union would ultimately find its future only in its past as Mother Russia. America was simultaneously redefining its relationship with the changing Soviet Union in confusion and hope. So, it is not surprising that the thought of peace with the Cold War enemy evoked an emotional response from the gathered Rotarians.

What invoked a greater emotional response from me was when Pyotr described how he had given me a list of medical supplies and equipment and how, within a few months of that, everything that the Belarus doctors needed and more began to arrive from the United States and from Europe. Pyotr gave me much credit for this fortunate situation, but in reality, I had only published the list. Something greater than I had apparently touched the hearts of those who read it. Readers had got in touch with the Peace Committee directly; no one had come through me. The twin emotions of guilt at not doing more and pleasure at having been an instrument for others' contributions pulled at me as I interpreted Pyotr's words.

When I returned to Minsk in 1993, Sasha was dead. He had spent the last six months of his life no longer sustaining anyone with his merry laugh but medicated to the point of stupor to mask the excruciating pain of death from radiation poisoning.

Children were still dying even though doctors were now better able to care for them. Pyotr, though, excitedly described a program he had put into place that took the children from Gomel to Germany every summer, thanks to the willingness of Germans to sponsor them. In this way, they reduced the children's level of exposure to radiation. That was a start. It was akin to having two fish and five loaves of bread to feed a starving multitude. What I did not know was that within six months of my visit there would be a modern-day repetition of that miracle.

In 1993, I was the president of the Global Studies Institute, a small organization dedicated to improving education world-wide, and was in Minsk at the National Humanities University to assist the authors from the Belarus Academy of Sciences (Anatoly's institution mentioned earlier). Joining me but arriving a few days after me was Dr. Rebecca Oxford, then from Columbia University. She couriered $5000 USD, at the time a considerable amount of money in Russia, to pay the annual salary of the Moscow representative of the Global Studies Institute, who was to meet her enroute at Sheremetovo Airport in Moscow. The salary was to be paid in cash, the only way to handle such matters back in the tumultuous days of the new *"smutnoe vremya."* Unbeknownst to Rebecca, I had fired the Moscow director upon my arrival in Moscow, having determined that he had done none of the work assigned. However, I was willing to let Rebecca pay him for the past year. In those days, there was almost no way to contact someone traveling to Russia, so there was no way I could have stopped her from paying him. Oddly, he never showed up to receive his salary even though he had signed a receipt for it when I was in Moscow. Fortunately, Rebecca could not track him down. So, she arrived in Belarus with a wad of money. Again, fortunately, I had nothing else to do with the money so I handed it over to Pyotr for unrestricted use in his Peace Committee programs. Pyotr, in his typically humble demeanor, was highly grateful, and six months later I received a note from the president of the Belarus Peace Committee in which the exultant blare of trumpets could be heard behind every word. The money had been combined with additional money from an organization in Germany and with in-kind donations of labor, material, and land. As a result of the in-kind contributions and benefitting from a highly advantageous exchange rate for foreign money, the Peace Committee was able to move 52 families from the highly irradiated areas in Gomel to a new village it had constructed outside of Minsk.

Not one, but two, unexplained fortuitous happenings that required vast amounts of money took place within four years, during which modest funds and international networking touched a multitude of lives and saved a community. Was it all only good luck?

## Poverty

Captive to a many-childrened dynasty, Dad's family evinced a history of great failure to achieve potential. Dad was simply one in a chain of talented people with unrealized dreams. He grew up on a farm in the countryside outside the small town of Londonderry, New Hampshire, where most people thought that his mother, a talented pianist, would attend a conservatory—indeed, she was offered a scholarship— and become a national celebrity. In spite of such an auspicious opportunity and a great talent, she never left Londonderry. She spent the rest of her life mothering five children and coping with the loss of two others, premature twins who died soon after birth.

All I remember of Grandpa is that he was always asleep on the couch. A young father during the Depression, he was unable to feed the five children he fathered (well, wth the twins, actually seven). So, he pulled his older sons out of school when they turned 14, convinced that eight grades of education was enough, anyway, and sent them into the factories to bring home the bacon to the family. Thus began life-long on-and-off work as a shoe cutter for Dad.

One might be quick to condemn Grandpa for setting his children up for failure. Yet, learning that as a nine-year-old he had accidentally observed his own father commit suicide created for me a sense of sadness for a man who thereafter never fully engaged with life. He seemed to see no future for himself or his sons other than to focus on mere survival because emotionally he himself had not survived his childhood.

As for Dad, he had excelled during his short stint as a radioman in the U. S. Army Air Force in WWII, where he was promoted rapidly. However, Dad did not want a soldier's life. When the war ended, he moved to the riverside town of East Gloucester, New Hampshire, where he opened a radio shop that he expanded to servicing televisions when they appeared in the early 1950s.

Shortly thereafter, Dad met and married Ma, bought my grandparents' house, and moved his radio shop into the garage, which became an engaging place for Katrina and me to learn radio theory with Dad, in his happier days, as our tutor. That did not last long, however. Immediately after their marriage, Dad, who always said he wanted a dozen children, and Ma began producing children faster than Dad could produce money from radio work. So, at Ma's insistence, like his mother before him,

Dad gave up his love and his talent for the needs of his family and returned to cutting shoes. Even that, though, did not bring in enough money to feed his growing family. Six (of what would eventually be eight) hungry mouths later, we moved to a farm in the foothills of the White Mountains, from which Dad made a daily commute for the rest of his life back to the coastal shoe factories. Although that did not solve the income problem completely, the farm at least fed us, and our crackers-and-milk suppers from town life were replaced with more substantial meals.

I have often wondered why Dad failed in his television business when others with lesser talents thrived. Was he afraid to rise above poverty level? Was he incapable of learning good business practices? Was he afraid of being disliked if he were to ask a decent price for his time or insist that people pay their bills? I suppose I will never know the reason, but the fact was that he (and we) never rose above poverty level.

If we were to have a chance at even a tentative touch of the "things" of childhood that our peers had in scads, sacrifices would have to be made, and Ma did make them although I have also wondered if she did not at times resent having no more than a couple changes of clothing—one or two outfits for farm work and one for going into town—and no leisure money. Once a year we went on a day's vacation to a local beach. In a moment of splurge, Ma worked out a deal with the church pianist to give us piano lessons. As the oldest, I benefitted the most from the financial sacrifices and scraping, including not only the piano lessons but also transportation to regional and state music competitions, where I usually placed but not at the very top. By the time the boys reached my age at each phase of childhood, there was rarely money left for them. The last piano player was Willie. After Dad's death, my younger sisters were raised in the pure poverty that all welfare children experience.

Given this background and my inclination toward humanities, not business, I was probably not destined to be a financial genius. After all, I had no models. As Robert Kiyosaki and Sharon Lechter note in *Rich Dad, Poor Dad*, we learn very different approaches to finances, depending on our fathers' approaches, predisposing us to emulate their successes or repeat their failures. That we all in the 8-pack were at least able to climb from the lower class to the middle class is testimony, more than anything else, to our willingness to work hard enough to overcome the poor example from our childhood.

When I first applied to colleges, I knew that financing an education would be a problem. The poverty that had greeted me at birth had nipped at my heels most of my life like a frightened but swaggering Chihuahua attempting to bolster its own self-confidence. Nonetheless, being an incurable optimist, I assumed that college funding would appear from somewhere. It did. As a result of high SAT scores and my having been selected for *Who's Who among American High School Students*, the University of New Hampshire (UNH) wrote to me and promised me four years of education, fully covered by scholarship. I considered UNH, but it was an unacceptable option because it would keep me near home. More than anything else in going to college, I was looking for an escape from home.

So, I applied to Penn State University even though the entrance requirements for out-of-state students were extremely rigorous (top 10% of the incoming student body) and out-of-state tuition way out of reach. Penn State had accepted me but had not yet responded about the possibility of financial aid when I received the unsolicited offer from UNH. At the advice of my high school guidance counselor, I sent Penn State a copy of the letter from UNH. Someone from the Penn State financial aid office wrote back to me and told me not to worry, that all my education would be paid through a combination of scholarships, loans, and work study. Soon thereafter, the financial aid office put together a package that took care of my first year in full, with the indication that subsequent years would be similar—but they weren't.

From a financial aid point of view, I made the catastrophic error of marrying Donnie my sophomore year instead of waiting for graduation. (My children were appalled to learn that pragmatics, not romance, prompted the wedding. We wanted to share rent, and no one in those days would lease to an unmarried couple.) The financial aid officer at Penn State who told me that being married would not make a difference was wrong. It did make a difference. While my marriage has lasted 38 years, my scholarship petered out in less than 38 weeks. "Giving scholarships to married women," the older, male financial aid officer who had taken over my account said, "is a waste of money. They just sit at home, doing nothing with their lives but living off men. So, go home, and take care of your husband."

I went home all right but not to take care of Donnie. He seemed to be handling that well enough on his own. Rather, I assessed my situation, looking for an out-of-the-box solution to the dilemma of having only a few weeks of financial aid left and two years of courses to complete. The answer came quickly—I have trouble thinking *in* the box; sometimes, I have trouble even finding the box!—so it did not take long to figure out that the 78 semester hours I still needed in order to graduate would break easily into 39 semester hours during each of the following two quarters, both of which were paid for by already-granted aid. Thanks to an advisor who paid little attention to students with A averages, considering them skilled enough to make their own decisions, a non-computerized course tracking system at the time, and a secretary willing to keep secrets, I was able to enroll for triple the maximum course load, tiptoe under the radar with my 3-page grade reports, and graduate after only 2 2/3 years.

Then Gram gave me a small "loan." With that and income from cocktail waitressing in the evening and go-go dancing at night, I even had enough money to fund the first quarter of graduate school.

"Don't pay the loan back," Gram said. "Pass it on." I have done that on many occasions in my life, passing along as well the philosophy of not paying back but passing on whatever kindness is shown.

Gram was quite unlike Ma, and sadly Ma did not return Gram's affection until Gram was in the hospital on her deathbed. A woman of hefty proportions and traditional haircut so unremarkable that I do not even remember it, Gram was a kindly matriarch. When she spoke, one obeyed. The liberating thing for me, though, was that she did not hit. Moreover, she listened, and when she spoke, she had fun ways of expressing herself, like looking for something "all over hell's kitchen." Throughout my preschool years, she fascinated me with nursery rhymes that she never tired of telling over and over and, when I was older, with an old gramophone that we wound up to play records that would gradually slow down, turning the singer's peppy voice into a drawn-out wail as the winding ran out. The games, songs, and rhymes that Gram taught me are ones that I now find myself teaching to my own grandson. When Ma would call me her "plain Jane," Gram would respond, "Pretty is as pretty does." During my penny-starved early college days, Gram would write to me every couple of weeks and include a package of Dentyne gum under whose wrapper she had inserted a five-dollar bill. So, it was not surprising to me that Gram was the one who would come to my rescue when I had fallen on the petard of the financial aid officer. Gram came to my rescue years later, too, moving in after third child, Shane, was born and doing my housework for a month. "No one should come home from the hospital the day after a baby is born; you are in no condition to do housework" she scolded. "You play with the baby. I will take care of the house and the kids." And she did.

Ironically, I might not have attended graduate school, had I not lost my undergraduate scholarship. Had I taken the slow route through school, Donnie, being a year older, would have finished significantly ahead of me and taken me to Montana from where his first job with the U. S. Forest Service beckoned. By graduating nearly a year and a half early, I had to wait for him for three quarters. During that time, I took all my master's courses, this time only doubling the course load. My teachers, advisor, and department chair all understood my financial dilemma and did their best to help me by letting me finish as many of the requirements each quarter as I could handle. So, I left for Montana with Donnie, with only my master's thesis left to complete, which could be done from afar—and was. Talk about getting the last laugh on the financial aid officer!

The Chihuahua had not disappeared, however. Although I did beat it from time to time, I never vanquished it. By the time I became a special needs parent for the third time—this time with the welcoming of Shura into our house, at least for as long as he was able to stay in California—poverty and I had become old friends.

From childhood, poverty fell very low on the discomfort ladder for me. There was food after the move to the farm, and there was clothing because my grandparents worked at a textile mill. I, too, worked there as a teenager. We girls learned to make our own clothes, and some of our creations even became popular styles at school. All of us learned to harvest crops, preserve food, make butter and ice cream, and cook. As soon as we could reach the pedals, we learned to drive a tractor and took turns mowing and raking hay. We also learned how to yoke the oxen and use them to plough the fields in the spring. In the summer and fall, as soon as we were old enough to recognize the difference between a ripe vegetable and berry and an immature one, we were put into the fields, both our own and those of neighbors who hired us to work at three cents a pound for harvested peas, beans, and blueberries. Thus, we acquired good skills and a strong work ethic. In this respect, our parents did well by the 8-pack for they poverty-proofed us. One can never be truly impoverished if one has skills, talents, and diligence—and, as the Russians say, 100 friends.

As a poverty-proofed adult, I have rarely felt an overwhelming need for money. Whenever I have truly needed money, it has fallen into my lap. Even when I did not ask anyone for it, even when I did not know that there was Anyone to whom I could turn, the money to stave off potentially dire consequences often appeared from unexpected sources just in the nick of time. A guidance counselor would suddenly be in need of having several items of clothing hemmed. (Only much later did I realize that her requests for hemming had less to do with my sewing skills, which were marginal at best, and more to do with her desire to help one of the poorest students at the university.) Ma's cousin, sent me a $20 bill on a number of occasions, saying only that she had felt that I was in need of a little cash—and always she was right. Scholarships appeared out of nowhere. I remember receiving a $300 scholarship from the Class of 1942 for which I had not applied. When I asked what I should do with the money, I was told it did not matter—buy 300 milkshakes if that is what appealed to me. I bought clothes.

Thanks to intervention after intervention, the Chihuahua would grow weary at times and lay down to rest, allowing me to make a good life, including travel to foreign lands without a cent in my pocket. Well, more accurately, I usually did have some cents (although many might have questioned my sense). The first summer I spent in Russia I took $20 with me and returned with the same twenty-dollar bill.

The little Chihuahua followed me into marriage and throughout most of my married life although I was able to bootstrap my children into a higher socioeconomic level than I had experienced as a child. They have become members of the middle class (except for the handicapped ones who, because of their extensive medical needs/expenses, have not been able to remain above the poverty line).

One of my present-day friends who read an early draft of this book told me that she could not imagine my having lived in poverty because on the surface all seems so swimmingly well now. What few know is that I am still often one step away from financial disaster. Every so often Donnie and I have to dig ourselves out from under a new financial avalanche. It is that tenacious little Chihuahua at our heels again! For example, I scrupulously saved $14K for transition costs from Jordan back to the USA in 2006. Fearing difficulty accessing our Jordanian bank account once we arrived in the States, I asked Shane to put the money into his bank account in California. Before I returned, however, the University of San Francisco Hospital, to whom Shane still owed thousands of dollars for five kidney surgeries that had been required earlier for our grandson, immediately found the "spare change" and, with court permission, withdraw every penny.

That is only one example of the kind of bad financial luck that we have experienced every few months over the past 38 years of our marriage. The result has been nearly no ability to save money for a rainy day or to take a vacation. Rather, we are content with getting through each month with enough money in the bank to take us to the next pay day and the ability to help our kids when they run into financial difficulties. Since the seven-dollar beating and Ma's candy gobbling in my childhood, a desire for money and possessions has never arisen (although Donnie would always like to have "just a little more.")

Sometimes just a little more might have been nice. For example, lack of financial resources on my family's side meant that I had to finance my own wedding. Since we were both college students at the time, to say that any plans Donnie and I drew up had to be simple is an understatement. Our wedding was to become my first foray into learning how to do much with nothing, a skill that has stood me in good stead as a wife, mother, and traveler. The selling of our used textbooks funded our wedding rings. I had really wanted to keep those books, books being one of the things that I value, but choices and priorities had to be made. Books could be borrowed; wedding rings could not. Being underage in Pennsylvania made some decisions easier and cheaper. We eloped to nearby Maryland; elopement cut costs considerably. Gram realized that we probably did not have the resources to set up housekeeping, and so her wedding gift to us was a treasure trove of household equipment: mop, broom, dustpan, pots and pans, cooking utensils, and the like. We very quickly came to appreciate her pragmatism.

A year later, after graduation from college, we moved to Montana, and the Chihuahua came along. During the summer, we enjoyed a cozy apartment above the apartment of the elderly matron who owned the building. However, once snow had wrapped up the mountains, Donnie was out of work. I was due with our first child, Lizzie, who fortunately was born early—appropriately, on Labor Day. Two weeks later, I picked up a job substitute teaching English, drama, and Spanish at the local high schools. My $20/day on-again, off-again checks for subbing, though, did not come close to replacing Donnie's Forest Service income, and so we quickly realized that we needed to find a creative alternative to paying rent.

The Chihuahua watched as Donnie and I negotiated a deal with a local rancher who wanted to spend the winter in warm Florida. We would keep an eye on the ranch in exchange for free living space in an A-frame he was building in one of his fields. We moved into a wooden matchbox with tar-paper covering just before the rainy season hit and spent a few weeks with a wall-to-wall pots-and-pans floor covering to catch the water that leaked through the roof. Lizzie was allowed to ambulate only in a round walker that protected her from the steaming pot-bellied stove in the middle of the only room we had. The kitchen sink was a dish pan, and the faucet was a sand-point well outside from which we drew water by lowering a bucket nailed to a long pole. The outhouse was unique; that is probably the most accurate description I can give of it. The doors had not yet been built, so Donnie fastened overlapping burlap bags to the frame as a form of enclosure. Nonetheless, because the little building had been built too narrow, his knees would poke out through the opening where the burlap bags came together. We did have a garden, and that eased our food bills. Donnie chopped the wood for the wood-burning stove, on which we also cooked our meals, and trouble-shot electrical problems whenever the light bulb at the end of a 500-yard series of electrical extension cords running from the ranch house across the field and, through a crack that meant that the door was always open, into the interior of the A-frame, burned out. To those who have never met the Chihuahua, this lifestyle might seem repugnant. We, however, remember it even now with fondness. You gotta love that "Chihuahua." It brought us so many memorable experiences!

Later, the Chihuahua helped to bond a growing family. As more children joined the family circle without an accompanying proportionate increase in salaries, there simply was not enough money to go around. So, one evening a week, we would hold a family meeting to make important decisions: since we could not afford both at the same time, should heat or electricity be considered the priority for the coming week? Sometimes we all decided that a particular child's specific need for something for school or a fee to participate in a particular activity was more important than either. Of course, given Noelle's neurogenic bladder, before we could spend a dime on food, we had to spend a dollar on pampers. That was a given, and no one resented it. School tuition came first when the kids were little and the gifted ones in need of special programs. Later, home-schooling helped meet both their learning needs and the requirement to manage financial exigencies.

All of this experience was great preparation for life in Siberia both for oldest child (and, therefore, most poverty-proofed), Lizzie, and for me. The Chihuahua, fortunately, did not come with us to Siberia, but he did not have to. Making-do was and is an inseparable part of Siberian life.

Poverty did not keep me from realizing my dreams of teaching and traveling. Nor were *my* dreams the only ones realized.

In 1987, Donnie was also able to fulfill his one and only childhood dream: hiking the Appalachian Trail (known to through-hikers as the A. T.) from Georgia to Maine. Certainly, his life had prepared him well for such an endeavor. At Penn State, he earned a degree in forest science, and in the early days of our marriage, he worked for the U. S. Forest Service in Montana and Idaho. As a result, he was well equipped to manage survival needs and well versed in forest lore to pass along to Shane, who, at the age of ten, became the youngest through-hiker in A. T. history.

Our entire family became outdoorsmen very early on, thanks to Donnie's attraction to the forest. Even before her birth, Lizzie became used to the rhythms associated with backpacking, hiking, and kayaking. When she was six weeks old, we wrapped her in multiple layers of down and wool, double sleepers, long underwear, coat, and blankets, and headed for a weekend of nineteen-below-zero snow camping at Yellowstone National Park. (Ironically, today, after a childhood in the snows of Montana, Moscow, and Siberia that should have prepared her to react otherwise, Lizzie shivers when the temperature dips below 32 degrees.)

Shane quickly became a backpacking partner for Donnie. The other children joined the dream as a support team. Hiking the A. T. became a family project.

In late March, Donnie quit his job, outfitted himself and Shane with the proper hiking gear, and spent a few weeks hiking the local hills in preparation. In early April, all of us headed south to Florida to visit Donnie's grandmother prior to dropping Shane and Donnie off at Springer Mountain, Georgia, the southern head of the A. T. It turned out to be a prescient trip since Donnie's grandmother died two weeks later. He would not learn this, however, until he emerged on the other side of the mountain and called home to let the rest of us know that the first miles of the hike were completed. That meant that he missed her funeral. More important, though, he had seen her while she was still alive, and she had seen him and her great-grandchildren. Had there been no plan to hike the A.T., very likely Donnie would not have had a chance to see his grandmother for a last time for her death was natural but unexpected.

For the next six months, Donnie and Shane hiked up and down the Appalachian Mountains. They took the trail names of Huff and Puff. Huff (Donnie) was considerably overweight when the hike began; hence, the name "Huff"—which is what he did with every step in the beginning. Puff (Shane), on the other hand, seemed to float over the hills like a puff of thistledown. Every couple of weeks, the other children and I would shop for backpacking food, bundle it up, and if I could squeeze an additional $20 out of our meager income, include a pack of Dentyne gum with the money slipped underneath its wrapper as Gram used to do. Sending these packages was the only leisure activity that we were able to accomplish during the 6-month period that Donnie and Shane were hiking—that and my production of a periodical newsletter, "The Trail Notes of Huff and Puff."

Since Shane was technically skipping school, the care packages also contained his next reading assignment: Thoreau's *Walden Pond*, Hawthorne's "Evangeline," and other literary works focused on the regions through which he was hiking. He also kept a journal of his experiences. Many years later, in moving, I came across the journal and saw there a note that illustrated how the experience had bonded his father and him. He talked about running out of food because "Huff" had not hiked fast enough, and so they trekked to a nearby stream where Donnie put together a makeshift fishing pole with forest remnants, dug up worms, and produced two fish for their dinner. Shane's comment following the description of Donnie's innovative approach to forest survival was "And to think that this is *my* Dad!" (Shane today is also quite an innovative survivalist, skills he clearly started to acquire on the trail.)

While fulfilling the dream brought many intangible benefits to the whole family, not just Donnie and Shane, some people (particularly those who did not know us) might have considered it a foolish financial move. Trying to raise a family of four even for six months on one salary in the Washington, D.C. area was considered nigh onto impossible, and it turned out to be impossible for us, too. I took on a night job with the AAA Supernumber, helping stranded motorists nationwide find road service. It was the ideal moonlighting job for me. I could work while the kids were asleep. Lizzie was old enough to babysit, and we were in a safe apartment building in which the supervisor was very good at keeping an eye on the tenants. I managed to catch 3-4 hours of sleep between my job at the State Department and the beginning of the AAA nightshift. When I got off AAA work, I would return home, wake up the children, get them ready for school, then go to work at State Department. The extra money from AAA paid for the food we sent to Donnie and Shane and for the mailing of it. My salary from State Department covered our regular bills and expenses, which we were able to lower considerably by changing our diet: macaroni and cheese became our daily meal. Meat was a rare event, and we would celebrate our occasional hamburger or hot dog dinner. Donnie and Shane hiked 1000 miles (80%) of the trail before the winter set in and a fall from a rock outcropping damaged Donnie's knees, sending them back home with a wonderful experience behind them: a dream fulfilled and a father-son bond built. As for me and lack of sleep, I would tell friends, "Sleep is overrated." At times during those six months, friends would wonder how we would survive these six months. How we would do that, I agreed, was unclear. However, as always, I had great confidence that somehow we would, and somehow we did.

Poverty has a different feel when you have chosen it, rather than it having chosen you. The ability of poverty to limit the achievement of one's personal or professional goals is controlled only by how one defines poverty. Not long ago a definition went around the Internet that pretty much coincides with my view. According to that definition, "if you have food in the refrigerator, clothes on your back, a roof overhead and a place to sleep, you are richer than 75% of this world" and "if you have money in the bank and in your wallet and spare change in a dish someplace, you are among the top 8% of the world's wealthy." By that definition, I am rich.

That little Chihuahua is not a bad little guy at all. His nipping at one's heels reminds one that money is not the most important thing in the world. As the Russians say, 100 friends well outweigh the value of 100 rubles, especially when there are young Siberians to be rescued. Learning to outwit the Chihuahua teaches creative, out-of-the box thinking, skills that can improve any family situation, help dying children to survive, and enhance any career, introducing one to work opportunities all over the world. That is what the Chihuahua of poverty has done for my life. What a great gift was sent to me!

## *Akademgorodok*

Back on that Easter morning where I had been introduced to the congregation as a Good Samaritan, I went home with Shura's family and his godmother, Natasha Petrova, after the church service. There all of us prepared for a gala evening as I became acquainted with Shura's family through Natasha's and Shura's excited, nearly frenetic attempts to introduce me to all aspects of the life that Shura had experienced prior to coming to the United States.

Natasha was slight in both stature and build, with straight long hair, resembling an American hippie of the 1960s not only in dress but also in temperament. She worked as the Siberian director of Open Society, a non-profit educational foundation with branches in dozens of cities of the former Soviet Union, sponsored by George Soros, the internationally famous Hungarian-turned-American investor.

During the years, 1993-1997, at the request of the Ministry of Education and the Ministry of Higher Education, I conducted seminars for educators in Russia and a number of the former Soviet republics. George Soros paid for many of these seminars, and, after the Ministry of Education translated one of my books into Russian, he paid for its printing and distribution throughout Russia, Ukraine, and Belarus.

It was through one such seminar that I had become acquainted with Natasha and through her with Shura's situation. In 1993 at a seminar I was conducting in Krasnoyarsk, a delegation from Novosibirsk, of which tiny Akademgorodok was considered a distant suburb, came to Krasnoyarsk to study with me. The delegation was headed by Natasha.

Natasha and I are not all that unlike one another. Although extraverted, we can both at times appear to be quiet but fight tooth and nail, take on any individual privately or publicly, and valiantly wave the flag wherever needed for a cause that we consider right. Natasha used her professional positions to improve the delivery of education and the social conditions of life—and she fought against her bosses and co-workers when she thought that they were wrong. I used my position as mother to bring change to public school districts that disadvantaged handicapped children, to change the behavior of hospitals that gave up on dying children, and to provide child care assistance to parents in rural areas as well as to parents of children with physical impairments. Where Natasha used an organization in which she held leadership roles, I founded new organizations. We both served as advisors to those capable of making change. She assisted George Soros, who spared no money in his attempts to improve the education and hence change the political system of the former Soviet Union. I, while a graduate student at Renboro University, assisted the office of the governor of the state of Pennsylvania in its attempts to improve the quality of life and social support for children with developmental delays.

Meeting Natasha, then, was like meeting a sister, and it took nearly no time before I found out that she was a sister in other ways, too. The heads of regional delegations, an American colleague, and I sat at the center table at meals during the 1993 Krasnoyarsk seminar. It was not long before Natasha and I struck up a personal conversation. Learning that she was not only from Novosibirsk but from Akademgorodok itself, I asked her if she happened to know Dr. Aleksandr Ilich Fyodorov.

Academician Fyodorov, was the highly respected head of the Philology Section of the Institute of History, Philosophy, and Philology at the Siberian Branch of the USSR Academy of Sciences (SOANSSSR). In 1985, he had served as my *kunsooltant* (advisor) when I was conducting dissertation research at the Philology Section and had become a dear friend.

"Of course, I know him," she replied to my question. "He was my *nauchnyj rukovoditil'* (graduate student advisor) when I was at NGU (Novosibirsk State University)."

I was happy to hear that Natasha knew him because I had a favor to ask her. "Would you tell him that I did receive the letter he sent to me last month?" I asked. "I did not get a chance to answer it before leaving to come here because my daughter, Noelle, was in the hospital. However, I will answer it upon return, and I can help him with his request."

"Certainly, I will tell him," she responded, then added, "Why was your daughter in the hospital?"

"Nothing dramatic," I said. "She has spina bifida and so ends up in the hospital periodically for one thing or another."

"Spina bifida?" Now Natasha was genuinely interested in the conversation. "My godson, Shura, has spina bifida. He is already a talented artist, but he is frequently in the hospital. The doctors are now telling us that his days are numbered, mainly because of infections and gangrene in his legs for which we have no antibiotics."

Then and there plans were made to try to bring Shura to the US for care. I promised to find out what was possible. The rest is, of course, history.

In addition to Natasha, Aleksandr Ilich, whom I addressed by name and patronymic (Aleksandr, son of Ilya) in the traditional Russian way of showing respect, had promised to come to the party at the Ivanovich home. I had not seen him in ten years. He was now 70 years old, beyond the 67-year average life span of Russian men of that time. I had been told that the intervening years had not treated him well.

Outside, the long rays of the setting sun turned the snow-powdered buildings, nestled in the birch-and-*kedr* forest, pink-red, like scenes on Christmas cards. It may have been Easter, but in Siberia, a land of long winters, it felt like Christmas, New Year's, and Easter all rolled into one—a most splendid holiday feeling. I waited with the anticipation of a child sitting before a Christmas tree on Christmas Eve for Aleksandr Ilich to appear.

A few hours later, we were all seated on the couches that typically doubled both as beds and as table benches in Soviet homes. Pulled up to the couches were three small tables, heaped with *sibirskie pelmeni* (dumplings with a special Siberian shape and flavor), *pirozhki* (little fried or baked meat pies), *borshch* (beet soup), *shchi* (cabbage soup), cucumbers, pickles, caviar, herring, raw salmon, salami, bread, wine, and, of course, vodka and cognac for toasting. Toasting is a very serious matter in Russia, with toasts being long and plentiful, each toast requiring that everyone completely drain his or her shot glass and then quickly down a pickle as a chaser. Shura's parents, Lara and Lev, their seven children, Natasha, Aleksandr Ilich, and I, in that order, sat down around the tables, eager to share an evening meal and talk. Talk we did! In true Russian style, we ran into the early hours of the morning. There was so much to share—with Shura's family his life in America, with Natasha commonly held professional interests, and with Aleksandr Ilich ten years of each other's lives.

I felt like I already knew Shura's family although this was the first time I was meeting them. I had, of course, met Lev in Moscow when we discussed the plans for bringing Shura to the United States. I met Lev a second time when he brought Shura to our home and lived with us for a month. The two of them shared a bedroom, both for solidarity and because even our large 13-room house was bursting at the seams with our four children and the other people we had taken in.

After Lev had left, Shura had told me story after story about his idolized older brother, Sasha, his younger brothers, Pyotr, Andrei, and Mikhail, and the two little girls whom he adored, Yulia and Maria—all of whom I was now seeing with my own eyes. The matriarch of the home was Lara, and she was indeed in full control of all seven children. A teacher in the local schools, she taught Shura at home and was the person who instilled strong faith in all the family. Many phone calls took place between Lara and Shura when he first came to our home, and subsequent phone calls took place between Lara and me when medical, historical, or behavioral issues needed to be worked out. Meeting Lara was the high point of the trip back to Siberia for me. I could hardly wait for the next day when she and I, two mothers of one child, could spend hours exploring Shura's medical history and childhood pictures.

Sitting beside Aleksandr Ilich at dinner, I felt transported to ten years earlier. I had been prepared for a worst-case scenario when people told me that he had not survived these intervening ten years well. However, when he arrived, he was dressed in a clean, well-worn green suit of the type that Soviet academics typically wore—and wore and wore until they wore out, availability of new suits always being unpredictable. He was tidy, with a forced spryness, and radiant with smiles. Surprisingly, he was freshly clean, not a typical attribute of Siberian folk for good reason. All three utilities—heat, hot water, and electricity—were rarely available on the same day. So, I felt singularly honored by the effort he had made in preparation for our meeting. Clearly, given the trusted reports of his emotional and physical difficulties, he had not only put on his best suit of clothes but his best suit of emotions and energy, as well.

I had become somewhat of a celebrity in Akademgorodok, and Aleksandr Ilich clearly enjoyed telling stories of what I was like in "the old days" when my proficiency in Russian was labored and when I knew nothing about Siberia. Indeed, in the intervening years, I had changed much. Russian and English had become equally accessible communication systems for me, and I had come to consider Siberia an alternate home.

Aleksandr Ilich told about the harshness of the winter of 1984-1985. He described how he rescued me from the University of Novosibirsk cafeteria, where the only meat on the menu was squirrel. Of course, squirrels in Siberia are not the tiny, gray delights of American parks but rather something closer to brown rabbits in size and color, so one harvests more meat from them.

Aleksandr Ilich also told about how Lizzie and I did not know how to cross-country ski. Since everyone in Siberia learns to ski as soon as they can walk, his descriptions of our attempts to learn—skiing ahead of me, Lizzie would fall and I would often end up in a heap on top of her—evoked hearty laughter. He talked about how readily I fit into the daily routine at the Academy of Sciences and carried out the role of a junior academician and how Lizzie was given her own desk and assisted me in research. This so astonished all of the academicians that I had to disabuse them of the notion that American schools teach 12-year-olds to conduct academic research. Aleksandr Ilich was clearly pleased and proud that someone he had helped years earlier had returned that help to a much-admired young member of the Akademgorodok community, and his quiet storytelling was a side I had not seen earlier from this man of few words.

Alas, his wife, Natalya Timofeevna, a scholar and academician in her own right and the more verbose of the two by far, could not be with us. I recalled how she used to scold me that Lizzie's down ski suit could not possibly be warm enough for the 75-below-zero Siberian winter because it felt so light. My taste buds remembered well the tasty *shchi* and *borshch* she made for Lizzie and me; hot soups were highly appreciated on Siberian winter days. Natalya Timofeevna would spend hours in an evening telling me in her clearly marked northern Russian dialect about her days in

Leningrad during the WWII blockade that the German Army began in September 1941 and ended in January 1944. The melancholy-infused stories brought back to life person after person, friends, acquaintances, and strangers, more than 600,000 Leningrad residents in total, who died from starvation. Survivors suffered lack of fuel, water, and electricity. Transportation ground to a halt. Children, since they were least likely to be noticed by the Germans, were sent to sneak past the blockade to nearby Lake Ladoga to bring back water. The children often died accomplishing this task. I remembered with relief her story of how she herself was eventually evacuated via the *Doroga zhizni* (Road of Life) that ran across Lake Ladoga eastward toward Siberia. The dolor of Natalya Timofeevna's absence sat with us throughout the evening, at times speaking in loud tones.

"She suffers from *skleroz* (Alzheimer's) now," Aleksandr Ilich told me. "She does not even recognize me much of the time."

I felt sad for him. He had always been devoted to her and now attended her faithfully even though she no longer knew who he was. What a lamentable denouement for what had been the brilliant mind of a significant contributor to the famous 17-volume *Encyclopedia of the Russian Language* and author of many books and articles!

Had it not been for the joint connection of Natasha and me with Aleksandr Ilich, the topic of spina bifida would not have come up. Had that topic not come up, I would never have learned about Shura. And, of course, I would not be at Shura's house with Natasha, Aleksandr Ilich, and his parents on this Easter Day evening, discussing all of the things that happened to bring him to the United States, all of the things mentioned above, and all of the connections that had to be made in order for his life to be saved. Tenuous connections, very tenuous!

(These tenuous connections would become even more significant. Two years after our lunch in Krasnoyarsk, Natasha would develop cancer and herself need the services of the University of Virginia Hospital, the medical facility that ended up caring for Shura.)

Our reverie of past events, of my personal and professional experiences in Siberia and elsewhere post-Siberia, and of the remarkable journey of Shura from Siberia to the United States that brought him from near-death to full health concluded all too quickly. The dinner at Shura's house ended without our noticing how uncomfortable the minimally padded Soviet couches had become. Even as midnight approached, it seemed far too early still to say good-bye to Aleksandr Ilich.

It was to be the last time I would see him, and somehow I sensed that at the time. His health, I knew, was not good. As the evening waned, so did his appearance of sprightliness. From discussions of his health, it was clear that much of his evening vigor came from the excitement of seeing me again, ten years after he had seen Lizzie and me off at the Novosibirsk Airport. Further, my opportunity to return to

Russia has always been iffy. Especially during the Cold War years when the United States was considered an enemy nation and few Americans were allowed behind the Iron Curtain of the Soviet Union, one always assumed that the current visit might be the last. So, the evening had a bit of a bitter ending although the hours of conversation and reminiscing had been sweet.

Now I am grateful that I had the opportunity that night to bring some sunshine to a lonely and kind man who had led a life other than he wanted. Sent to the U.S.S.R. Academy of Sciences in remote Novosibirsk rather than to the metropolitan Leningrad where he had done his doctoral work, he worked in an esoteric field, contributing nonetheless in brilliant ways to the general work on linguistics being conducted by colleagues in Moscow and Leningrad. He spent his last years caring for a beloved wife and lifelong colleague who no longer recognized him, while professionally stymied in getting his most recent books published because of lack of paper in the new Russia. Still, once upon a time he had met an American and through that connection had been a participant in a miracle that touched the hearts and deepened the faith of many people living in the wooded steppe of the Ob River. That knowledge buoyed him that evening and, I am told, for some time beyond.

Aleksandr Ilich and Natasha departed for their homes, and it was time now for bed. Going to bed in Russia is always a complicated matter because Russian apartments are small. The couches used for sleeping are not sofa beds, not by the greatest stretch of the imagination, but couches with wooden frames, which are not all that uncomfortable if one is used to the Russian style of sleeping on a thin mattress and under a featherbed-like cover. The cover was actually quite warm. A two-ply sheet with a diamond-shaped hole cut in the upper layer was stuffed with a blanket, making a Russian-style featherbed—without the feathers, of course! The combination was very comfortable, much warmer than most blankets on American beds.

With seven children, a huge family by comparison to the typical one-child Soviet family, the Ivanoviches did not fit into one apartment, and so the Soviet government had given Lev and Lara two apartments in order to accommodate all the children. I slept on a large couch with the little girls in the "primary" apartment with Lara and Lev. Surprisingly quietly for boys, Shura and his brothers went to bed in the second apartment across the hallway.

Seven children in Siberia was a handful, and splitting them between two apartments could have been fraught with troubles. Peace reigned, however, in this powerfully bonded family. It was the faith of Lara that sustained the faith of the family, a remarkable feat in the atheistic Soviet Union. It was the faith of the family that remained confident that God would send someone to help Shura. They just never expected that God would send them an atheist from the West!

I stayed with Shura's family for a couple of weeks. The time was far too short, but it was enough to give me a good sense of how Shura had grown up. It was still the school year. So, Shura's siblings had to go to school the next morning, and his parents, of course, had to go to work. So did I.

Part of what made my participation in the trip possible was the request by the Soros Foundation for me to give lectures to local educational establishments. So, in the mornings, I, too, would get up early and prepare for a full day of activities. I split my time between two programs: the Russian Orthodox Gymnasium (high school for college preparatory students) where Lara taught and the public schools system's health education instructional program. I worked with both groups on the same topic: how to adapt lessons to individual students' cognitive needs so as to maximize each instructional hour. As always, I enjoyed working with the teachers, so much so that none of us really noticed the snow falling outside, or when it did not snow, the dipping of the temperature to tens of degrees below zero. I would never complain about the snowy weather, anyway. The snow is a big part of the charm of Siberia.

In the evenings, the children, Lara and Lev, and I would all gather around the kitchen table and eat Siberian *pelmeni*. I watched Shura make ice cubes in a tray he designed. Putting ice into his drinks was one of many American behaviors that Shura had assimilated during his time in the States. It was not one that was readily accepted in Siberia because Russians do not put ice into their drinks; they consider it bad for the stomach. We talked about the ways in which Shura's behavior had Americanized and the ways in which his heart was still Siberian. Like mine.

## One-Way Tickets

My role in Shura's story took first root ten years earlier when I came to Akademgorodok as a young graduate student to work under the direction of Aleksandr Ilich at the Siberian Branch of the USSR Academy of Sciences. This was unheard of at the time. Americans simply did not spend time in Siberia during the Cold War. I was, in fact, the first to conduct research at the Philology Section of the Institute of History, Philosophy, and Philology, thanks in large part to the intervention on my behalf by Aleksandr Ilich.

Getting to Siberia was no easy feat. In 1984, *Inostrannyj otdel*, or *Inotdel*, the foreign student office, at Moscow State University (MGU), where I was enrolled as a graduate student in the dialectology program, controlled every movement of the dozen or so visiting scholars in the USSR, the sum total of American students/researchers that the Soviet government allowed behind the Iron Curtain that year. It did not help that I had brought Lizzie with me, and she would need a visa and ticket, too.

When I asked *Inotdel* for permission to go to Siberia, I was refused. "No one goes there," I was told. "You can do your research at Lenin Library, and you can consult with the dialectologists at the U.S.S.R. Academy of Sciences in Moscow."

While they were right about no one going there, they were wrong about my need. I had to go there to do the research for my dissertation: *The Semi-Dialect of Russian in the Ob Areal Region.* I had read everything available at Lenin Library during the fall semester, and I had conferred extensively with the dialectologists at the Academy of Sciences' Moscow dialectology section under the direction of Academician Dr. Sofia Bromlei, a kind woman who deserved every ounce of respect she had earned as the country's eminent dialectologist. Her erstwhile plea for me to change my dialect of interest to one less complicated linguistically and politically fell on deaf ears. I was fascinated by linguistic change in Siberia, and studying the dialects on site was the only way to explore that change and the reasons for it. To do so, I needed to be in a city along the Ob River to collect data from the people who spoke the dialect. The most obvious choice was to be placed at Novosibirsk State University (NGU) and work with the Siberian Branch of the Academy of Sciences.

Fall semester came to an end. Snow fell in Moscow, and blizzards raged in Siberia. "This is not a good time to go to Siberia," argued the officials at *Inotdel*.

"I'm from New England," I told them. "I like snow. I was born in a blizzard, and for nearly every birthday during my growing-up years, I was treated to a blizzard. So, please, *do* throw me in that briar patch!"

My university advisor, Dr. Sofia Konstantinovna Pozharitskaya, who had earlier managed to get me pulled out of the simplistic Russian for Foreigners classes and enrolled in graduate school in the dialectology program along with my Soviet peers, stepped up to the plate for me once again. Sofia Konstantinovna knew that the most valuable dictionaries of Siberian dialects had been compiled by Aleksandr Ilich, with whom she was acquainted from national dialectology conferences. She contacted him, and he agreed to help. Armed with his assistance, she went to *Inotdel* and told the officials that a room had already been reserved for Lizzie and me at NGU and that Aleksandr Ilich was adjunct faculty there so there should be no problem in this being considered a university placement. The latter connection was important since I was a doctoral student, not a professor, and therefore could not be placed directly at the Academy of Sciences.

*Inotdel* reluctantly obtained the visas. The woman who headed the office looked—and acted—like the broad-shoulder, orders-barking female lead of the Russian movie, *Komendant (Commandant)*. Tall, blonde, and not particularly good-looking, she seemed particularly irritated with me that I had brought Lizzie to Moscow with me although she had never seen her. On several occasions, this *"komendant"* had said, "Perhaps we will get the visa for you, and you will leave the child here in Moscow" and "*Inotdel* does not take care of children; your child is your responsibility." Her attitude was out of keeping with the typical Russian love for children. Likely, it reflected her annoyance that an American had managed to sneak behind the Iron Curtain—and bring a child with her.

She threw up a final barrier. "There is a problem with tickets," she said. "We can reserve only one-way tickets to Siberia for you and your daughter. If you purchase them, you will have to negotiate return tickets from there if you can."

"I'll take them," I said, not realizing how difficult it would be to get return tickets. I was simply not going to accept any barrier, including one-way tickets. I reasoned that we were not being exiled to Siberia. We were going there by choice for a reasonable purpose. I was confident that we would find our way back to Moscow. We did, albeit with some difficulty and only *after* our visas had expired.

I was grateful to Sofia Konstantinovna and Aleksandr Ilich for everything they did to bring me to Siberia. Now, reflecting on Shura's story, I have to wonder if it was only by the chance help of kind people that I was able to break down all the walls of resistance and travel to a land frozen not only by climate but also from external contact during the frosty days of the Cold War. Had I not gone then, I surely would not have gone later. Had I not been assigned to that branch of the Academy, I would not have met Aleksandr Ilich, who became an important link in Shura's story.

Working at the Siberian Branch of the Academy of Science is one of the most fascinating and rewarding things I have done. The academicians were stellar researchers, and I was in awe of their contributions to the field. When I finished my time there, I had to give a 45-minute report to the collective body of academicians and invited professors from the university. In presenting the research I had completed on their dialect, I found myself in an unnerving position in spite of all their kindnesses to me while I was working there. Their treatment of me like any junior Russian academician, a treatment that has little in common with the manner in which American academics relate to each other, made the awkwardness worse. My presentation was followed by questions from all those in attendance. The questions fell like pelting rain from a cloudburst, one after the other in rapid-fire order, some of them piercing, others insightful, few of them easy. That discussion was followed by a 45-minute public evaluation of my report by Aleksandr Ilich, who later sent me a written evaluation of my performance to pass along to my supervisor (not that I had a supervisor who could read it since it was written in Russian). If nothing else, the time there did much to help me build a bond with the people and land of Siberia and, equally important, improve my Russian language skills.

The need for speaking Russian saddened Aleksandr Ilich. When we went to his home for lunch and dinner, nearly every day he would spend our walking time chatting in English. He had learned English during WWII from reading technical manuals for the American airplanes he was flying as a navigator. Once at his home, of course, we spoke Russian with Natalya Timofeevna. At the Academy, we also spoke Russian even though all the academicians used English books in their research. Aleksandr Ilich would chide them on missing the opportunity of a lifetime: to speak English with a native speaker.

One of the senior academicians put the problem into clear perspective. "One native speaker in our lifetime shows up here, and you think we could possibly speak English to her? No, this is not only beyond my capacity but also beyond importance for once she leaves, we will not hear English again." Under conditions of the Cold War, he was right. It would take the dissolution of the Soviet Union before Americans and other Westerners would begin to show up in Akademgorodok.

Akademgorodok turned out to be a breath of fresh air after constant KGB surveillance in Moscow. There, I often wished that there was some way for academics to play the game that I am told military attachés had played for years, if not decades, with their KGB tails. An attaché would be very careful not to lose his tail, something that Lizzie and I never learned for we were very skilled at losing anyone following us, some of it through scatterbrained approaches to learning our way around the byways of Moscow and some of it through real skill when it was important that we not be followed for fear of getting a friend or a helpful colleague into trouble. In gratitude for always being able to follow the attaché without difficulty, the KGB agent would give the attaché an occasional "day off." The day was designated by the attaché walking slowly along the street and, when no one was looking, placing a bottle of vodka or cognac on the sidewalk. If the KGB agent picked up the bottle, the next day would be the day off. Each departing attaché would tell his replacement, and so the game continued, at least until the end of the Cold War.

When Lizzie and I first walked down Morskoi Prospekt, the 6-block-long main street in Akademgorodok with which intersected Prospekt Lavrentyeva, named after Mikhail Alekseevich Lavrentyev, the first Chairman of the Siberian Division of the USSR Academy of Sciences, we immediately felt the absence of Moscow. The elevated militia posts on poles at the beginning and end of each street were unmanned, and people talked freely about anything they desired. Surprised, I asked Aleksandr Ilich about this.

"What can the Soviet government do to us here in Akademgorodok?" he asked. "Exile us to Siberia? We are already here!"

Dear Aleksandr Ilich! He had helped us so much. He became our best friend in Siberia—my research advisor, father figure, and teacher. What I learned about Siberian language and culture had come first from his books, which I had read at Lenin Library. Then in person he filled in many missing pieces for me, providing a foundation that I would build on for years and am still building on.

He was like most Siberians that way. In a land where everyone has to fight against the harshness of the climate, being one's brother's keeper takes on literal meaning and action. Even strangers would help us out. One taxi driver, in particular, I remember with intense gratitude.

Lizzie and I had been in Akademgorodok for a while when I realized that we had better go the airport, the only place we could get a return ticket to Moscow. Our visas would run out soon, and we had come on those one-way tickets proffered by *Inotdel*. With the airport 75 kilometers away, we would have to go by bus. Of the two buses in town, one went to Novosibirsk, originally named Novonikolayevsk after Tsar Nicholas II, the third largest city in the Soviet Union. The other went to the Novosibirsk/Tolmachevo Airport. Both cost 75 kopecks for me and 25 kopecks for Lizzie, exactly one ruble all told. That was good. I had only 10 rubles left to my name. I had traveler's checks, but the bank in Akademgorodok was unable to cash them. I was hoping that I would be able to do that at the airport. Having obtained the departure schedule for the bus, Lizzie and I set off for the airport.

At the airport, getting the tickets was not as easy as I thought. All tickets to Moscow were sold out until after our visas expired, and there was no way to extend a visa while in Akademgorodok. Well, what we were to do? Purchase the tickets for the earliest day possible and worry about the visas later! (When we got back, Aleksandr

Ilich told us not to worry about the visas; no one would be checking—and besides, what would they do? Send us to Siberia? Like everyone else in Akademgorodok, we, too, now were already there! And so we overstayed our visas, with no questions ever asked.)

Once we had purchased the tickets, we returned to the bus stop. It was not there. The stand where the bus had pulled up earlier was a drop-off spot only. There was no pick up. I checked out all the other bus stops. At a tiny airport like Novosibirsk's Tolmachevo, there aren't many. One bus driver noticed my obvious confusion and opened his door,

"*Kuda khotite?*" (Where are you looking to go?)

"*V Akademgorodok.*" (To Akademgorodok.)

"*Akh, nu, avtobusa netu.*" (I see, well, there is no bus.)

"*Dolzhen byt! My syuda na avtobuse iz Akademgorodka priekhali.*" (There has to be! We came here by bus from Akademgorodok.)

"*Da. Syuda priezhaet, no tuda ne vozvrashchaetsya.*" (Yes, the bus comes here from there, but it does not return there.)

Along about that time, the driver of a taxi parked nearby came over and asked if he could help. I explained our dilemma: we had come to the airport by bus from Akademgorodok, never dreaming that there would not be a bus back. He offered to take us. I would have agreed with alacrity. However, all I had to my name was nine rubles since the airport had been unable to cash our traveler's checks. Certainly, a 75-kilometer-trip would cost at least 30. I hesitated, then explained my dilemma to him. He smiled and said that he would take us for nine rubles. (I had forgotten about Lizzie being with me and how most Russians will do anything to help children.)

Taking us to Akademgorodok along the road between Tolmachevo and Novosibirsk and then along the Ob River was a long trip in and of itself. When we came across unexpectedly derailed cars from the Trans-Siberian Railroad, which crossed the Ob two blocks from our dormitory at Novosibirsk State University and then sped eastward across the open steppe, the trip became considerably longer. We had to turn around, go back to the airport, and find back roads to Akademgorodok. The trip wound through the woods and passed a Strategic Rocket Forces airbase that we were not supposed to know about, especially in the days of the Cold War, as we wended our way back to Akademgorodok for more than two hours.

Along the way, Lizzie and I chatted in English. Surprised to hear a foreign language, the taxicab driver asked us, "Are you speaking Czech?"

We said no and admitted that we were Americans, speaking English. The trip immediately became more interesting to him. He had never met an American before and was full of questions—just as many questions as the Soviet media was at that time full of propaganda. The driver's good deed turned out to be very educational for him. He returned the meter to its starting point three times, and when we reached our dorm at NGU, he proudly announced that the meter read nine rubles. We handed him nine rubles, along with a pack of American cigarettes that we often carried as a bribe, Russian cigarettes being distasteful and unhealthily unfiltered. To that, we added American coins for his nephew and a few other pieces of Americana that we happened to have on us. He was pleased. We were pleased. The Russian Good Samaritan may have lost 20 rubles, but he gained much that day that he has probably never forgotten. At the time, I told Lizzie that we were really lucky to come across this particular taxi driver. Now I wonder if we really owed our rescue only to Lady Luck leading us to one kind Siberian Samaritan.

Eight years after spending wintry days in Akademgorodok, researching Siberian dialects under the tutelage of Aleksandr Ilich, I found myself in Krasnoyarsk, another Siberian city, lecturing to administrators and teachers at the request of the Siberian Ministry of Education, which hoped to make some radical changes in its educational system. Krasnoyarsk, an industrialized city with a population of one million people, located an hour south of the famous Divnegorsk hydroelectric dam on the Yeneisei River, east of the Ob, and in the northern *taiga*, contrasted vividly to the 8-block town of Akademgorodok. The people, though, were the same sort of warm, kind, and supportive colleagues, and I was able to establish a working bond that lasted over a period of several years of come-and-go lecturing there.

At one point, I was given a choice of conducting a seminar in Krasnoyarsk, St. Petersburg, or Moscow. I chose Krasnoyarsk, and when I arrived there in the middle of the winter without gloves, having forgotten about the tens-of-degrees-below-zero temperatures, one of my friends who met me at the airport pulled the mittens of her hands and handed them to me, saying, "We knew you would choose Siberia."

Of course, she was right—and why not? Any Siberian I know will hand you the mittens off his or her hands in the middle of the winter!

More frequently than with any other institution in Russia, I worked with Universe School. Headed by Dr. Jacob Freeman, an unusually innovative school principal, Universe School was a K-12 laboratory school for the University of Krasnoyarsk, overseen by the Department of Educational Psychology, where I had upon occasion lectured to the faculty.

Jacob turned out to be a lifesaver. On my first trip to Krasnoyarsk, which I made jointly with a colleague, I ended up in Moscow with two huge boxes of books and handouts for the seminars that a colleague and I were to conduct there. At Domodedovo Airport, the domestic airport serving Siberia and the southern cities of the former Soviet Union, I found to my consternation that nowhere did I have my ticket to Krasnoyarsk. It had either been left at the counter when I checked in for the Moscow flight in London or I had forgotten it at home. Computerization of ticketing was not a feature of airlines in Moscow at the time. Since I had no way to prove I had a ticket, I would have to purchase a new ticket, as well as pay overweight charges for the books. The total amount was high. My colleague and I put our resources together. It was enough either to purchase a roundtrip ticket or to pay for the books and purchase a one-way ticket. My colleague wanted to leave the books behind. I was comfortable with taking my chances on being able to get out of Siberia. So, we took the books, and once again I went to Siberia on a one-way ticket.

As anticipated, I was rescued. When Jacob learned of the situation, he purchased a return ticket for me with Universe School funds. That was not quite fair in my mind, and so I made a deal. Instead of returning the cost of the ticket later, I would find an equivalent amount of hard-to-acquire Western books that he needed for the school library and send them to him. This was definitely a win-win situation, especially since I found many of the books at library sales and was able to purchase multiple times the value of the ticket in books for an amount equivalent to the cost of the ticket. More than that, when people heard what I was doing, neighbors, colleagues, friends, and even libraries donated books, resulting in a treasure trove for Universe School. Seeing how so many people benefited—the school children from the books and the donors from a sense of contributing to a worthy cause—I considered myself very lucky to have lost that ticket! Or was it really luck?

A few years later when I was at a conference in Kemerovo, a Siberian mining town, I continued the tradition of one-way visits to Siberia. Shane was with me on that particular trip, and I was quite pleased to have a round-trip ticket for each of us in hand. When we got to the Kemerovo Airport, I bragged to Shane, "This is the first time I have been in Siberia on a roundtrip ticket."

A stickler for details, 15-year-old Shane looked carefully at our tickets, then up at me. "Don't be so sure, Mom," he said. "These tickets are for yesterday."

As usual, Someone watched over us, and we made it out of Kemerovo even though we did not have everything we needed in our possession. In this case, I asked to speak to an administrator of the airlines. Because there was a child involved, the airline waived its rules and let us fly space available on the next plane out. Even officials in Russia make special cases when children are involved.

## Moscow

Watching Lara with her children brought back many memories of my days as a Soviet parent—of Lizzie. Nothing was easy for Soviet mothers, and nothing was easy for me, either. Just getting Lizzie into school was a matter of pitting an American mother against Soviet bureaucracy.

We had taken the normal approach in the beginning: asked the American Embassy to submit paperwork for Lizzie to be enrolled in any appropriate Soviet school. Now, of course, this was not a "typical" request in those days. American children very rarely attended Soviet schools, and so the embassy rarely was involved in obtaining approval from the Ministry of Education to enroll them.

Clearly, getting Lizzie into school was not going to be easy. After three weeks, the American Embassy had made little progress with the USSR Ministry of Education, but the Cultural Attaché was able to tell me that the paperwork was on the Minister's desk. Armed with that knowledge, I prepared for the battle ahead. "Don't worry," I told him. "I am certain that the Soviet government is used to working with diplomats, but I doubt that it has ever met a mad American mother."

I asked our friend Sveta, who had enrolled in Moscow State University and moved from Krasnodar with her daughter years earlier, about the process of enrolling a child in school in Moscow. It turned out to be a matter of getting a *napravlenie* (enrollment permit)from the Main School Directorate. Of course, I needed a school to which to send Lizzie. Friends recommended School #77, somewhat distant from the university but conveniently located near Mosfilm Studio for the many students in the school who were actors in the famous studio's movies. So, I dressed Lizzie in a pretty pink dress since we had not yet been able to obtain a school uniform for her, tied her hair in big pink ribbons, and took her to meet the director of School #77.

The director talked to me for some time, determining why I wanted to enroll Lizzie in her school, while the teaching staff looked at Lizzie's American textbooks to determine what grade to put her in. That decision caused some consternation: Lizzie had skipped two grades at home, and her textbooks indicated that she should go into seventh grade in Russia, where the children would be two years older than she. Although I explained that she was used to studying with older children, skipping grades was just not done in Russia. I left the decision of whether to put her in an age-appropriate level or an ability-appropriate level to the school director. She chose the latter after a brief discussion with Lizzie, whose Russian language skills impressed her, even more so after I told her that Lizzie had been studying Russian for all of two weeks.

The next step was to go to the Main School Directorate and, with the concurrence of the director of School #77, to get the *napravlenie*. Off I went, towing Lizzie in pink dress and ribbons. There we met a kind, elderly lady who sympathized when she heard that Lizzie had not been able to go to school for two weeks. Quickly she pulled down a book from her shelves and flipped open to a map of the Soviet Union. "Where is she transferring from?" she asked me.

"*Iz Vashingtona* (from Washington)," I answered.

She searched in vain for the name Washington on the map. Then the light dawned. "Etot *Vashington* (*That* Washington)?" she asked.

When I nodded, she informed me that I had come to the domestic transfer division and that I needed the foreign division. Since she had already filled out the forms, she handed them to me in order to make the work of the foreign division easier—and that ultimately made obtaining the *napravlenie* easier.

In the foreign transfer office, I explained the need for the *napravlenie*. When asked about the permission from the Ministry of Education, I noted that the paperwork from the US Embassy was on the desk of the minister. Rather than prompting further action, this caused the bureaucrat with whom I was talking to hesitate. I quickly realized that I was not going to get the *napravlenie* unless I could find some way to convince this woman to give it to me. "I am sorry to seem impatient," I told her. "It is just because Americans love children and value education. I hope you understand."

Of course, she understood. These were very strong *Russian* values. "We do, too," she responded and signed the *napravlenie*, remarking under her breath, "I wonder if we will ever get the ministry paperwork."

Whether she did or not, we never found out. However, Lizzie did spend some amazing months at School #77, getting to know her classmates and forming some close friendships. She excelled in her science and math classes, as she did back home, was unsure about her applied arts classes, especially sewing and mechanical drawing, and found her foreign language course, English, understandably quite easy but her grammar and composition course, Russian, understandably quite difficult.

Thanks to Sveta, I knew what to do to get Lizzie into school. Thanks to Sveta, Lizzie was adequately prepared for school. Thanks to Sveta, I grew to know Soviet society and, more important, Soviet people very well.

Sveta and I had become acquainted two years earlier. When I showed up in 1984 in Moscow with Lizzie in tow, Sveta already knew who she was and eagerly awaited the opportunity to meet her and introduce her to children's life in the Soviet Union. To Sveta's delight, while waiting to get Lizzie enrolled in school, I still had to go to my own classes at the University of Moscow, where I was taking a graduate course in dialectology. Concurrently, I was conducting research for my dissertation at the *Dissertatsionyj zal* (the dissertation archives) of *Biblioteka imeni Lenina* (Lenin Library) downtown. So, Lizzie would have been alone for long periods of time had not Sveta, a graduate student in the field of philosophy, watched out for her. Sveta also gave Lizzie indirect lessons in Russian that stood her in good stead in her early days in School #77. Sveta knew no English so all communication was in Russian, and Lizzie picked up the language by necessity. When she started attending school, Lizzie already had a comfort level in communicating and sufficient tolerance of ambiguity in the language not to panic when she did not understand.

Sveta and I were bonded by our daughters, Sonya and Noelle, and by Sveta's brother, who lived in the same *sektor* (wing) of the university that we did. Although I never met Sonya, who had moved back to Krasnodar to live with her father shortly before I became acquainted with Sveta, I felt like I knew her because she, like Noelle, suffered from hydrocephalus, colloquially known as water-on-the-brain. Although Sveta never met Noelle, she felt like she knew her because both her brother and Noelle coped daily with paraplegia. Until I showed up with Lizzie, we had only pictures through which to share our families. Now I had a real child with me, Noelle's sister, Lizzie. Sveta promised to bring her real McCoy, Sonya, from Krasnodar so the children could play together. Like most graduate students, we had great plans for ourselves and for our children.

The three of us had not spent many hours together, however, before Sveta was diagnosed with tuberculosis. I urged her to stay in Moscow where the medical care was more advanced and where I could keep an eye on her. Her husband demanded that she return to Krasnodar where he could take care of her and she could be with her daughter. She returned to Krasnodar, begging me to come visit her there. I had no visa for Krasnodar and no hope at that time for getting one because I would have had to indicate that I was planning to visit a friend—at a time when Russians were not supposed to be friends with Americans.

"No problem," said Sveta. "Just jump on the train and come without a visa. No one will know you are not Russian." Well, perhaps my generic appearance and my Russian-language skills would allow me to pass for a Russian. However, Lizzie with her grey eyes, auburn hair, dimples, and freckles would not pass, in spite of her school uniform, for a Russian child. So, I did not go that time.

Two years later, when I came back to Moscow to provide consultation to the American ambassador on language programs, I applied for a visa to Krasnodar and sent a telegram to Sveta, telling her my plans. (This was, of course, before the days of Internet, cell phones, and other marvelous forms of instant communication.) Sveta, upon learning that I was in Moscow and doubting that I would be able to get a visa for Krasnodar, hopped immediately onto a plane and flew to meet me in Moscow, but she never informed me that she was coming. In the interim, I *did* get a visa for Krasnodar, and off I went to Domodedovo Airport to fly to the land of the Kuban, the middle land of European Russia. The plane from Krasnodar had landed, and in a spurt of efficiency, the airline officials had us already lined up to load onto the plane as the last of the passengers from Krasnodar were disembarking. Like in the plot of a B-rated movie, as I shuffled behind the other passengers to get onto the plane, through a window in the panel that separated embarking from disembarking passengers, I caught a glimpse of Sveta. I stopped and pounded on the window. She turned and rushed over.

"I'll fly back," she mouthed. "Meet me tonight at the town square." That was all she was able to get out before we were both pushed away from each other by the stream of passengers behind us, pushing us forward.

Sveta did not make it back to Krasnodar that evening. For hours, I waited in vain at the town square. At least, the weather was not severe. Over the next few days, I became acquainted with Krasnodar, a city that represented the mix that could be seen throughout Russia: a modern Intourist hotel for visiting foreigners and houses without plumbing for residents. I remembered Sveta telling me how she had to go to the end of the street to pump water for use at home. Now, Sveta was in Moscow, and I was in her town. I sent a telegram to Zina, a mutual friend living in the outskirts of Moscow to whom Sveta had introduced me in 1982. I knew that Sveta would have checked in with her. In the telegram, I asked them both to meet me at Arbat Restaurant in the center of town at 7:00 on Friday. I flew back to Moscow on Friday, and once again found myself waiting for hours for Sveta. Finally, around 9:00, I called Zina at home. She answered the phone.

"We just got the telegram," she explained, "only ten minutes ago. We are coming. We will be there in an hour."

"I sent the telegram three days ago," I remarked, but my remark should not have been in surprise.

"Yeah," said Zina. "That might be, but you know the KGB has to read it first and then would try to deliver it at a time that could be said it was delivered but late enough that you would miss meeting with us. It is good that you called."

We did meet, and like the later meeting with Aleksandr Ilich, it was to be the last time I would see my friend. Only then, I had no inkling of how ill she was. The call from Zina, telling me that Sveta had died, came in the middle of the night two years later. Given the hour and such tragic news, I was certain for days that I had dreamed it. Unfortunately, it was no dream.

I have written poems for Sveta on several occasions. Recently, I wrote one on the occasion of the twentieth anniversary of her death. How young she died! More important and more unbelievably, so much has changed in those twenty years that one would not today recognize Sveta's *rodina* (motherland) as the same country. The worries we suffered are now only a dim memory from the social history of the former Soviet Union.

*Не «прощай», Света, а «пока»!*
*/На 20-ую годовщину смерти*
*Моей молодой подруги советской/*

*Ох, как я помню московские вечера*
*И наши чувства, как будьто все прошло вчера.*
*Под громкой музыкой радио шептали,*
*Недопустимые мысли выражали.*

*Ох, как я помню наши поделившие*
*Идеи и надежды на будущее,*
*На дружбу вечную, жизнь удачную,*
*И работу и степень кандидатскую.*

*И помню как мы сидели с ее братом*
*Живущем в блоке с нами рядом.*
*Талантливым, он был, и безумно милым,*
*Жизнерадостным, жизнелюбивым, мирным.*

*А сейчас призасыпанный землей лежит*
*Из-за бессмысленной смерти—перитонит.*
*И помню неутещающие слезы*
*И вечно повторяющие вопросы:*

*Почему? Как? Чем объяснить? Чем утешить?*
*Ну, сегодня же что значит перитонит?*
*Вопросы никак неотвечаемые.*
*Ответы никак непонимаемые.*

*Я помню как мы все теснее сблизились,*
*Как мы, русская с американкой, дружились.*
*При холодной войне кто это подумал бы?*
*Но у нас больше смерти общего, увы!*

*Она родила дочь, а я сразу за ней.*
*Головная водянка у наших дочерей*
*И парализированные ноги.*
*К тому же у обеих и припадки.*

*Помню как Света от горя с ума сошла.*
*Я не могла помогать. Я была в США.*
*Я помню как от тюберкулеза она,*
*До своего времени, увы, умерла.*

*О Свет, все изменилось после распада!*
*Скрывать дружбу как мы скрывали не надо.*
*И не надо бояться как мы боялись.*
*Создать открытое общество старались.*

*Но сейчас на том свете, не на этом, ты.*
*Туда пошли подряд, друзья мои, все вы.*
*В то время была я в далекой стране,*
*Справляясь только матом о суровой судьбе.*

*Но настоящая дружба не умирает,*
*Только организм приятеля изчезает.*
*Твой дух, который жил, все еще живет*
*У меня в сердце и мыслях и даже расстет.*

*Ветераны мы холодной войны.*
*Ветераны мы жестокой судьбы.*
*Но надо иметь ввиду с другой стороны*
*Что уникальную дружбу имели мы.*

*Translation:*

*"Not Good-Bye, Sveta, Just Ciao for Now."*
*(On the 20th anniversary of the death of my young Soviet friend)*

*Oh, how I remember the Moscow evenings and our fears,*
*As if everything had happened only a day ago,*
*How we turned up the radio*
*And whispered disallowed ideas into each others' ears.*

*elizabeth mahlou*

*Oh, how I remember our thoughts shared*
*And hopes for the future bared,*
*For eternal friendship, a life that would please,*
*Good jobs and careers, and Ph.D. degrees.*

*I remember how we sat with her brother;*
*We three lived in dorm rooms next to one another.*
*Talented he was and really kind,*
*Filled with the joy of living, the love of life, a peaceful mind.*

*And now buried under a mound of earth he lies*
*Because of a senseless death—peritonitis.*
*I remember uncomforted tears*
*And eternally repeating cries:*

*Why? How? For what reason? How to survive each day?*
*After all, how fatal is peritonitis today?*
*Questions that had no answers.*
*Answers that could be understood no way.*

*I remember how we worked and played, hip to hip,*
*How we, Russian and American, celebrated friendship.*
*During the Cold War, who would have thought this?*
*Alas, we had more in common than death.*

*She gave birth to a daughter, and so did I.*
*Both had hydrocephalus (on the brain: too much "water"),*
*And both suffered from epilepsy, sigh!*
*Paraplegic, moreover, was my daughter.*

*I remember how Sveta went crazy with grief.*
*I could not help. I was in the USA.*
*I remember how tuberculosis took her life,*
*Alas, prematurely, before her day.*

*Oh, Svet' everything has changed since communism's fall.*
*One no longer has to hide a friendship as we did.*
*One no longer has to fear as we did.*
*An open society is before us all.*

*But now you are in that world, not this one here.*
*One after another, my friends, you went there.*
*I was in a faraway land,*
*And only cursing helped me cope with a cruel hand.*

*But true friendship does not die.*
*Only the body we no longer espy.*
*Your spirit, which lived then, lives now*
*In my heart and in my mind and even grows.*

*Veterans of the Cold War were we.*
*Victims of a cruel fate were we.*
*But one must hold to another view:*
*We had a unique friendship, so true.*

My poems about Sveta were not without effect on others. A teacher, with whom I was working at the time, had not seen a close personal friend in many years and had the opportunity to meet her in Bulgaria. This was a bit risky when the Soviet empire reigned since Bulgaria was held closely in check by the USSR. Still, both Easterners and Westerners could travel there, making Bulgaria about the only crossroads available for those who wanted to meet. Bella confided in me where she was going and whom she was going to meet in case something happened. She gave me her phone numbers and other ways to reach her if she did not show up at work at the end of her scheduled annual leave.

"I would never have dared to take such a risk without you," she told me. "I am a *refusenik* (someone who defied the Soviet government) and am here in the US as a refugee. For my own safety, I should not go to Bulgaria, but after listening to your poems about Sveta, I realize that friendship has a sacred character to it. We do not come by true friends easily, and we should not abandon them under any circumstances. I will go and see my friend, see how and if I can help her, and I will rely on God to take care of me and bring me back."

She returned on time. Her decision, she said, had been the right one.

Once again, something bad—the death of my friend—had been turned into something good—Bella's courage to see her friend before it was too late. Once more, the theme of my life repeated: bad turning into good, into a chance for one person to help another, even for one person to help many. And once again, ironically, an atheist had inspired someone's trust in God.

# University

I was 14 when we moved from our New Hampshire village to our Maine farm. The farm, for me, was about apple orchards, berry fields, and playing baseball.

I would sit for hours under one of the many apple trees, occasionally surveying the 50 acres of woods that extended beyond our lower fields, and read a book. One book after another. Books! More books! They were my first love, and they are still my greatest love.

Through books, I was able to escape from the parochial thinking that taught my parents that it is all right to beat children. "Spare the rod and spoil the child" Ma would recite to me when I asked "Why are you so mean?" Ah, God again, I would think, and, like Ma, not understanding that the "rod" was that of the shepherd, meant to guide the flock, rather than a literal rod meant to inflict pain, I added one more point for atheism as a life choice on my scorecard. Through books, I learned that not all children grew up with the rod. Through books, I learned that I was indeed sane but perhaps my parents were not fully so.

At times, I lived in my own world, peopled by characters from classical literature. I read all the classics, or at least all the classics I could put my hands on. I also read some religious classics. Although I dismissed the allusions and even straightforward presentations of the various formulations of the Abrahamic religions as more of what I had experienced in church—creative nonsense devised by highly imaginative authors to justify and, in some cases, atone for the daily cruelties and selfishness found everywhere in the world, not just in my neighborhood or among the congregation with which I shared pews for more than a dozen years.

From books came my sense of morality, my philosophical curiosity, my inclination toward dialectalism, and my understanding of polemical thinking. In this way, the farm prepared me well for the university, which would become my escape from the burning house of my childhood.

Equally important, reading under the apple trees taught me to love nature. In nature, I found an alternative universe. A walk in the woods would allow me to slip away from the painful heat of the burning sun and experience the soothing coolness of a late afternoon breeze, chasing playfully through the trees. The berry fields held a similar attraction for me.

We had acres of berries, both those that grew naturally and those that were cultivated. Blueberries, strawberries, raspberries, and blackberries. The cultivated variety of each was large, disappeared down the throat not much differently from a large pill, and gained favor with buyers. The wild ones were small, left a long aftertaste of sweetness on the tongue, and gained no favor with buyers who judged a berry by its size, not by its flavor. In addition to the wild berries, from the edges of the fields we gathered wild, dark, concord grapes, the kind that one cannot find on store shelves, small and round, and oh, so sweet and tart at the same time.

Picking berries and grapes was one of life's sweetest pleasures for me as a child because one picked alone and was left for a while with the quiet delight of vines and sun for companionship. Picking berries was also a pleasure because some of them ended up in my belly, not in the box.

Baseball was the third positive aspect of the farm for me and a significant part of my growing-up experience. Baseball made me happy—and I do mean baseball. Although the girls at school played softball on their side of the playground, when I was free of the gender restrictions out in the country, I would round up all the boys in town. We would play baseball in our apple orchard, designating specific trees as bases. When I played ball, I could run away, from home to first base, from first base to second, and farther. Somehow, running away from the baseman trying to tag me out was metaphoric for me. Running made me free. Escaping from being tagged out breathed life into me. The other team was, at times, wrapped in the clothing of the adults in my life, and I ran as fast as freedom to escape them.

It was more than the other team that I needed to escape. I had to run all the way to college if I wanted to get away from the adults who hurt me. Running all the way to college meant getting good grades. Like in baseball, I ran as fast as freedom in school in order to get the grades, giving up my during-school and after-school play time. When others were "hanging out" on the school grounds between classes or waiting for the school bus, I was working at the Dairy Queen (during the school year) or in the textile mill (during the summer) to earn money for college and to pay for Russian-language lessons, a language in which I had a special interest for no known reason and which was not taught in our high school. I ran and ran—through every book in the school library, public library, and then the nearby University of New Hampshire library. I ran so fast through my courses in high school that I graduated third in my class. This was certainly not the norm for children of farmers and shoe cutters. Scholarships rolled in, fattening my meager savings to the point that my dream of becoming the first person in my family to attend college became a reality. Yes! Free at last!

My freshman year, Dad drove me to Penn State University. He dropped me off, said good-bye, and punched me in the arm. Ah! I knew he loved me: he hit me.

My halcyon university days began with that loving punch in the arm, the closest Dad could come to a physical display of emotion. There was pride in that punch as well. Dad of the genius IQ, who loved books, classical music, and intellectual sparring, who had had to leave school in the eighth grade, who was drafted into WWII, and who never finished his education, had a daughter in college. I was a real first-generation college student, the first in our entire extended family. As such, I was the fulfillment of one of Dad's dreams. Beginning with his teaching me Latin when I was nine, radio theory and repair when I was ten, and tractor driving when I was thirteen, he never cared that I was a girl. That is perhaps why I never cared either and often found myself in a room filled with male colleagues as I made my way up the ladders of a series of male-dominated career fields.

I accepted Dad's punch in the arm as affection, said "good-bye" to him with just that one word, and turned my back on my old life. He walked toward the car for the 3-day drive back home, and I walked in the opposite direction toward my dorm room with a sense of release and pending adventure. The only things I would miss were the debates that Dad and I had every day as he drove me to and from high school and the whippoorwills.

The whippoorwills had been long gone, however, by the time I reached the university. They remain only as wispy shards of the memory of a two-year-old that briefly surf the synapses of my adult mind. At the time, we lived in a little white house at the edge of the path that led to "the Alley," the home of the poorest people in our small town, a place that today would be called a ghetto. Between our tiny house and the alley lay an enchanted path, at least in the mind of a two-year-old, which ran through a small clump of trees that appeared to me to be a forest. The "forest" carpeted the bank of Trout Falls River, which separated our New Hampshire village from the farmland of our neighboring state of Maine. In that forest lived delightful birds whose song, "whip poor will," repeated over and over.

As a child, I often wondered what poor Will had done to deserve being whipped. At the same time, I understood, even at that age, that he may have done nothing. He just might have had a mother like Ma. I don't know how, as a toddler, I had figured out that Ma was a force to be avoided, but I do remember creeping to the top of the stairs one night, thirsty for a bottle. I could see the red-and-white checkered tablecloth, covering our blue enamel table. On top of the table was a bottle of milk, next to an old toaster that had two sides that could be pulled away from the bread when the toast was ready to eat. Beside the milk sat Ma, talking to Dad. I understood instantly that although I was thirsty, that milk was not mine to ask for. I crept back into the bedroom, trying to make no noise.

Soon, however, Dad was upstairs, and, as on other nights, he picked me up and put me on his lap. We sat very, very still, listening to the rhythmic calling of the birds outside the open bedroom window. I felt very sad for poor little Will, who had somehow offended these birds. At the same time, I loved the rhythmic sounds coming from their throats, the still of the night, and the gentle arms that held me steady on Dad's lap. After we moved from the little white house, the nightly ritual stopped. I missed the whippoorwills. Even today the song of the whippoorwill reminds me what might have been had we not moved from the enchanted path and the whippoorwill forest and had Dad been able to stand up to the rages of Ma.

One might not consider a university a likely location for a battlefield. Nonetheless, those of us who have spent much time in academia beyond the undergraduate level realize that all kinds of battles take place there daily. Universities are hotbeds of interoffice politics, academic jealousies, and demonstrations of the fact that people who are powerless in general will use whatever little power they have not for the sake of others but for their own vainglory. In no place is this latter principle more glaringly obvious than in the case of doctoral students and the university faculty members who have been entrusted with the task of guiding them into becoming peers. Many Ph.D. holders can tell horror stories of graduate-school days that rival the movies in engendering frustration, fear, and subservience.

Possessing the rugged individualism that Ralph Waldo Emerson attributes to all New Englanders, I may get frustrated, but I am rarely fearful and never subservient. My teaching-fellow peers at the University of Renboro, which I shall call the university where I did my doctoral work, must have sensed that. Or, perhaps they felt my readiness to jump into any fray for a good cause, an example of the rage gene, semi-controlled and specifically focused, in action. In any event, on one fine day that turned out not to be so fine for my graduate-school future, they approached me about discussing the ineptness of the teaching fellow supervisor, Philip, with the department chairperson. Philip certainly was not qualified to teach any of us how to teach. Most of us had had far more teaching experience than he had had. Moreover, some of my peers complained that Philip had included their ideas and work in his own publications without attribution. We might have "put up and shut up" until we finished our dissertations and found ourselves positions as his peers at other universities. However, he graded us. He determined whether or not we continued receiving our teaching fellowships. Not having much knowledge or experience upon which to base his decisions, he used his limited power to make our lives miserable. So, my peers asked me to talk to Jill, the department chair, on their behalf.

In spite of my pugnacity and tenacity in a fray, I did have respectful, cheerful, and trusting relationships with most of the people in my personal and professional life. Moreover, having spent my undergraduate years as a member of the Student Council at Penn State University, I knew how to approach faculty members about serious issues. So, talking to Jill was not difficult.

The result of our conversation was better than I could have anticipated. Jill had observed a number of the problems I described and decided to turn over supervision of the teaching fellowship program to Pat, an excellent speaker of Russian with teaching experience and good mentoring skills. Philip, while angry with me, seemed relieved not to have to deal with teaching fellows.

I willingly took on Philip because, unlike my peers, I was not afraid for my academic safety (although I should have been). In those days, as in these, I trusted in my own capability to take on nearly any challenge. I trusted that while life was not always fair, Life (with a capital L) would not let me down. I trusted that Good in the long run would overcome Evil. I suppose for some people trusting in these things would be the same as trusting in the Divine, but the Divine, in my mind at that time, did not exist.

What was the result of such trust? The immediate result was major failure. Philip set about nursing a grudge that he never weaned, one that grew along with his abundant supply of milk of malevolence. When my dissertation advisor left the university, Philip, as the only remaining professor with expertise in my area of research, became my dissertation advisor. The door to retaliation opened wide. First, he announced the loss of the records of my comprehensive exams and told me that I would have to take them again. I appealed to the dean's office, where a record of my grade on the exams had been kept. Then, after I had completed my research in Siberia, Philip told me he would not accept my dissertation topic because no one in the USA was an expert in Siberian dialects of Russian and he would not accept Soviet academicians as committee members. Gamely, I changed my topic to one that he thought he could handle: acquisition of listening comprehension skills. At my prospectus defense, Philip tried to halt my writing on that topic—*after* I had completed all the research for it. Fortunately, he did not prevail. The committee accepted my research. All I had to do was finish writing the dissertation. Or, so it seemed until Philip found a loophole: the topic I was writing on had not been the topic intended at the time I took my comprehensive exams and so no related questions had been included. I would have to take another exam that Philip would conduct. He alone would determine whether or not my knowledge was sufficient enough for the university to support my completion of the dissertation. I appealed to the dean. The dean supported Philip. Unwilling to get into the personal aspects of the matter, the dean ruled that examination of a missing topic could be required *post-facto* if directly related to the dissertation and that one faculty member could make the decision about the adequacy of my responses. Clearly, Philip would not pass me no matter how well I performed on the exam. In fact, he told one of my fellow graduate students that I would graduate only over his dead body. The handwriting was on the wall. There no longer was a place for me at Renboro University.

One perhaps could not blame Philip for his attitude. He was an untenured assistant professor, trying to navigate his way through labyrinthine university politics, demanding requirements to publish, and needy graduate students. I was idealistic and disputatious. I did not consider the effect of my conversation with Jill on his career. While he did eventually gain tenure, it was not without a fight of his own, and I obviously did much to damage his reputation. So, why should he help me?

In making it impossible for me to complete my degree at Renboro, Philip could never have imagined that the long-term result of our battle would be my significant success. Years later, I had been traveling throughout the various countries of the former Soviet Union when, through the suggestion of a mutual friend, the rector of Pushkin Institute, the leading Russian university in my academic field, offered to let me enroll and complete my Ph.D. there. It was the first time that a native of the United States would do so. Pushkin Institute is a far more respected university than Renboro and afforded me the opportunity to earn a first-class doctorate. Moreover, my experience in completing my degree in Russia taught me much about Russian educational systems and helped me completely master the Russian language.

Philip had no idea that when he closed the door on my dissertation, he had facilitated my walking through a door that very few Americans are privileged to open. Harm intended was somehow miraculously turned into a great triumph. Whoever would have thought?

# Impossible Dream

In Shura's case, a long-range plan must have been at work because without the Russian university experiences that improved my language skills and introduced me to Russian dialectology, I would never have studied Siberian dialects of Russian as spoken in the Ob areal region. Had I not come to Akademgorodok for that, I would never have met Aleksandr Ilich. Had I never met Aleksandr Ilich, Natasha would have been just another head of a regional delegation—from a region that I knew nothing about, rather than from a region I had come to love passionately. One has to have great respect for the Master Plan Developer! Shura's parents certainly did, and so did many of the people who contributed to Shura's story. It was a story that was faith confirming and faith building for nearly everyone, except, ironically, for the person who had been placed at the nucleus of it: me. I became the unlikely center of a centrifugal force that revolved around a world stage with dizzying entrances and exits of heroes, heroines, and bit players as an incredible Author created an entire play, from casual opening through intense catharsis to tender denouement, to take care of one child. No role was without significance. It was a long time before I met the Author of this larger-than-life play, but that did not stop Divine Power from using me to offer comfort to Shura's family and put Shura on a path to health.

In the beginning, I was, of course, a stranger to Shura's family. Yes, Natasha had met me and trusted me. And yes, the family knew Aleksandr Ilich and trusted, even revered, him. Akademgorodok was, after all, very small; everyone there knew everyone else there. Aleksandr Ilich, of course, knew I could be trusted, and moreover, he knew Lizzie, so he had a sense of my parenting style. So, too, did one of the professors at Novosibirsk State University, who had taught Lizzie and me to cross-country ski in the winter of 1985.

Nonetheless, Lev came to Moscow to meet me a couple of months after Natasha and I had become acquainted in Krasnoyarsk. After all, he would be giving his son to a complete stranger, even if I did come with good recommendations, so he needed to personally feel that he could trust me.

Lev was an unimposing man, every bit as unimposing as I am to look at. Neither of us have any remarkable facial features: dark eyes, short hair, average noses. We would not be picked out as unique in any group photo, except perhaps for stature. Neither of us surpasses the bottom ten percent of our gender categories for height. Vertically challenged is what some folks like to call it nowadays. Short stature, though, does not preclude one from wanting to make one's world a better place. Lev and I were alike in that, too. His friends called him a dreamer, and mine called me an incurable optimist.

We had something else in common. He had founded Khronograf, a Siberian press dedicated to educating people on uncommon topics. My husband and I founded a small American press, also dedicated to educating people on uncommon topics. In 1994, Lev would publish a Siberian edition of my book on differentiated instruction in K-12 classrooms, a book that had been previously published by the Ministry of Education of Russia. Likewise, in 2003, I published a book through another American press, in which I included drawings by Shura. Publishing experience is what instantly connected us, but it was not what we had come together to talk about. We had come to talk about Shura, for whom Lev had big dreams and I had high hopes.

We met on the platform of Oktryabryaskaya metro station, the meeting of the Circle Line, Lev's point of origin, and the Kaluzhko-Rizhskaya Line, mine. Smiling and uttering no complaint about an old hip injury, he limped toward me with surprising alacrity. I waved. We recognized each other from Natasha's description.

The next train—trains came every two minutes in Moscow with metronymic regularity timed to the flipping of minutes on the seconds counter above the rails—roared up and momentarily paused, impatiently pawing at the tracks as the horde of waiting people swarmed to mount it. Then we moved swiftly from station to station, speeding toward the newly built Yasenovo station in the southern Moscow suburbs, where I was staying with Zina and her young teenage daughter, Ksenya, whom Lizzie had babysat ten years earlier, completely unaware that within a year, Ksenya would be living with us in California.

Lev's voice was soft but intense. His conversation had a single focus: Shura. A strong Russian Orthodox believer, he instantly felt that I was the answer God had sent to the prayers of his family and the members of his church. So, it took little persuasion for him to decide to hand his son over to me.

The handoff, however, was not immediate. The beginning of the journey was fraught with complications. I returned to the United States with a mission: to pry Shura out of Siberia into an appropriate medical setting in order to help him recover from his limb infections and grow into adulthood with resilient health. I would need money, a visa, doctors and a hospital, airline tickets for Shura and Lev, who would need to accompany Shura on the trip to the USA because of his disabilities, and a Russian-speaking family to host Shura while in the United States.

These tasks turned out to be harder than I originally thought, especially raising money. When all was said and done, Lev and the folks in Siberia were able to do a better job of raising money than I was ever able to do in spite of my success at fundraising at an earlier stage of my life.

When Shura's situation was nearly literally thrust upon me, my first step was to propose to the Board of Directors that the Global Studies Institute, where I was serving as president at the time, modify its charter to add a division for child health issues, expanding upon the educational purposes for which it was originally established. The goal would be to undertake fundraising for Shura and open the possibility of helping other children in similar situations should they be placed before us. The Board agreed to establish a Shura Ivanovich Fund, and we began a campaign of consciousness-raising and fund-raising.

Although I had acquired a reputation as a child of being the best salesperson for tickets for the town's annual baked bean supper, Girl Scout cookies, and the like, I quickly found out that I was no longer in a small New England village, where it was "Ruth's little girl" who was asking for pennies for a good cause. I was now living in the Central Coast area of California, where many people took to heart the saying, "charity begins at home." Some even reprimanded me for paying attention to a foreign child when so many local children needed help. Yet, I persevered. Why I persevered, I did not know. Somewhere, deep inside, was the conviction that I "had" to do this.

In Washington, D.C., a friend, Talia Gospod, whom I asked to help by selling copies of Shura's art books, also worked diligently to raise consciousness and money. She convinced the congregation at St. John's Russian Orthodox Church to which she belonged to become involved. She did not know why, either. She once told me that when I asked her to do it, she felt compelled to do it, that it was not a request she could turn down, but she did not really know why she felt that way. A devout believer, she was a likelier candidate for use for divine purposes than I although it would appear that Talia's God could direct even an atheist to action.

Coincidentally, with Shura's later arrival I learned that Talia's deceased grandfather was the author of a famous book about St. Petersburg, a book with which Lev was familiar. Talia's father was a Russian artist, and her well educated and compassionate mother, Tusya, knew Russian art inside out. The connection to Talia and her family turned out to be a comforting one for Shura, who spent several delightful afternoons at Tusya's Arlington, Virginia apartment, discussing Russian art, a topic near and dear to his heart. These discussions prepared him to undergo surgery in a foreign land with greater ease, having spent some time with people who understood him and his passion. The number of interwoven coincidences in Shura's story was piling up. Only a die-hard atheist like I could have failed to see God behind them.

The next step was to expand the numbers and kinds of people involved in the process of bringing Shura to the United States. For that, we would need to rely on the kindness of strangers and some amazing grace.

It was at this point that I received an unexpected phone call. On the other end of the line was Dick Burns from Felton, California. He had just returned from a trip to Russia, where, coincidentally—I now wonder if there are any real coincidences in this world—he had met Shura's family. He could not help directly himself, but he did offer to assist. His offer was happily accepted, and he quickly involved his church, a Russian Orthodox congregation. (Because of this, just "coincidentally," when he arrived in California, Shura had a place to attend Sunday services.)

Early on, once it became clear that the circle of friends would indeed grow, we realized that we needed a way to communicate. So was born the Shura Ivanovich Fund weekly newsletter. Ultimately, the number of copies sent out each week to people committed to helping Shura would number in the dozens, many of whom I never met. Many people, given the opportunity to carry out a specific role, were willing to help, and the work of dozens of hands, each doing small things, quickly added up to big accomplishments. Unfortunately, though, it did not add up to big bucks.

Meanwhile, Lev had obtained contact information for Eastern Orthodox and Catholic Churches in several countries—Russia, France, Switzerland, Germany, USA—whose members had passed through Novosibirsk and had expressed an interest in helping Shura but had subsequently disappeared. He found most of the disappearing people and asked them to contribute financially to the Shura Ivanovich fund. Money came in. Not in basketfuls but in fistfuls of foreign currency (francs, marks, pounds, schillings) that would later take the bank in agricultural Salts, California, used to working nearly exclusively with local farmers, an entire afternoon to convert to dollars. These contributions were a start, but they would never pay for all the medical care that we would need. We needed doctors with big hearts and a generous hospital to waive fees. That seemed like an impossible dream.

An impossible dream to find the medical care we would need for Shura? That was only the start. Medical care, family, visa. It did not matter in which order they would be accomplished—or even if they were done simultaneously. Any one of these projects, all three of which had to be successful in order to help Shura, seemed like an impossible dream to everyone to whom I talked .

The impossible dream? I had dreamed that before. In fact, I knew all the words to that song from *Man of La Mancha*. The lyrics were:

> *To dream the impossible dream*
> *To fight the unbeatable foe*
> *To bear with unbearable sorrow*
> *To run where the brave dare not go*
> *To right the unrightable wrong*
> *To love pure and chaste from afar*
> *To try when your arms are too weary*

*To reach the unreachable star*
*This is my quest*
*To follow that star*
*No matter how hopeless*
*No matter how far*
*To fight for the right*
*Without question or pause*
*To be willing to march into Hell*
*For a heavenly cause*
*And I know if I'll only be true*
*To this glorious quest*
*That my heart will lie peaceful and calm*
*When I'm laid to my rest*
*And the world will be better for this*
*That one man, scorned and covered with scars*
*Still strove with his last ounce of courage*
*To reach the unreachable star*

Yes, I knew all those words. Moreover, I had experiences to go with all of them. The "Impossible Dream" was *my* song because it was my life.

I have never understood the word *impossible*, nor have I ever allowed the word *cannot* to enter the vocabulary of my handicapped children. *Cannot* and *impossible* would have kept me down on the farm, and while farms are wonderful places to take a rest and fantastic places to raise children, for me the farm was too far from the rest of the world. This is a world full of impossible dreams and unreachable stars that I know I will strive with the last ounce of courage to reach. It is a striving with which I was clearly born. Perhaps it was a striving that was put into me before I knew that I was me.

Mission Impossible lay ahead. Full of hope and excitement, Lev and Shura went to Moscow to apply for a visa.

The answer came quickly: No. The Embassy not only had no questions to ask of Lev and Shura but also had a strict policy: no one who might cost the USA any money would be allowed to come. No one who might end up staying in the USA would be allowed to come. We would not be allowed to prove that Shura did not fit into either category because the consular office was unwilling to talk further.

It appeared that trying to get Shura to the United States was going to be like tilting at windmills, a test of endurance if nothing else. Who would outlast whom? Would I outlast the consular officers, or would the consular officers outlast me?

I was born tilting at windmills. Using fantasy to cope with the emotional complications of abuse, I could easily have been Miguel de Cervantes's Don Quixote de la Mancha as I found dreams to be the reality of my life as a child. Dissociation into fantasy was my escape from a house burning with parental ire. Dreams were my escape from a house *de cuyo nombre no quiero acordarme* (whose name I do not care to recall), to quote Cervantes. These dreams poised me to flee from the burning house when the time came.

Dreams were the stuff of my adult life as well as my childhood. Ultimately, even without the financial resources to do so, I would fulfill many of them.

And so, armed with dreams, I took a long lance and began tilting at the US Embassy windmill. I went to the embassy with Lev and learned the problems first hand-hand. They began with the attitudes of the American consular officers, whose unhidden hostility toward the pushing, pulsating line of people outside the embassy, wanting to emigrate or visit the United States in the early 1990s when that possibility became a reality for the first time in a long history, made me ashamed of my countrymen.

"Give up," I was told by my friends within the State Department. "There are rules, and no one is going to bend them. There is no way to get a visa for a sick Russian child; that child will be a drain on the welfare system of the USA and is, therefore, unwanted."

I was not about to give up, even given the seemingly unreachable star of finding a hospital and team of doctors to donate care for Shura. I had contacts at two hospitals capable of treating Shura. Administrators at neither felt any compassion at all. They wanted money. Specifically, they wanted $50,000 in cash up front and coldly informed me that I should expect to pay at least $500,000 for the initial medical care. At the rate at which only copper money was trickling into our Global Studies Institute coffers, my cause was clearly not one shared by the rest of the community and the collection of a half-million dollars in the short time that Shura appeared to have left did not seem likely. The star of hope was shining on our endeavors, but it was oh, so far away—truly the unreachable star. Was this a dream? Or was it a nightmare?

# Pop

Nightmares I was used to. My maternal grandfather, Pop, introduced me to them. Especially deep, dark, and enduring was his death. That he died was not troubling. It was a relief, an end to long-term sexual abuse. What was troubling was that I let him die—not by intentional act but through failure to help because I was focused on my relief, not on his need. At some psychological level, I knew I was not guilty of killing him. Nonetheless, undeserved guilt dogged me for more than 40 years.

Pop had a special affection for the girls in the family. In fact, we three older girls in the 8-pack just whet Pop's appetite, and soon he was also abusing our cousins.

We girls had only one conversation about the matter, and I remember it clearly even now. Danielle, Katrina, and I were in the bathroom. Our parents were asleep. In this conversation, we were comparing notes about what happened when Pop babysat us. It turns out that he had prurient interests whenever he came close to any of us girls. I wanted to tell Ma, but Katrina urged me to say nothing. "Ma will kill you, really kill you this time, if you tell her that her beloved father is anything but perfect. How many beatings do you think you can survive?" she asked.

Katrina was always worried about staying alive. I was willing to risk anything for "the principle of the matter," but in this case, it was clear that the risk would be useless because Ma adored Pop. Danielle agreed with Katrina. So, giving in to the petrified urgings of my sisters, I said nothing to Ma. Instead, I listened to her extol Pop with warm heart and misty eyes and tell us how lucky we were that he was willing to baby-sit us whenever she and Dad wanted to go out.

With Pop, one wore pants and made oneself as scarce as possible as quickly as possible. Avoiding Pop, however, was not always possible, nor was wearing pants in a community where girls were expected to wear dresses. On one visit to my grandparents, it seemed safe to wear a dress since there were ten of us descending upon our grandparents and we were all going to sit around the kitchen and talk. Still somewhat naïve—after all, I was only nine—I mistakenly assumed that there could be no danger in that. However, as soon as we arrived, Gram said to me, "Beth, go see what Pop is doing in the basement. He made a bureau for you and is painting it. See if you like the color."

"Oh, Gram," I replied. "Whatever the color is, I will like it." I spoke bravely and strongly but trembled inside, feeling alone in that room of eleven people.

"No, no, go down and look," Gram insisted. I came up with a myriad of creative excuses not to go into the basement, each one more lame but more urgent than the one before. Gram would not entertain them. She thought that there was something "good" for me down there. She did not know that it was a lion's den, and the lion was lying in wait for me (or for any girl relative who might be innocently thrown to him). Dismissing my pleas to stay upstairs as a childish desire to remain with the grown-ups, she led me down the stairs and handed me over to the lion.

Perhaps she will stay, I thought hopefully but incorrectly. "Here is Beth," she announced to Pop. I felt like I was being "served" to him as some kind of entrée. I know that Gram had no idea what would happen next, what always happened next. After all, we always emerged from the lion's den healthy on the outside albeit bruised inside. The kinds of mauling we experienced were well hidden.

I turned to go back upstairs with her, but she firmly turned me over to Pop, standing me next to the half-painted blue bureau, saying "Perhaps you would like to help Pop paint." Painting, I thought, is not what Pop ever has in mind for me.

As soon as Gram disappeared, I became numb for an instant. I was once again in the lion's den alone.

Pop lay down his paintbrush and in one quick movement, deftly slid his paint-covered, rough fingers into my body with a practiced hand. "You are a good girl," he whispered. "Gram does not let me touch her, but you understand. I need you to understand. It is important that you be a good girl for Poppy."

Malice did not enter the picture for "Poppy," just unfulfilled physiological need, pushing, pulsating, and demanding attention ever more urgently until Pop, the some-what naive, generally kind-hearted, basically uneducated boy-man of the fields and forests, became nothing but urge personified. As he pulled me closer, I felt the hardening in his pants, something that no 9-year-old girl should know anything about.

Although I was physically pinned, my mind was free, and I desperately searched for a way to distract him long enough to get away from him and back upstairs. "Gram said she would be right back down," I said to him, hoping that he would be afraid of getting caught. Gram was a matriarch of formidable proportions, and she was able to control Pop like no other.

That argument was ineffective, however. "Don't worry," he murmured, as he be-gan nuzzling my neck, "we can finish before she comes back. It won't take long. She won't know. I just need you to help me take care of this." With those last words, he rubbed his free hand along the protrusion in his pants, and, growing excited and breathing heavily, he fumbled with his zipper.

At that moment, my eye fell on the paintbrush. A weapon!

"Look, Pop," I said. "Here is the paintbrush. Gram wants us to paint. If no more gets painted, she will wonder what happened. I am going to paint."

I was able to catch him off-guard as his zipper jammed, and I quickly twisted away. I, too, had become practiced at these encounters. Dipping the paintbrush in paint, I quickly began to paint the bureau, putting dark blue where light blue belonged. That distracted him long enough to say, "Stop! You're messing up the paint job."

At that point, I handed him the paintbrush, saying "You finish it!" With that, I ran upstairs.

"How do you like the bureau?" asked Gram.

"It's very nice," I answered. Right, nice! I hated that bureau for the next nine years that it stood in my bedroom.

My bedroom, with or without that bureau, was no haven. Whenever Pop babysat us, I never slept. If I did, I would awaken to 250 pounds of Pop on top of me. Sometimes I would hear him coming up the stairs. Bald and bowlegged, round and rugged, he was by any measure a big man, and climbing stairs caused him to breathe heavily. In those cases, if it were not winter, I would climb out of my bedroom window onto the second-story roof and hide under one of the old-fashioned New England eaves, pulling back against the angle created by the intersection of the eave with the side of the house, hoping that no neighbor would notice that "Beth is on the roof again" and solicitously call Pop. With eight children and ten rooms in the house, it could be anyone's guess as to where I was—or, at least, that was my thinking. Pop could not squeeze through the tiny attic window, and, anyway, he was scared of walking on the slippery tarred shingles of the steeply sloped roof. Many times, his fear was my salvation.

When he could not find me, he would amble off to the bedroom that Katrina and Danielle shared to tuck them in. Familiar with his special tucking-in routine, I felt like a coward that I watched him leave in relief and did not come to the rescue of my sisters. Of course, my 50 pounds was no match for his 250, so I just crawled under the eaves and hoped that the two girls could protect each other or that he would not bother one while the other could see. After all, he usually worked in private.

When I became a teenager, I brought even greater joy to Pop, who always expressed delight in seeing me. "Pop really loves Beth," everyone would say.

"With love like that," I would think, "let him love someone else!" On the other hand, I did not want anyone else to have to deal even once with what I had to deal with on a weekly basis.

One morning, Dad had to be at work early and dropped me off at my grandparents' house in the city before school. I was still tired from one of Ma's late-night beatings and fell asleep while waiting for a friend to stop by to walk to school with me. That was a serious mistake. Gram had already gone to work, and when my friend stopped by, Pop told her that I would be out sick that day.

I woke up to the sound of the bedroom door being locked from the inside. Lying on my stomach and watching through half-closed eyes, I saw Pop remove his pants. I had a very good idea what was coming next and realized that there was no way out because Pop was between me and any exit. Then, nearly immediately he was on top of me, trying first to remove my clothes, then, when that failed, to turn me over. I clung desperately and wordlessly to the sides of the bed. I have no idea where I got my strength because for a young teenage girl to win a strength contest with a former lumberjack and blacksmith was unrealistic, but win I did. Unable to "awaken" me or turn me over, he was pondering his next move when the front doorbell rang.

"Saved by the bell!" I thought, as relief washed over me. "Literally!" Who rang that bell and why? That was a wonderful mystery, but not one I was going to waste any time solving.

As Pop went off to answer the unexpected doorbell, I did not wait to see who was at the door but quickly grabbed my school bag, raised the window, jumped to the ground, and ran off to school—having thwarted yet another attempted rape. I arrived at school a little late but elated: I had won a show of strength in more than one sense of that expression.

I had to thwart many such attempts. Ma was constantly putting me in Pop's charge. Whenever I complained, Ma would hit me. Whenever I suggested an alternative babysitter, Ma would hit me. Whenever I tried to reason that perhaps I was old enough not to need a babysitter, Ma would hit me. And in every instance, Pop would show up with a smile to watch over me.

The greatest opportunity for Pop arose when Ma decided that it was time for me, having turned 16, to learn to drive a car and that Pop would teach me. Even though I would not need many lessons because I had been driving a tractor for many years, I imagined being with Pop alone in the car on the isolated roads in our farm community and knew that this opportunity spelled disaster. I refused the lessons. Ma demanded. I still refused. Ma called me a bitch and a brat. I still refused—I was used to being called names, anyway. Ma hit me and spat in my face. I still refused—and reciprocated Ma's attack with an equally forceful hit-and-spit counterattack. I knew I could win this battle because no one could make me get into the car. I had free will even if free will came with physical and emotional abuse. Both were preferable in my mind to sexual abuse. So, I learned to drive a car only after Pop died.

Thank God, Pop did die. Katrina, Danielle, and I were teenagers at the time, and we were the only ones with him when he departed our universe. He was supposed to be babysitting us. He made some popcorn for us, a talent he had that all his grandchildren enjoyed. (Even bad people have some good traits.) Then he sat down, took a deep breath, put his head back, and stopped breathing. I watched with the dawning realization and hope that he was dying. When he did not take a next breath, I told my sisters that something was wrong with Pop. I was pretty sure that they knew what was going on, but none of us alluded to that reality in front of each other. Later, my sisters told me that they had indeed figured out what was going on and were hoping very strongly that the gurgling they were hearing was Pop's last breath.

At the time, unspoken thoughts were the safest ones because of the steps I chose to take next. Rather than getting Pop's heart medication out of his pocket and putting it into his mouth, I walked slowly to a neighbor's apartment. There was a part of me that said this was wrong. At some level, I felt that any human life should be saved. In Pop's case, since he was incapacitated, I was the only one who could save him because I was the only one who knew about his nitroglycerin. Another part, however, said that this was right. Nature had determined that Pop's life was at an end, so why should I do something artificial to prolong it, as well as prolonging the abuse of the other girls in the family and myself. Later, I rationalized that I had not denied Pop his medicine because he had not asked for it. Instead, I had left it in the hands of Nature, and Nature ultimately had given the female side of the family a reprieve.

The neighbor was not home. I returned to the apartment, hoping that Pop was still dead. In the intervening minutes, Dad had arrived to pick us up, had determined that Pop was indeed dead, and had made all the proper phone calls. I could finally breathe a sigh of relief. I watched the coroner carefully as he checked Pop, wanting to be sure that Pop was as dead as the chair he was still sitting upright in and would not, like a zombie in a horror movie, suddenly come to life and terrorize us again.

Dozens of town folk showed up at church for Pop's funeral. He was clearly very popular in town, and, like my parents, he had attended church services ardently. As Pop's immediate kin, my family sat up front and center. We were all decked out in our Sunday-nice clothes. With folded hands, outward demureness, and inward relief, we waited for the final sentence in the last chapter of Pop's life to be spoken. That sentence shocked all of us victims of Pop's sexual addictions: "This man has been a pillar of the community and a great example to all of us in his godliness. May all the men in our community follow his example!"

I could only imagine a town gone wild with orgy and wondered where the morals were. How could a minister of the church say such things? Those words were nails not in Pop's coffin but in mine, in the coffin of atheism that I had been building for myself for 15 years. From that day forward, for me, any concept of God was also dead. I had no idea whom or what the members of the church were serving, but in my mind, if the minister was promoting sexual abuse of children, or equally bad, did not have any idea of Pop's proclivities, I wanted nothing to do with him, the church, or what the church represented. It gave the final impetus to my fateful youth sermon a few months later. At that time and for many years afterward I did not realize that one cannot judge God by the people who enthusiastically attend church, publicly proclaim their faith, or sincerely love God but suffer from weakness of the flesh.

The trauma did not end with Pop's burial. Afterward, I lived with the conviction that I had murdered him. Even though I rationalized that Nature took him, he was not old (age 64) and could have lived longer had I brought him his medicine. I knew that, and so did Gram.

"You are 15 years old," she admonished me. "You are capable of knowing what was going on, and you knew where his medicine was. Why did you not give it to him?" She looked at me questioningly. I think deep down she knew I had intentionally not given him his medicine, but she had no understanding as to why I would withhold it from him. It was not a question that I ever answered for her. The truth would only have hurt her, and she had done nothing to deserve such hurt.

The instant Pop died I forgave him for his sexual appetite that would not be satiated by someone of his own age and was only whetted by children who were helpless in his grasp. To some extent, I felt vindicated that I had taken charge of the situation and "gotten back at him" by not giving him his medicine. Someday I would forgive myself for my helplessness, for my reluctance to tell someone who might have been able to put a stop to it, for taking the coward's way out and letting Nature deal the death blow. Someday, I would do that, thanks to a divine lesson, but not right away for such a day does not come quickly nor such an act easily.

Uncle Charles had a special affection for the boys in the family, but, unlike Pop, he did not limit himself just to the family. Apparently, my brothers were not enough to satisfy his appetite. He began to find boys elsewhere, especially after my brothers became big enough to fend him off, grew up, and left home.

My brothers told Ma, but she did not react. Then, years later, they asked Ma, out of deference to them, to stop socializing with Uncle Charles, who would drive Ma wherever she wanted and bring her to his house for afternoon chats with him and my aunt. Ma refused, telling them to "get over the past" because she deserved a "comfortable old age."

Fortunately, some people did care about what Uncle Charles was doing. One of the boys he abused knew him from church, where Uncle Charles was a deacon and therefore considered a trustworthy person. (I guess those who trusted him simply because he was a deacon did not hear my youth sermon in which I said atheists were far more trustworthy than deacons!) At any rate, one teenage boy who ended up on the receiving end of Uncle Charles' sexual favors told his parents. Outraged, they filed a lawsuit, and the boy was to testify against Uncle Charles. As the trial approached, the terrified and embarrassed boy resisted, but his parents insisted: for the sake of others in the future, he needed to do this, they told him. On the eve of the trial, the boy committed suicide.

Although other boys had been involved, none were willing to take the witness stand. My aunt's reaction was relief. This reaction caused a breach between my aunt and some members of my family, especially one of my cousins, whose daughter by her first husband had been raped by her second husband. She was appalled by my aunt's reaction. Ma, though, supported her. At least, the church did something this time. It removed Uncle Charles as deacon and identified him as a pedophile.

Of all the situations I found myself in as a child, the ones involving sexual abuse were the most humiliating and enraging. Where, indeed, was God when children were being initiated into sex in the most obscene ways? I suspect that watching what was going on might well have made God regret giving free will to the human race, but that was a done deal and so our fate was sealed. Still, I do believe that I would not have survived had God not given me strength of all kinds at the times when I needed it—not only not only emotional resistance but actual physical resistance. How could a young girl's physical strength outmatch that of a lumberjack and blacksmith? And what about that unexpected doorbell? God that day was in the doorbell. God also gave me an eave to escape the sexual advances. For those times when I could not reach the eave in time, God gave me the ability to separate mind and body.

God gave me another kind of strength, too: the strength to let a dying man die. Then God gave me the strength to live with the knowledge that I had allowed my own kin to perish. At the time, I did not wonder where my strength came from. I certainly would not have attributed it to God (and might well have been quite angry with God for not intervening more had I thought there was a Divinity "in charge of" the universe. Instead, I was both too caught up with fighting off Pop's advances (and those who pushed me toward him) and too relieved when I no longer needed to do that to analyze the situation at all. The analysis came years later.

As an adult, I found my first sexual experiences as unpleasant as they were pleasant. The image of Pop intruded, prompting a revulsion that rivaled normal arousal. With time and Donnie's patience, Pop receded, finally, into an emotional grave where he lost his last shred of control over me.

Dispassionate understanding helped. Even as a teenager, I could understand Pop's inability to control his sexual urges because I careened through childhood in the attire of unsatisfied emotional cravings. Much later I would come to understand that I *was* loved as a child. I was loved by God. Those understandings made forgiving Pop and ultimately myself possible.

# The Burning House

A poem penned by my brother-in-law, William Smith, in 1998 is the best concise description of my childhood home. Bill appropriately titled the poem "The Burning House."

*I dreamed a dream of a burning house*
*With brothers and sisters and a cold bitter spouse.*
*The halls were all crooked, the doors were ajar.*
*I heard all their cries from the road in my car.*

*I put on the brakes and came to a stop*
*While an old jackrabbit went hippity hop.*
*I looked back again, and the house was ablaze.*
*The people inside just looked in a daze.*

*The curtains were tattered, the roof was not straight.*
*The hinges were knocked off the broken front gate.*
*The paint was all weathered, and the shutters hung loose.*
*A shadow on the barn door looked like a noose.*

*A kid outside shouted, "There's a fire there, you see".*
*But Mama kept screaming, "Come back here to me".*
*"No, I cannot, 'cause your house is on fire".*
*But nobody listened as the flames grew still higher.*

*Once in a while a child would run out,*
*But Mama and Papa would just scream and shout.*
*The kid in the yard would utter a scream*
*As a child ran back in as if in a dream.*

*Soon the house burned right to the ground.*
*The kid in the yard made not a sound.*
*I opened the door, and she sat on the seat.*
*She didn't look back because of the heat.*

*I stepped on the gas, and we sped away.*
*I opened my mouth, but what can you say?*
*"They had to go back," was her soft reply.*
*All of them chose their way to die.*

*I turned on the light; she was just seventeen.*
*She was the prettiest girl I'd ever seen.*
*I'll never forget the night I stopped there,*
*'Cause I married that girl with the long, flowing hair.*

The remarkable part of our family's story is that, unlike others, such as David Pelzer (*The Boy Named It*), no one in our family escaped from the abuse but together all eight navigated years of life-threatening beatings, as well as sexual and emotional abuse, relatively safely. The "girl with the long, flowing hair," Danielle, has worked as a psychiatric nurse for more than 20 years. Although I personally consider homeless, hungry people to have had a more difficult experience growing up than I did, Danielle insists that child abuse is more deleterious to normal emotional development than physical needs not being met. She says that she has encountered only one case of child abuse more severe than what we experienced as children and that case had resulted in the person developing multiple personalities, something that is well documented in psychiatric literature as an outcome of horrendous child abuse and something that we were blessedly spared.

We all ran back into the burning house time and again because in the 1950s and 1960s there was no other place to go. In rural New England back then, neighbors found you and pushed you back into the fire. Out in the country, families were self-reliant, and police were far from ubiquitous and almost never interventionist.

In the end, it was not teachers, social workers, or police that saved the 8-pack. It was the 8-pack that saved the 8-pack, especially psychologically.

With increasing years, my confidence in my ability to win against Ma grew, and therewith the dynamics of our relationship changed. With no help in sight, I began to take Ma on physically. What Dad lacked in courage, I had in brazenness. Once I became embroiled in a fight with Ma, fear played no role. I only cared that I win. I truly did not care whether I lived or died in the attempt.

Fearlessness I had. Fearlessness got me into trouble many times, but in the long run, fearlessness saved me, and sometimes my siblings, from the burning house. (Many years later, Rollie told me that as a child he always looked upon me, not Dad, as his real father for I was the one who taught him how to survive.)

Perhaps the moral lessons from classical literature played a role in fueling my fearlessness. Characters in my life at times seemed somehow to merge with the heroes and villains in the classics. Of course, I was always the hero, and Ma was always the villain, destined in my mind to lose for I was never willing to contemplate a world in which evil (Ma) could possibly permanently triumph over good (me).

I did not know where my inner strength came from. I just accepted that I had it. I do not know where my self-confidence came from. I just accepted that I had it. That self-confidence spilled over to school and anything else I decided to put my hand to. After all, if I could survive Ma, I could survive anything. If I could fight Ma, I could fight anything. If I could win against Ma, I could win against anything.

That ego-soaked pride that kept me alive in the burning house is no longer needed, but the downside of its birth is that it continues to live a life of its own. While few who work or socialize with me would likely consider me hubristic or egotistical, deep down I still respond first with a fist, albeit it a veiled one, and later with a handshake. Many of the people who work for me have observed this in a slightly different way. At one point, I noticed that nearly everyone who came to speak to me made two appointments, one for five minutes and one for 20. When I queried them about it, they told me that my first response tended to be negative and later I would re-think. So, they would give me a "heads up" in a short first meeting in order to get a positive response at the follow-up, normal-length meeting. Knowing this, I have tried to keep that fight-first response, so well honed in childhood, under control. Some days I even succeed.

The ability to survive the burning house did have an upside. It gave me the capacity and courage to help others. It appears that I learned to be a Good Samaritan in the fires of my childhood.

Even when it became possible to escape from the burning house, the bond of the 8-pack brought some back into the house. Rollie is an example.

As a teenager, Rollie got into trouble with the local law officials. He had taken his devil-may-care attitude (the end result of extensive abuse to a happy-go-lucky attitude) from home into the community. He had not done any real harm, but he had mouthed off to the sheriff on several occasions, calling him a "copper" on one occasion. In a big city, he would have been considered a restless, harmless teenager. In the country, he was more noticeable as a troublemaker since most country folk are pretty tame, or at least they were in those days.

Ma was at wit's end and used an extra dose of the only disciplinary tool she had at her command: severe beatings. In a fit of anger, she hit Rollie very hard in the nose and broke it. Clearly, the broken nose could not be hidden, but Ma did not take Rollie to the doctor. She did not want to have to explain what had happened. Rollie, in turn, declined the concerned offer of one of his teachers to have him removed from home. He was paranoid about being removed from the 8-pack, as any one of us would have been. We were a group, tied together in our sense of sanity by a lifeline that ran to each of us. No, Rollie could not leave, but he could become increasingly outspoken and pugilistic in his own defense.

Ma was embarrassed. After all the dedication and hard work she had put into raising her children, Rollie had "gone wild" on her. Of course, the neighbors understood. Like Beth, Rollie was a "difficult" child. They sympathized. How unlucky she was to have two difficult children. Ma felt she had to "do something" about Rollie.

At the time, Donnie and I had already been married for four years, had a toddler, Lizzie, and were living in Montana. I heard about the situation with Rollie, checked with Donnie, and made an offer to Ma to have Rollie live with us. Rollie was 17 at the time, and I thought he could work in the day care center we ran because he was very good with kids. Then perhaps we could get him enrolled in college to go into social work, medicine, or something else where he could work with children and put his talents and interests to good use. I wanted to find a way out of the burning house for Rollie permanently, a good way out.

Ma agreed. Rollie agreed. He came to Montana and worked in the day care center. The children at the center adored him. We began to explore university options near us, but after being in Montana less than a year, Rollie suddenly told us that he missed our two younger sisters, over whom he had always watched. He said he wanted to go back home to be with them.

Years later we learned the whole story. It had two parts. As he lay dying, Dad had looked at teenage Rollie, who was in the hospital room with him, along with Katrina, and had asked him to accept responsibility for the safekeeping of Sharon and Victoria, ages 5 and 2 at the time. Clearly, Dad had worried that Ma would hurt them. He could not will them away from Ma, not in those days and not with his affection for her. Willie, in many ways a carbon copy of Dad, was too gentle and cerebral to stand up to Ma, and Keith was too young to take on such responsibility. So, Rollie was the only choice. Rollie had taken the request seriously. Not only had he missed the little girls while living in Montana but also he had felt guilty about not keeping his promise to watch over them.

So, Rollie went back into the burning house. Deliberately. Ma had not been able to kill the full extent of his generosity toward others, and while he might not admit it, being an atheist himself, he may well have been used as a divine instrument to prevent more harm from being done to the little girls. Sharon and Victoria today are convinced that they received less abusive treatment than we three older girls experienced. I believe that is true. Perhaps Ma had mellowed by then. Perhaps the social welfare system that provided medical assistance to them appeared to her to be looking over her shoulder, creating a deterrent to using her customary excessive force in disciplinary matters. And just perhaps Rollie did help both by actively protecting them and also by drawing Ma's fire toward himself and away from them.

The second part of the story of Rollie's return had to do with protecting our little sisters in a different way. Like the rest of us, more than anything Rollie wanted to leave home and leave the abuse behind, but he could not. Cousin Billy, he learned, had developed a special affection for Sharon and Victoria, who all too young learned the lasting sorrow of sexual abuse. For the short while that he was back, Rollie's presence curtailed, but did not prevent, abuse that ultimately went on for years. Few of the details have been shared with me. That is the way it is with family rape and sexual abuse. No one wants to talk about it. No one wants to admit that it can happen in his or her family, but I have found that it happens in far more families than most people suspect. Chris Newlin, the executive director of the National Child Advocacy Center, points to statistics that show one in four girls and one in seven boys under the age of 18 will be the victims of sexual abuse.

Rollie lasted less than two years in the burning house before Ma decided that she "could not deal with him." So, she turned him out of the house and locked the door on him. Miles from civilization in an area that had no public transportation, Rollie spent 40 days living in the woods, stealing food from stores that bordered on the forest whenever he could. Eventually, he was able to call out to one of our cousins, and our aunt went to the forest and found him. She bunked him with our cousin's boyfriend until Katrina learned of his dilemma and offered him a home with her in Ohio, where she was attending Ohio State University. Rollie moved in with her and this time did not return to the burning house.

It is inconceivable that with the exception of the one teacher who wanted to help Rollie the adults in our lives—doctors, teachers, and neighbors—did not notice the marks on our bodies. Perhaps they noticed but said nothing because community involvement in child abuse cases was not commonplace in the 1950s. Then, too, the community respected and feared my parents. Dad served as a member of the School Board, and Ma was known to humiliate others publicly and cause trouble for those who opposed her or what she wanted. In addition, Ma did do much charitable work in the community. This positive image was reinforced by the fact that we children came to school looking well cared for. So, most of the community viewed her as a good mother saddled with difficult children. While there are still times I would like to blame members of that community for callousness, selfishness, and a variety of sins beyond just holding them accountable for ignoring children in trouble, perhaps they really were deceived by our outward appearance and what my parents told them.

# Embers

Teachers did much to counteract the negative input I was getting on a daily basis at home. School became a special place, one that I tried to keep untainted by what was going on at home. Nonetheless, there were times that fear of "home" intruded on "not-home."

One such instance I remember well from my sixth grade, as do any of the students who attended elementary school with me. On this particular day, I had to stay in from recess because I had a cold. The teacher put me in the cafeteria with some clay and told me I could play with that during recess. Now, playing with clay was not my idea of fun. I would have been much happier sitting in the corner with a good book or out playing baseball with the boys. Nonetheless, I tried my best to amuse myself and create a sculpture to while away the time. I chose to make a monkey, but I was quite unsuccessful in getting the clay to look like anything other than a lump of clay. Artistic talent has never found its way into my repertoire of skills, and after a good deal of time spent in fruitless endeavor, I threw the clay into the air in frustration. To my horror, the strength I used was enough to make it sail upward to the ceiling and stick there, way out of reach of anyone except the janitor, his ladder, and a very long pole—and even then, with difficulty, given the high New England school ceilings. The teacher was not amused.

"What would your father say?" she asked me and was absolutely confounded by my immediate hysterics.

It was not what my father would say that brought on the hysterics. It was what my mother would do. Reminiscent of my infant crying that unsettled a city square, my screaming could be heard all over our small-town school, and the principal decided that I should be released to go home. That was the worst decision possible, and my hysterics increased. Not knowing what to do, she asked two of the boys in the class to accompany me home, a matter of a two-block walk. They could not hold me, fear being a great multiplier of strength, and so four boys were selected to carry me home—one on each arm and one on each leg. By then, the other students in the school were visibly upset by the commotion, and the principal cancelled classes for the rest of the day. (The day that Beth shut down the school became a legend in town.)

In spite of such moments, it would be incorrect to conclude that my childhood was all misery or that, at the time, I even considered it overall a miserable place. My inherent unflappably positive outlook on the world prompted me to treasure small pleasures. These included the vanilla ice cream cones with jimmies from Pete's store around the corner from where we lived. Dad had an account there, and Ma would send Katrina and me to pick up groceries, sometimes giving us a nickel for an ice cream cone. They also included the annual trip to York Beach, Benson's Wild Animal Farm, or Story Land. Danielle points out that it was the annual obligation to show the world that you provided entertainment for your children, but I took it as a day's respite and as a great opportunity, especially at Story Land, to learn. Talking to the people who portrayed characters in books I had read thrilled me. At Story Land, when I was 9, I was offered the opportunity to work as Heidi by the man who was playing the role of the grandfather. There was no Heidi that year. I knew the story inside out—and even fit into the costume. When Ma and Dad found me alone with Heidi's grandfather, they scolded me for wandering away. Grandfather made the job offer. For a fleeting moment, I had visions of a carefree, exciting summer, but my hopes were instantly shredded by Ma's sneered "you leave her alone." I looked at Heidi's Grandfather. He shrugged his shoulders, and there was something in that shrug that told me that he suspected what my life at home was like and was sorry that he could not pull me out of there for a little while. That shrug stayed in my memory for a long time as a vivid validation that my parents were somehow wrong and I was somehow an okay kid.

The second child in the family, Katrina, was quite different from me. She was light-skinned and blue-eyed. And she was quiet, even from birth. She won some kind of pretty baby contest when she was small, and Ma talked about that for years. "Beth is my plain Jane," she would say, "but Katrina is my beautiful baby."

Katrina was Ma's favorite, or so it seemed to me. (Katrina would later say that I was the favorite.) Being a favorite (whether Katrina or me) did not protect either of us from the daily beatings although Katrina often managed to avoid conflict through obedience. When Ma required something of her, Katrina did it. (I would argue.) Whether it was at home, in our own fields, in our neighbors' fields, or for a business, Katrina worked diligently. (I would wander off to read a book.)

Katrina was the only one of us as a child to show Ma any kindness. Although she fully expected to die at Ma's hands, she nonetheless had great compassion for her. She appreciated the fact that Ma went without clothes and, when we lived in town, without food on many occasions so that we could be properly dressed for school and have enough to eat. One year around the time of Ma's birthday, Katrina noticed that the habitually limited household funds had resulted in Ma having no clothes that could be worn in public without shame. Somewhat older than we had been when my parents beat me into turning over the seven dollars in my bank account for a pair of shoes, we all had jobs on a neighbor's farm where we picked peas, beans, and berries for pennies. Katrina gathered all our pennies and bought Ma a nice skirt, blouse, and sweater for her birthday.

Likewise, sometimes Ma would pretend to have a heart attack, which she said we were causing, and Katrina would attempt placation. The rest of us would simply laugh. (We were not very old when we learned that Ma's heart attacks were shams).

"Ma," Danielle, the future nurse, would tell her, "stop faking. Your heart is not on the right side of your body."

"I am really serious this time," Ma would reply, changing her hand position to clutch the left side of her chest. "You are going to be sorry when I am dead. No one is going to want all of you brats. You are going to be without a home. You had better hurry up and [do whatever it was she wanted done at the moment]."

"Ma, don't worry!" Katrina, on the other hand, would try to calm her. "We'll do it. We'll do it. Just lie down, and let us do it." And she would turn to the rest of us, urging us to do whatever it was that Ma wanted done at the moment.

Years later, Rollie would say that Katrina was the real mother in our house. Most important, he credits her with teaching the rest of us compassion.

When Dad died in 1973, leaving Ma alone with the five youngest of the 8-Pack, it was Katrina who dropped out of college and helped Ma, who had only once for a two-week period worked somewhere other than on the farm. She taught Ma how to write a check and run the "bacon" side of a household. She also hooked her up with the county and state welfare offices so that the youngest of the 8-pack could be fed, clothed, and medicated, as needed. So, not only did Katrina teach compassion; she also practiced it.

Katrina escaped from the burning house right after I did. For her, though, the escape itself was painful. Given the ferocity of our abuse, she had never expected to live until adulthood. When she found herself still alive at the age of 18, she was taken by surprise. As a result of her experience in being lost in a sea of career choices, she decided on career counseling as a profession and has helped many university students in New York, where she now lives, successfully navigate a plethora of options.

Katrina never married, but she stayed in close contact with Keith, who also never married, and has spent much time with him over the years. In more recent years, she has become close to Lizzie, now a professor in New York. As for offspring, Katrina's students are her "children." So are her nieces and nephews. They all are fond of her. She still represents the compassionate element of the family.

Danielle married and joined the Army, in that order. Her wedding is forever etched into my memory because that night was the first of the last thirty days of Dad's life. For some reason, I felt it at the time, yet I would not have been able to articulate the feeling back then. It was a simple wedding. Don and Danielle had to finance it since Ma and Dad had no money for things like that. Hence, as with Donnie and me, simplicity mattered. Donnie and I had had no reception, but Don and Danielle had included that traditional event. What transpired there, I do not know for we never made it to there. Dad, caught in the clutches of walking pneumonia, had trouble concentrating on the line of drivers in front of him. Seated in the back seat of Dad's car, Donnie and I were amazed to watch him turn right when all the other cars turned left. When he realized that he was no longer in the line of cars proceeding to the reception, he turned around but could not catch up with the last car. Without an address, we had no idea where to go. So, we headed home. Dad and Ma railed at Don and Danielle, claiming that they had intended to keep them away from the reception. How reminiscent of the many times growing up that they had blamed us for their failings!

In the Army, Don and Danielle trained as Army nurses at Fort Sam Houston in Texas and then were stationed first in Hawaii and then at Ft. Lewis, Washington. Subsequently, they returned to school in Spokane for an M.S. in psychiatric nursing, and Danielle found a job as charge nurse at a Seattle hospital. Shortly after completing her graduate work, she divorced Don, who turned out to be abusive. (The literature on abused children shows that they frequently choose abusive spouses although in Danielle's case I don't believe she had any idea that her husband could possibly be abusive until after they were married, but perhaps that is the way it usually is.)

Danielle remarried, this time to the author of "The Burning House" poem. Bill helped Danielle move out of the closet of fear in which she so often hid. Together, they raised and home-schooled two girls, Heidi and Heather, whose only knowledge of abuse came from Ma, who once came to visit.

While visiting, Ma flew into a rage when six-year-old Heidi sat on some freshly laundered clothes Ma had just finished folding. Bill walked in as Ma was beating Heidi with a hairbrush.

"Get your coat, Ma," Bill told her with an amazing amount of self-controlled dispassion, "We are going to the airport."

Ma looked up, surprised. "My flight is not until next week."

"That is your problem," Bill replied. "I am taking you to the airport right now. You are no longer welcome in this house." Bill dragged her to the airport, and that was the last time his children ever saw their grandmother until Heidi, fully grown and married, attended her 80th birthday party in 2008.

For years, Danielle was unable to return to New England. As a nurse, she would have had to report Uncle Charles to the authorities were she to have been in the state where his crimes were being committed. Once Uncle Charles was prosecuted, that barrier was eliminated, but as with me, there was nothing to attract her back to the charred foundations of the burning house until the 8-pack decided to gather for an old woman's 80th birthday party.

In many ways, Willie was like me. We both found a retreat in books and both often got in trouble for having "our noses in a damned book" when Ma wanted us to be doing something else. We both often used our lunch money to buy books.

In other ways, Willie was not like me at all. He looked like Dad, and perhaps for that reason Ma favored him. We all were envious that he seemed to get less physical abuse than we did although he did not escape other forms of abuse. Of all of us, he was the most strongly affected by emotional abuse. Today, he aptly describes his emotional captivity in the following way: "Every time I manage to cast off the emotional baggage that Ma saddled me with, she comes along and says, 'Wait a minute! You have forgotten something!' And with that, she hands the baggage back to me."

Willie did have support in his scholarly interests. His high school science teacher went out of his way to help him, purchasing supplies for experiments in the intersection of science and parascience, an area which Willie found absorbing. As part of his research, Willie visited me for a week at Penn State and spent most of his time at the university's huge and wondrous Pattee library. These particular experiments led to his being invited to present his results at a regional meeting of physicists. Surprised by Willie's youth, one physicist asked him what his affiliation was. Willie responded, "Heck, I am just a farm boy from down Maine," a comment that he was to repeat years later when he ended up at Boston Children's Hospital with my son, Doah, and was mistaken for a doctor.

Willie stayed the longest in the burning house. After Dad's death he taught Ma to drive the car, but for the most part he drove her wherever she needed to go. He also helped Sharon and Victoria with their schoolwork. He limited his own educational opportunities and gave in to attending the nearest university, where the professors were not up to managing his serious scholarly inquiry. One even promised him an A if he would just stop coming to class because the professor found his questions intimidating.

Of course, Ma always complained that Willie never did enough for her even though he spent 11 post-high-school years repairing the farmhouse, running the farm, and doing Ma's bidding. Unable to beat him physically because he had grown up, she beat him emotionally.

Erica, Willie's wife, rescued him from the burning house. They met while acting in a community theater production. Erica recognized that Willie had many talents. She also recognized what Ma was doing to dull those talents. Like the other in-laws, she saw past the smoke from the burning house, something that we of the 8-pack always found difficult, perhaps because when you are in a burning house long enough, the flames seem normal and perhaps because we so much wanted to live in a normal house that we redefined "normal."

Willie did not escape far. He lives on the top of the hill nearly overlooking the valley farm on which we grew up as children. Although he has the mind of a scholar, scholarship was not to be his lot in life. He spent most of his middle years as a toy-maker, creating wooden toys for schools in a workshop on his farm. Ultimately, a dreamer like Dad, not quite fitting into this world, he bounced around from one Dad-like job to another until recently when he more appropriately began working for the county conservation district, spending his spare time as an organist for the Anglican Churchof Kenya, where he and Erica have found a spiritual home.

As much as he loves geology, Willie finds even greater happiness in the life-long genealogical research that he began conducting in his early twenties. He clearly knows more about the founding of New England, the founding fathers, and the rise and fall of families than any published historian. Pushed to publish his work, he admits its value—and stops there. Perhaps one day the research will become public. In the interim, he finds his happiness in his research and in a deep faith in God, shared and enriched by Erica, the oh-so-necessary counterbalance to Ma because Erica respects and loves him, two emotions that were surely alien to him when first encountered.

As a child, Rollie could get himself into trouble even in his sleep. I remember 6-year-old Rollie sleepwalking to the bathroom. (Rollie walked a lot in his sleep, and I have to think that he had troubled dreams from all the abuse he experienced.) In this instance, sound asleep and feeling the urge to relieve his bladder, he stumbled into the bathroom at the top of our staircase, turned in the wrong direction, and peed down the stairs. Poor Rollie! Yanked out of the bed into which he had tumbled after his sleepwalking, he was treated to several minutes of invigorating slaps.

I know more about Rollie's adult emotional experiences than about those of my other siblings because when Doah was a senior in high school, we ran into serious problems with the California school system at the same time that I was offered a long-term consulting stint at NASA. Rollie, living in Ohio, offered to take Doah in for that year. During my many trips from Houston to Columbus to visit with my son, I had long, emotionally exhausting discussions with Rollie about the effect of our abusive childhood on him. He told me that he dreams about Ma's death by torture every single night, and every night the torture is of a different kind but of equal intensity.

Rollie did not get to this place of hatred simply because of what happened to him as a child. He, like me, actually "got past" the childhood and even took Ma in at one point when she was without a home, just as I did on two occasions. And like me, he has regretted it for a lifetime because she hurt his children.

The final straw came when he encountered her pulling his youngest son, Jason, out of the chair by his hair. Rollie jumped in, disentangled Ma and Jason, and held Ma in a grip that would not let her move.

"Go pack!" he said. "You're leaving."

"I'm not going anywhere," she responded. "I have a right to discipline that brat."

"You don't have a right to lay a hand on *my* child," he responded.

"I certainly do," she said. "He is my grandson. You don't know what he did to my printer. He needs to be punished for that."

"My son is more important than your damn printer," Rollie responded. "Now go pack unless you want to leave without any of your things." And, once again, Ma ended up at an airport days in advance of her scheduled flight.

Beginning with his teenage days in the woods, Rollie seems to have drawn the short end of the straw on far too many occasions. After moving in with Katrina when she was attending Ohio State University, he fell in love with and married someone I will call Agnes. Agnes had a brother who was in the house finishing business and taught Rollie the trade, one which he has plied to this day and one in which his three sons, now grown, have joined him. Agnes left Rollie as a result of a mental breakdown, the cause of which is still unknown. So, Rollie finished raising his boys by himself and helps out Agnes financially from time to time with money that he does not have.

In spite of Rollie's tough life, he always seems to have something to laugh about and thinks that *my* life is one that he would not want to have to live. (Perspective is a perplexing thing, for sure.) Doah is always pestering me to send him back to visit his Uncle Rollie. Rollie is like the pied piper with children. Might one liken this to the Phoenix bird in a rough sort of way? From the ashes of child abuse comes the children's hero?

Keith was the proverbial bouncing baby boy. I should know. I lugged him to my fourth grade class for show and tell when he was a few months old. In fact, I lugged him everywhere, and at night he often toddled into my room and crawled into bed with me. "Biffy" he called me, not being able to say "Bethie."

Three years younger than Rollie, he looked very much like Rollie as a baby and was as fun-loving as Rollie. His easy-going nature, unlike Rollie's, never took on a sharp edge, but then, he never experienced the full range of abuse that Rollie did. Willie and Rollie, for example, made sure that Keith was never alone with Uncle Charles.

I was not present for all of Keith's upbringing. When Keith was eight, Pop died, and later that year I moved in with Gram, a decision made by the extended family who did not want Gram to live alone. (When I left for college, Danielle replaced me as Gram's live-in grandchild, and we both considered that experience to be a time of reprieve. Dad would stop by every night to see if I wanted to move back home, back to the burning house, but I did not even though I felt sorry for my siblings who were still there. The fresh air was too appealing.)

Keith clearly received a share of the physical and emotional abuse. None of us escaped that. Once Dad died, though, when Keith was a teenager, much changed. Ma was getting physically older and therefore weaker when it came to winning fist fights with her children. Dependence on welfare may have dulled her ego (not a lot, but even a little helped). After Katrina's semester of educating her on household management ended, Ma took over her own finances, failed abysmally, and Keith stepped in to prevent loss of all assets. Beating someone physically bigger than you and upon whom you are dependent is not a sensible course, so Ma was reduced to emotional abuse—a weapon she deploys upon unexplainable occasions against the entire 8-pack to this day.

Bachelor Uncle Keith became close to my children, all of whom love him. After high school, he moved to a farm in a neighboring town and for more than two decades has worked as foreman of a submarine pipe fitter unit at a shipyard. Although he never married, he is very family-oriented and spends many hours with his friends' children. How he remained easy-going, Lord only knows (and probably the Lord does know because Keith has always had a strong faith in and reliance upon God).

Of all of the 8-pack, though, Keith is probably Ma's best offspring. If he finds an urgent message on the answering machine, he does call her and, if something is needed, makes arrangements for someone to help her. Once a month, he stops by her apartment to see if she is still alive and what she might need. He is able to confirm to the rest of the 8-pack that "Ma is just as healthy and ornery as ever." So, we all know then that she is alive and well—and likely as happy as she is ever going to be.

About Sharon's childhood, I know even less than about Keith's. She was born my senior year, when I was living with Gram, and after that I was living out of state. Lizzie spent a few summers on the farm with my sisters (at the time I was unaware that Ma had no compulsion about beating her grandchildren although not as roughly as she had beaten her children). So, Lizzie came to know Sharon better than I.

One thing for sure is that Ma was indeed mellower during Sharon's and Victoria's childhood. The welfare connection explained some of it since social workers were more likely to notice and report abuse than school teachers of that era. Ma's advancing age explained more. Perhaps most, though, was explained by a kindly neighbor from town, whom we always called Uncle John, losing his wife, Aunt Kathleen, and moving in with Ma a year or two later. Ma was unable to mesmerize Uncle John as she had Dad, so Uncle John served as a protective force for as long as he remained in the household, which was only for a few years. Why he left, he told no one, not even Ma.

Unfortunately, Uncle John remained in the dark about Cousin Billy's tormenting of Sharon and Victoria. Not all the torment was sexual. Sometimes Cousin Billy engaged in simple bullying, such as the times he would pop up behind the little girls with the head of a dead pig and laugh as they ran away in horror. Uncle John never knew because Cousin Billy was clever in carefully choosing times and places for his torments. He also never knew because the younger girls, like the older girls, never told. They knew Ma would not believe them, and they, like so many rape victims, felt ashamed and embarrassed. These were not things one talked about in gentrified society—or any society in those days.

Although I did not share Sharon's daily childhood life, I did share some of her personality. In a near repetition of gene selection, she not only looked like me and sometimes acted like me but also she shared my childhood interests, especially in physics. Fortunately, times had changed since the days my high school physics teacher, in noting that I had the highest grade in a class of 40 students that contained only five girls, bemoaned my gender. "It is too bad you are a girl," he told me with the kindliest of intentions, "because you would make a great physicist."

Sharon did have that opportunity. She majored in nuclear physics at Michigan State University, graduated with a 4.0, and was highly recruited by graduate schools before changing her mind to work in the computer field with her husband. Also like me, she now lives too often on an airplane for reasons of work. Her husband? Ah, that is the story of her escape. Like Erica's rescue of Willie, Soren pulled Sharon from the burning house, but in an unorthodox and socially unacceptable way.

Soren was Sharon's high school math teacher. They fell in love when Sharon was in his class. She would sneak away to be with him, seizing stolen gasps of fresh air and breezes of emotional support while momentarily away from the burning house. In the country, such indiscretion does not go unnoticed, and soon their relationship became a scandal. Sharon left school. Soren was fired. At that point, Sharon moved to New York, where compassionate Katrina, unaware of the whole story at the time, rescued her, like Rollie before her, from the burning house. There Sharon finished her senior year and earned a full scholarship to Michigan State. Soren followed her to Michigan, and they married there a few months later. They have no children, and following their spectacular start, they have settled into a quietly enduring marriage for nearly twenty years.

At 15, Victoria began to fail her school subjects. Failure is not something that Ma accepts. Ma's children do not fail. Period. Ma's children have one purpose in life: to bring her glory. Failure is not glory. So, just as she found a way to remove Sharon and Rollie as obstacles to her glory, she found a way to remove Victoria. She sent her to me.

As a result, I came to know Victoria well, as much as a daughter as a sister for she had been born when I was 20, just two months after Donnie and I married. For Lizzie, Victoria was both sister and aunt. They attended the same school; they both babysat Lizzie's siblings.

Victoria was the last to escape the burning house, not only by age but also by circumstance. Abuse became a way of life for her, and she went from an abusive parent, who followed her from pillar to post, to an abusive spouse, whom she claimed to love in spite of the abuse. Those circumstances could not be more unbelievable had they been part of a fairy tale—or more likely, horror story.

Although not a scholar like me, Victoria, perhaps from the very act of living with me, assumed that she should attend college. She applied to a small college in Bristol, Virginia and was accepted.

All might have been very different had Ma not reentered the picture slightly before then. Having sold the farm because she could not maintain it by herself, Ma moved to Washington, D.C.. Oh, joy! She settled herself into a small apartment near me and took Victoria with her. Then, when Victoria moved to Bristol, Ma moved there, bought a house, and insisted that Victoria and her friends move in.

Co-dependence rampaged their relationship for years and ravaged Victoria's life. Gray, a classmate of Victoria's from high school, with whom she had fallen in love her senior year, followed her to Bristol, where they married, much to Ma's dismay. Subsequently, Gray joined the U. S. Army as a private in the infantry, and moved Victoria and soon-to-be born Austin with him. That effectively broke Ma's yoke.

The yoke of cruel circumstance continued, however. While stationed in Tennessee, Gray and Victoria met another couple, Tom and Susan. For some inexplicable reason—is love ever explicable?—Tom and Victoria found themselves attracted to each other and so did Gray and Susan. The odd fable of Victoria's life continued: the two couples divorced and married each other's partners.

After Tom completed his stint in the military, he took Victoria home to Michigan, where their son, Ashton, was born. Tom took up truck driving, beating Victoria, and browbeating Austin. Each time Victoria forgave him and blamed herself for "pushing his buttons."

Victoria's low self-esteem behaviors kept her tied to a co-dependent mother and a husband who came close to killing her. The day that Tom held a knife to her throat and a call to 911 saved her from imminent death proved a watershed. Tom served a 6-month jail term, during which social workers gave Victoria the choice of divorce or losing her children. She chose divorce. Since then she has been a happy and fulfilled single mother. That is not the marital status she would have chosen for herself or her children, but it was the one that became her lot. It has worked. Rollie lives within driving distance and like the pied piper and helping brother that he is, his door has always been open to Austin, Ashton, and Victoria, as it was to Doah and me.

Victoria flailed not only against Tom's physical abuse but also in her career planning. She had cut her education short in Bristol in order to follow Gray. Then, she had followed Tom. Now, as a single mother, she needed a profession. She tried nursing school before finding that she had talent at massage therapy, a trade she has happily plied now for going on ten years. Austin, amazingly well adjusted for the child of divorce and abuse, finishes high school this year, and happy little Ashton begins it.

All told, then, one might count eight escapees from the burning house, but when one has children living nearby, they also feel the flames. So, the total count would be about 19.

What the world saw during my childhood was something very different from what the 8-pack experienced: physical, sexual, emotional, and spiritual abuse. For that reason, Edward Arlington Robinson's poem, "Richard Corey," resonated with me from the time I first heard it in a high school English class:

> *Whenever Richard Cory went down town,*
> *We people on the pavement looked at him:*
> *He was a gentleman from sole to crown,*
> *Clean favored, and imperially slim.*
>
> *And he was always quietly arrayed,*
> *And he was always human when he talked;*
> *But still he fluttered pulses when he said,*
> *"Good-morning," and he glittered when he walked.*

*And he was rich - yes, richer than a king -*
*And admirably schooled in every grace;*
*In fine we thought that he was everything*
*To make us wish that we were in his place.*

*So on we worked, and waited for the light,*
*And went without the meat, and cursed the bread;*
*And Richard Cory, one calm summer night,*
*Went home and put a bullet through his head.*

Like Richard Corey, we came from what appeared to be an impeccably perfect family. Everyone in the community praised Ma for having smart children. We had better be or it would have been a lot of airplane rides for us; even for piano lessons, the beat for practicing was a combined metronome and hair brush on the hands. They praised her for having well-behaved children; there would have been even more airplane rides had we not been. They praised her for well-kempt children. That, to Ma's credit, was something she did well. We were always clean, and our hair was brushed and, for the girls, braided, not unaccompanied by hair yanking and mouth-slapping, but the results were aesthetic.

Who knows what was really at the core of Robin Corey's "glitter" and "quiet array?" We knew far too well that the surface and the core are as different as gurgling, cool rivers and boiling, hot lava.

Unlike Richard Corey, who "went home and put a bullet through his head," we grew up to have friends and families and to help people. We have shared unthinkable, even unbelievable torment that, thankfully, was not experienced by anyone else we know. Most important, to this day, we have each other and the self-confidence that comes from having survived brutality but not repeated it.

Unlike Richard Corey, we wanted to live. We rose above our experience, impoverished and in pain but intent upon survival. "Raging, raging against the dying of the light," in Dylan Thomas's words, we did not let MacBeth's "brief candle" go out.

I was the first to escape the burning house. I always knew I would. Through all the years of beatings, I looked only ahead. Thanks to the books, I knew that there was an outside world.

I did leave, and I go home very rarely. The old memories are no longer painful, but very little attracts me back to a place where I knew so much torment. Although the 8-pack meets occasionally, it is not at the old farmhouse. We now have many emotionally safe places to meet for today the 8-pack can be found spread across the United States in Maine, New York, Ohio, Michigan, Oregon, Washington, and California.

The fire in the burning house embered out. We overcame.

# The Consul

After Lev's visit to the American Embassy and the extreme negative response of the consul, Shura began to give up hope. It was about then that his parents and those of us who were trying to help him were wondering whether we should have told him about our plans.

To make matters worse, he was admitted to the hospital in Siberia with constant kidney and bladder infections, osteomyelitis, and gangrene in both legs, gangrene that periodically threatened to end his life. This certainly complicated matters. If he did not get better, we would not be able to get him to the United States even if the American Embassy in Moscow were to relent and grant him a visa.

While he was lying in a hospital in Siberia, with limited access to antibiotics, trying to overcome with sheer will power a disease that needed antibiotics for treatment, we continued to press the embassy for a visa. Hope dwindled and nearly embered in the others but still flamed brightly in me. With the same certainty that I knew I would escape from the burning house, I assumed that somehow, some way we would get the visa, and so Lev and I both traveled to Moscow once more.

Lev had arranged for us to meet the consular officer together. On the morning of the appointment, we approached the gates of the embassy. Although our appointment was for first thing in the morning, the line into the consular section of the embassy already extended several blocks. As we pushed our way forward, people kept pushing us back, telling us to get in line. Lev would explain that I was an American and had an appointment. I held up my blue tourist passport as proof. Some folks grudgingly let us pass. Others made rude comments about us thinking ourselves better than others. The animosity and jockeying for position reminded me of those science fiction movies in which inhabitants have to leave a planet before it explodes. I suppose, in a way, that Russia was exploding during the new *smutnoe vremya* (time of troubles), when there were limited jobs and a massive brain drain westward.

Finally, we made it to the embassy gate. On the street side of the gate stood a Russian guard, to whom we explained in Russian that we had a meeting with the consular officer, whom I shall call Joyce Anderson since I have long ago forgotten her name. Once past the Russian guard, the American marine guard on the side of the gate facing the embassy compound grilled us with questions spoken rapidly in machine-gun-like bursts. The name of Joyce Anderson, however, held sway, and soon we found ourselves face-to-face with that august person, except that she was not august at all. In her mid-30s, she had a nondescript face, a grating voice, and mousy-brown hair. She also had a peremptory manner. I could not tell whether she wanted to help us or put an end to what she considered our nonsense.

Lev and I had brought with us a *spravka* (certificate) from Shura's doctor in Akademgorodok, which summarized Shura's medical situation. I held the *spravka* out to the consular officer. "Let me explain what it says," I offered.

She snatched it out of my hand. "I have to read it myself," she said curtly.

Okay, I thought, good luck! Her Russian language skills, from the brief interaction she had had with Lev up to this point, were at a survival, not a professional, level of proficiency, and the piece of paper I had just given to her would typically require much higher general proficiency skills along with the knowledge of specialized medical terminology.

She read it over several times while the clock ticked on. Clearly, she could not understand it. Finally, she spoke. "Excuse me," she said coldly, as if we were causing her a good deal of trouble or at least annoyance. "I have to go study this."

Right, I thought, go study it. Look up *spinomozgavaya gryzha* in a Russian-English medical dictionary if you have one. You will find the term *meningeomyelocele*, which I truly doubt that you will understand.

She disappeared for nearly ten minutes. She was probably asking colleagues for help, but who among them would know the term, *meningeomyelocele*, the more descriptive name for spina bifida? Sure enough, she returned uneducated about Shura's condition. She pushed the paper toward me and said, "Translate it for me."

Without any comment, I explained what the *spravka* said and what *meningeomyelocele* encompassed. Lev stood quietly at my side. I wonder what he thinks about Americans right at this moment—this stray thought ran through my mind. I was embarrassed that a countryman would act in this way. Lev's face was expressionless, but I could feel his tenseness. He probably thinks that this is hopeless and that we will go away empty-handed—a second stray thought ran through my mind. I said nothing to him for fear of unbalancing an already tenuous situation, but I did believe that we would get some help with a visa this time.

Once Joyce had understood the situation, she commented that some of my former students who had risen to respected positions at the embassy had vouched for me and that she would consider issuing a visitor's visa if we completed the medical documentation and requirements. Essentially, what she wanted was to know that there would be no drain on the American welfare system, that doctors and a hospital would donate all care while Shura was in the United States.

At least, now we knew what was needed, and knowing gives hope. Our trek toward the unreachable star was back on track. Clearly, some fights were ahead of us. That was not frightening. We had already won the most important one. I now had great confidence in winning not only the battles but also the war. Little did I know at that time how many more skirmishes there would be before the war would be won.

Now that we knew what the embassy would require, we kept pushing. The "we" was mostly Dr. Uscinski, a leading pediatric neurosurgeon from Washington, DC, who had been Noelle's doctor when we lived there. Noelle's good fortune at having been treated by Dr. Uscinski turned out to be Shura's good fortune, as well. So many times Dr. Uscinski had been not only Noelle's knight in shining armor but mine as well. Of all the neurosurgeons who have treated Noelle, he is the one I remember the best and the most fondly.

My first encounter with Dr. Uscinski was in the middle of the night at Georgetown University Hospital to which we had rushed 11-year-old Noelle when her shunt, the device that controlled her hydrocephalus (water-on-the-brain), malfunctioned. Normally the shunt drained the cerebrospinal fluid that routinely built up inside her brain from that location into her abdomen. Now the fluid was remaining in her brain, pressing the brain matter against her skull, shutting down her autonomous functions. The resident neurosurgeon worried.

"Tell me how many fingers you can see," he directed her.

"Forget about the fingers," she replied. "Do something about my breathing." With those words, she stopped breathing and went into cardiac arrest.

Immediately, we were pushed out of the way as a bevy of doctors and nurses rushed resuscitation equipment to her side. Carts, tubes, paddles, all the latest in modern technology appeared instantly as if conjured by a magician. Soon, Noelle was breathing again, thanks to the support of a life machine. At that point, the staff made a call to Dr. Uscinski, who crawled out of bed at 2:00 a.m. to perform a shunt replacement on a patient he had never met.

"Tell me everything you know about Noelle's shunt and related conditions," he requested of me, having learned that all of Noelle's records were still at her previous hospital and not obtainable at that hour. I was glad that I had made the habit of memorizing all my children's records!

We were to go through three shunt revisions in the next six weeks. During that time, I came to know Dr. Uscinski quite well—and he us.

Dr. Uscinski looked at Shura's x-rays and knew that he could help him. He sent a fax to the embassy in Moscow, stating that he would donate his care. Finally, all was a "go"—or so I thought.

I checked with the embassy by phone call from the United States the next day. I was coldly informed that no fax had been received. Dr. Uscinski re-sent the fax, and again I was informed that it had not been received.

Suspecting that roadblocks were being deliberately placed in our path, I contacted a friend in Moscow who had a fax at her home. She agreed to hand-carry a copy of Dr. Uscinski's fax to the embassy if necessary. I called Dr. Uscinski and asked him to send the fax one more time, which, patient man that he is, he did. This new fax carried the notation that it was being concurrently sent to the other Moscow fax and would be brought to the embassy if not received. Surprise? The embassy reported receiving this third fax. *Now*, all was a "go"—or so I thought.

This time Joyce Anderson called me. She told me that while the embassy did receive the fax, it was insufficient to grant a visa. Dr. Uscinski, she said, had stated that he would perform surgery for free, but he had not said that he would do the examination for free.

I called Dr. Uscinski right away. He was puzzled by this interpretation of his fax. "Are consular officers required to have lobotomies before being posted to Moscow?" he asked in frustration.

I did not know how to answer. It certainly seemed like they went from having fully effective brains while in language training and other forms of preparation for their assignments abroad, but once they got there, somehow all their commonsense, let alone compassion, disappeared.

We were all frustrated by one more delay. Dr. Uscinski sent his fourth fax to Moscow, and we all held our breath, fully expecting yet another requirement to be levied upon us.

Meanwhile, I contacted all the airlines that flew into Siberia, which was not many. Flights from Siberia were expensive. Some airlines did not donate travel for charitable purposes; others had already given away all the available free tickets for the year. Hope was dimming when the American Councils, which had an office in Akademgorodok, offered tickets to Lev and Shura.

Next we had to to find an American Russian-speaking family that would take in a child with spina bifida. That did not seem to me to be a difficult task, but it turned out to be an impossible one. I contacted Russian family after Russian family. None understood spina bifida, and all were fearful of taking in a child with so many medical needs. So, I turned to the spina bifida families I knew. There was quite a number of those. Once again, family after family turned me down. While they understood spina bifida and did not fear the medical requirements, they were reluctant to take in a child who did not speak English. I pondered the problem at length, eventually realizing that a Russian-speaking family with spina bifida experience had been right under my nose all along: it was my family.

Everything, finally, was lined up: the doctors, the airline tickets, and a Russian-speaking family. Good to go! Well, except for the hospital, but that was a "small" (!) detail that I was not about to mention to the U. S. Embassy.

And then...we won! Joyce Anderson called me once again, this time to tell me that the visa had been granted. We had tilted at the windmill, and it had moved.

# Growing Up on the Boys' Side of the Playground

Taking on embassies, consular officers, bureaucracies—essentially all comers—began very early for me. In addition to physically fighting Ma in my teen years, I took on my classmates as the occasion demanded. The occasion demanded, for example, when I was riding home on the school bus one seventh grade afternoon the year before moving to the Maine farm. As usual, I was in the back of the bus with the boys. Girl talk and girl games of the 1960s interested me far less than boy talk and boy games of those days. The boy's side of the playground was where I felt most at home. Boys liked to climb trees, like I did. Girls of my era did not. Boys liked to play baseball, like I did. Girls used a boring, slow-moving, soft ball. Boys liked physical interaction, as did I. Girls of my peerage preferred dolls and chatting. As an adult, I, not Donnie, would physically wrestle with our elementary-school sons.

Usually, we were a bit rowdy at the back of the bus. On this occasion, however, we went beyond just being rowdy. Something sparked a desire in one of the boys to challenge me, and then it caught on with all six of them. They always teased me because I was an avid reader. I saw no contradiction between being a ball player and a reader, between using my legs to race down a field and using my eyes to race through a book. They did. So, one of them grabbed my book bag with my beloved books and held it above his head.

"Give it back!" I demanded and jumped for it. I was the shortest person in my class, so I was always jumping to compete with the height of my classmates—not only of the boys, of the girls, too.

The lad laughed and tossed the book bag to another boy, Mike, sitting two seats away. "Come get it," Mike teased. The boys were not being mean *per se*. We always teased each other. It was the way of the boys' world in which I lived. I also teased, but I never teased about books. Books were my friends. Books were an escape from my tormented home life.

"You bet I'll come get it!" I rose to that challenge as I rose to most challenges in childhood: readily and pugnaciously. Jumping into the fray required no prompting. Those boys had my books. I wanted them back.

I climbed over the seat between us, grabbed the book bag, and pushed Mike onto the bus floor. (Mike was a wimp, anyway. He was just trying to show the other boys that he could be macho. I was actually more macho than he!)

"Hey! Quit it!" Mike's seatmate, Martin, rose to his defense, grabbing my book bag away from me again.

"That's it! You've had it!" I warned Martin, grabbing the bag back, and knocking him to the floor. That caused the other four boys to jump to the rescue of their gender, and a free-for-all broke out, mostly shoving and some fisticuffs.

"What is going on back here?" Roger, the bus driver, suddenly standing beside us, demanded to know. We had not even noticed that the bus had stopped! Oh, oh! Instant silence!

"Off! Get off, all of you!" There was not much we could do but get off the bus. As we stood on the roadside, Roger informed us, "I will have the school contact your parents to pick you up, and they will have to find a way to get you to and from school for the next week. You cannot ride this bus unless you behave properly." Then, he looked directly at me and said, "As for you, Beth, I will tell your father personally."

Oh, boy! Roger and Dad were friends, so Dad would get an earful. At least, it would not be Ma. I was pretty certain that Dad would not beat me for this. He would understand about my books because he, too, loved books. Ma might try to beat me, but I was getting much better at holding my own with her. In general, whether with peers or with Ma, I was gaining good skills at fighting, and I was winning more contests than I was losing. Perhaps that is why my emotional reaction to being kicked off the school bus was not fear, but anger. I had been winning the fisticuff contest with those six boys, and I was mad that Roger did not let the contest come to its natural conclusion. I was certain that I would have won!

Dad was not impressed with my physical prowess when Roger called to tell him where he had put me off the bus and that he should find another way into school for me for the next week. Fortunately, Martin's mother took pity on me and drove me to school along with Martin.

The attitude I demonstrated on the seventh-grade bus took many years to convert to a word-based defense system, such as that used by Rollie, who never struck with anything except words. As for me, especially after we moved to the Maine farm, I grew up to be a Maine woman, crafted ruggedly independent from farming the fields, pitching hay, and watching over many younger siblings. Maine women are raised to do everything Maine men do on a physically bold, defiantly self-sufficient, conquer-the-elements plane, in addition to caring for children. Perhaps the epitome of the stereotypical Maine woman is portrayed best in a popular anecdote.

> *Three men were sitting together bragging about the obedience and care-taking of their wives. Each strove to show the other that he had given his new wife duties that were greater in number and more complex in difficulty than those of the other men.*

> *The first man had married a woman from Arizona. "I told her that I expect her to do all the dishes and all the cleaning," he said. "Well, it took a couple days, but on the third day when I came home from work, the dishes were done, and house was spotless."*
>
> *The second man had married a woman from Louisiana. He smiled. "That's small potatoes. I told my wife the same thing. I also told her that she had to do all the cooking, as well. Like you, on the first day I didn't see anything. The second day, though, things were better, and when I came home on the third day, the house was spic-and-span, the dishes were clean and in the cupboard, and on the table was a marvelously delicious supper of blackened catfish and vegetables."*
>
> *The third man had married a woman from Maine. He began his tale. "I told my new wife that her duties include cleaning galore—the house, the dishes, everything. I also told her that I wanted the lawn mowed, the laundry washed, and hot meals every day." The other men allowed as to that being considerably more than they had asked of their wives.*
>
> *The third man continued, "On the first day, I didn't see anything. On the second day, I didn't see anything, either. By the third day, though, most of the swelling had gone down, and I could see a little bit out of my right eye, just enough to fix myself something to eat, load the dishwasher, and call a landscaper."*

In every joke, there is usually a spark of truth. I suppose Shakespeare might have called Maine women shrews. If that is true, there would nonetheless be no taming of them, as Maine men have learned long ago. I suppose that shrew trait led to my willingness to step up to any fight and brought me some difficulties on the seventh grade bus. However, in general, pugilism saw me through home trials, the few school challenges I encountered, and later a life of challenge. Of course, the older and more knowledgeable I became, the more my weapon of choice became words rather than fisticuffs. Book reading gave me an understanding of words, and I soon found that I had an innate talent in their use. The divine gift of words made the fighting that I was to have to do throughout my life more effective than any physical prowess I had developed on my own.

Growing up on the boys' side of the playground and surviving the burning house made me unafraid to knock down the barriers raised against any member of the family. Sadly, many of the barriers Noelle and Doah had to surmount were created by professionals meant to help parents like me. These professionals' efforts were often in vain, however, because they thought that they had all the right answers—and often they had not even asked the right questions. And so, I often said "no" to them.

When a mother says "no" to a doctor, typically all hell breaks loose. I experienced that loosing of hell on many occasions, especially with Noelle. Her circumstances taught me how to skirt the fires while speeding through hell.

The first serious "no" that I said to a doctor was to quite a famous one. President of the American Pediatric Neurosurgeon Association at the time, Dr. King was accustomed to charming parents into breathing a sigh of relief and handing over their children and expected the same from me. Just turn all medical decisions for my child over to a doctor who does not live at home with us? I don't think so!

Noelle's epileptic episodes created the rift between Dr. King and me. Noelle had one *grand mal* seizure, concurrent with a shunt malfunction. Experiencing multiple seizures under such conditions can be expected. Fortunately, Noelle experienced only one seizure. Nonetheless, Dr. King felt compelled to put her on medication. The one he chose was Phenobarbital.

Nowadays, no doctor would use Phenobarbital to control seizures. It is too risky and has too many side effects, in particular mood swings and interference with learning capacity. Noelle had been a good learner prior to being on Phenobarbital; she also had had a pleasant temperament. Almost immediately both these attributes changed. Her grades dipped to Ds; soon she was failing all her kindergarten work. At the same time, she would sometimes be hostile, other times weepy, and yet other times overly cheerful—in totally unpredictable and inexplicable ways. She was referred to a psychologist for help with her mood swings. As was my wont during the years of childrearing, I buried myself in medical journals, researching information about Phenobarbital, the only thing that had changed in her life and, therefore, the presumed culprit. I learned that my suspicions were justified. In article after article, doctors and medical researchers described similar effects on other children.

Certain that Dr. King would be unwilling to consider a parent's research, I unilaterally decided to remove Noelle from the medication. I talked to several friends in the medical field about how to do this safely and, of course, read some medical texts on the topic. Slowly reducing the daily dosage in order to prevent withdrawal symptoms, I was pleased to see Noelle's moods stabilizing. So was her teacher. In short order, she was released from psychotherapy as a success story. Her grades, too, responded, climbing from F to D to C to B and occasionally A, as the amount of Phenobarbital in her system dissipated. When she was down to ¼ gram of Phenobarbital per day, a non-therapeutic level, I threw out the rest of the pills. Noelle was back to normal: good grades, good moods. All was well with the world.

All was well with the world, that is, until Noelle's next clinic visit with Dr. King. When we signed into the clinic, the nurse told us that the time had come to check

Noelle's blood Phenobarbital level, and I had to inform her that Noelle was no longer taking Phenobarbital. The nurse was shocked, and, of course, she immediately informed Dr. King. We were whisked into a private room for counseling, i.e. interrogation and lecturing. I responded, trying to convert Dr. King's berating into an exchange of information and ideas. He was dogmatic and bellicose. His tongue spurted fire. Logic had no place in the exchange.

"How can *you* make a decision to stop medicating your daughter?" he demanded to know.

"Well," I said, "I felt compelled to do so by her violently negative responses to the medication. I did not ask because I know you would have insisted that she continue to take the medication no matter what."

"That is correct. She belongs on medication," he pronounced.

"But," I countered, "she had only one seizure, and that one was directly connected to a shunt malfunction."

"You don't know what you are talking about," he came back in condescension. "She has epileptiform activity. She must have this medication."

"Dr. King," it was now my turn to inject a note of condescension into my tone (after all, he started it), "as her parent I choose to put up with an occasional seizure should her epileptiform activity result in one. That is preferable to her extreme mood swings and bad grades in school."

"Her mood swings and bad grades have nothing to with the medication, Mom." Condescension now saturated his voice, and derision surrounded the word "Mom".

"Commonsense and logic indicate that they do." Condescension now saturated my voice. "Have you read the research on the side effects of Phenobarbital recently published in *The New England Journal of Medicine*?" Condescension had now reached an apex.

"*The New England Journal of Medicine* is not a reputable journal, and you should not be reading it." His face reddened, perhaps from a guilty conscience in lying about one of the most respected journals in the medical field.

This conversation was going nowhere. I just looked at him and shook my head in disbelief at his words. His way, right or wrong, I would not accept.

As I simply looked at him, wordlessly, his tone changed to solicitation. "Don't you love your daughter?" he asked, implying that if I loved Noelle, I would do everything he recommended.

"Certainly, I love her," I responded. "That is why I won't give her the medicine."

He slammed his fist into the wall and nearly screamed at me, "You don't know what you are doing. You are endangering your daughter. You cannot simply stop giving her Phenobarbital. It is an addictive medicine. Its withdrawal must be monitored. You will be back here in tears very soon at what you have done because your daughter will now start having seizures every day. Are you ready for that?"

"Doctor," I responded, wanting to scream, too, but calmed by the realization that now I really did have the upper hand, "I forgot to mention that I did reduce her dosage very gradually, probably even more gradually than you would have done, and, oh, that was nearly six months ago. I am happy to report that she has had absolutely no seizures since then."

"Come with me," he abruptly ordered the nurse who was in the room with us. Together they left.

When he returned after nearly half an hour, I had already re-clothed Noelle who had not yet had her examination. I had heard enough and was ready to leave. There were other neurosurgeons in Renboro, and Dr. King was no longer my first choice.

Dr. King was still angry but in better control of his emotions. "Look," he said, "I have little more to say. Since you refuse to follow my instructions, I do not think I will be able to care for your daughter any longer."

"For once, we are in complete agreement," I told him. My ability to resist his arsenal of emotional weapons derived from successfully withstanding Ma's 18 years of emotional intimidation. Thanks to my upbringing in a burning house, there just simply was not any kind of fiery intimidation coming from a doctor that I would not be able to withstand. March into hell, through hell, and out of hell? Yes, I had done that before. And, yes, indeed, once more good had emerged from bad, the continuing story of my life!

I was confident in saying "no" to Dr. King because I knew that I, too, had valuable information about the medical situation from living with Noelle and that Noelle would not be harmed by my decision. I was also confident in saying "no" because this was not the first battle I had had with doctors over inappropriate medication. Years earlier, in 1977, at Children's Hospital of Boston, a complacent urology resident was following Noelle after our move to Boston. (We lived there only two years, 1977-1978, but that time provided the contacts that were needed three years later to save Doah's life.) Unlike the other myelodysplasia clinic children, who had been followed there from birth, Noelle had never been prophylactically medicated for urinary tract infections. The resident gave me a prescription for an antibiotic to be taken on a daily basis.

Concerned because the resident would not listen to my argument that Noelle had never had a urinary tract infection, upon returning home I turned to Dr. Moffett, her pediatrician, whom I trusted. Dr. Moffett shared my concern about medicating someone who was not ill. He suggested a compromise: we would not give her the medicine, and he would monitor her urine weekly, daily if necessary. If she developed a urine infection, she would immediately receive medication.

Armed with this compromise, I returned to Boston Children's Hospital. The same resident greeted me, and I had the questionably "pleasant" opportunity to offer the compromise.

"You did not fill the prescription I gave you?" he asked incredulously.

"No," I answered. "Prophylactic medication makes no sense to me. I wanted to check my reaction with Noelle's pediatrician, who knows her better than you do."

Hell broke loose again. The resident insisted that we medicate Noelle. When his exhortation yielded no result, he threatened to tell Dr. Colodny about this. Ouch! That threw an arrow squarely into my soft spot. Even before we knew that Dr. Colodny would save Doah's life three years hence, he was already a godsend to us. He had examined Noelle upon our arrival in Boston and had determined that the colostomy that had been done shortly after her birth to control a rectal prolapse was not needed, that the prolapse could be treated in non-surgical ways, such as diet. The colostomy had been a constant irritation both to Noelle and to us. The colostomy site was frequently sore, raw, and even infected in spite of our best efforts to keep it clean. Seeing our efforts yield such poor results frustrated us. When Dr. Colodny successfully took down Noelle's colostomy and prescribed a diet regime that worked, we put him on a very high pedestal. So, when the resident threatened to tell Dr. Colodny that we were being uncooperative, he unsettled me.

"Okay," I told him. "Tell Dr. Colodny. If he wants Noelle on prophylactic antibiotics, we will give them to her." The resident smiled, relieved, and made a comment about the prescription he had given us.

"I don't have that anymore," I said.

"Why not?" he asked.

"I threw it away," I told him, probably too cavalierly. I could tell that my attitude did not sit well with him, but he shrugged and went to find Dr. Colodny.

He returned about ten minutes later with interesting news. "Dr. Colodny agrees with you," he reported. "He said that if Noelle has not had any urinary tract infections in the first two years of her life, she can probably safely forego prophylaxis, but he would like the pediatrician to monitor her urine weekly."

"We will be happy to comply," I cheerfully told him.

Another fiery experience had been cooled, and we forgot about the experience until 20 years later. Julie, the director of the spina bifida clinic, where Shura was ultimately treated once he reached the Unied States, of course, learned about Noelle in the process of treating Shura. She also learned about my refusal of prophylactic antibiotics for Noelle. Julie had written an article on the topic based on research that showed that years of prophylaxis in childhood produced antibiotic-resistant adults. Ironically, the doctors who prescribed prophylactic medication in order to keep spina bifida children healthy in the short run had significantly endangered them in the long run.

"How did you know not to give Noelle antibiotics?" Julie asked me.

"She wasn't sick," was my simple and logical reply.

Looking back on all the conflicts we had with doctors over how best to raise and treat Noelle, I marvel that we had the gumption to say "no" on so many occasions. So do other parents of our acquaintance. Most say "yes" to doctors on nearly every issue. Perhaps parents cave in because they do not want to feel guilty if something goes wrong. It is perhaps easier to blame the doctor than oneself for a decision that works out poorly. From where did our ability and instinct to question doctors arise? From where came the courage to stand up to doctors who berate, belittle, and expect to be worshipped, adored, and obeyed? How lucky we were in our confidence to make decisions for Noelle and later for Doah! The repeating question comes to mind, however: could all of this have been pure luck? Or has Noelle been watched over? Did our self-assurance come from our stubborn natures? Was it developed in my case from a difficult childhood? Did it come from learning and education? All three of these sources probably contributed, but what pulled them together and allowed us to stand up to medical authorities time after time after time in full confidence that everything would work out well? What allowed us to walk through these kinds of hell without fear of being burned? Did my confidence in the ultimate goodness of life have a Source that I did not at the time recognize?

## Stealing Doah

I have lost beloved acquaintances to untimely deaths: close friends such as Sveta, who rarely saw a light moment; friends such as my co-author Linda Woodward, with whom I was in the process of writing a book that has not and probably now will not see the light of day since she died of cancer unexpectedly; young, future colleagues with high potential such as the 24-year-old Siberian psychologist and talented illustrator of one of my books, Evgeni Khasan, who died in a car crash; and some of my former students like Rick Husband, commander, and crew members of the shuttle Columbia on its last voyage. These instances, though, are not out of the realm of the ordinary. People die, sadly even at young ages, as a normal part of the life process. Although I miss all of them, I have never obsessed over the death of a friend, and I have never feared dying. We are born; we do what we can to make this world a better place during the years we have on this planet; we die—that was my philosophy of life if I had any philosophy at all.

Or so I thought, until Doah was born. Our fourth child, Doah entered this world with 18 birth defects, including mental retardation and a subglottic stenosis (a growth under the glottis, or voice box, which quickly increased in size, nearly occluding his trachea and therefore precluding him from breathing normally). At the age of six months, the doctors performed a tracheotomy, and for the next 12 months he breathed through a small tube.

In cases like Doah's, one wins a good fight only by continuing to take step after step, no matter what. Told that Doah would die for certain, the trail ahead of us to bring him into adulthood seemed hopeless and far, indeed—except that I simply have no idea what the word *hopeless* means. To me, where there is life, there is hope. Clearly, though, to maintain that hope, we would have to do something about the attitude of the doctors and hospital in which Doah was being followed.

We did not have to think long. Matters quickly came to a head at Renboro Children's Hospital, to which I have given a name change for obvious reasons, one of which is the sincere hope that today the staff and administration at Renboro does not exhibit the same attitudes or practice the same policies as they did 30 years ago. Our knock-down-drag-out fights with what we considered Renboro's misguided medical personnel pitted parent against doctor in a war that was not going to serve Doah well.

In June 1980, that cold war heated up rapidly. I refused to sign papers for a fun-doplication, an operation that would repair Doah's hiatal hernia at the risk of losing him because of his breathing difficulties. Doah's pediatrician, Dr. P, was one of our strongest supporters. He would come to the hospital, mediate disputes, and provide me with his medical opinion. Dr. P researched the surgical procedure. He learned that the operation in 1980 had only a 25% survival rate in cases like Doah's and, if the patient survived, there was only a 50/50 chance that the surgery would take care of the problem. In any event, the surgery would have to be repeated every few years. (Over the years, the surgery success rate and survival rate has approached nearly 100%, but the surgery does still have to be repeated every five years.) Given these statistics, the pediatrician agreed with us that surgery was not wise.

Bent presumably on their pursuit of medical training and the chance to do what was then a relatively new procedure, the doctors insisted that Doah have the surgery. Part of me wondered whether they just assumed he was going to die, anyway, and therefore he was a good candidate for "training" surgeons on a new procedure. In any event, the doctors did not accept my refusal to sign papers authorizing surgery and took the case to court, requesting that the court grant custody of Doah to Renboro Children's Hospital so that they could do the surgery. We were not told about this court proceeding; apparently, we were going to be deprived of the opportunity even to be in courtroom and defend our rights as his parents. I found out about this intention because I read promiscuously—books and journals and articles and medical records: all Doah's surgical reports, all the nurses' notes, all the medical entries of any sort. And that is where I found it. In Doah's four-inch-thick file was a scrawled note about our being unfit parents because we would not sign for the surgery and the date of the court proceeding. The date was only two days away.

What to do? A daring plan entered my mind: steal Doah from Renboro Children's Hospital and take him to Boston Children's Hospital where Noelle had been treated three years earlier. I trusted the doctors there because they listened to me. The doctors I knew there even liked me—well, maybe all except that urology resident. I quickly found out more about Noelle's former urologist, Dr. Colodny, and learned that while he was at that time specializing in lower GI problems, he had at one time worked in the area of upper GI problems. He could be Doah's doctor, I reasoned. That thought comforted me, but we still had to get to Boston.

We developed a step-by-step plan to steal Doah from his hospital room. I shared the plan, but not the details or the timing, with Dr. P. He looked at me thoughtfully. Then he said, "I cannot condone what you propose. However, if you do happen to end up in Boston, please be aware that Bob, the son of my partner, is an intern there. He can provide the link back to us and make the transition of records and information smooth." He disappeared from the room and came back in a couple of minutes with Bob's phone number. That was all that I needed to put our plan into action.

The next day, the doctors were in court, and we were at the curb outside the hospital. Donnie kept the car running in a "standing only" zone. What I was about to do would not, could not take a long time, we reasoned.

I walked into the hospital as I had on any other day. I carried no clothes for Doah; they were in the car. I would not have time to dress him if I were to whisk him out unnoticed.

I took the elevator to the fifth floor and walked to Doah's room. Visible from the elevator, the room was catty corner from the nurses' station. The nurse on duty looked up and said hello, and I responded, just as if it were any other day.

I walked into Doah's room. Good, there was no one else in there. Doah was plugged into an array of machinery. The machines did not provide life support. They simply monitored Doah's condition. I could unplug them without doing any harm to him, but they would set off alarms at the nurses' station. That would have to be the last thing I did. I looked in the supply cabinet where his medical "things" were kept and found the hand-held suction machine that was there for an emergency cleaning of his trach tube in the event that the electricity went out and he experienced a mucous plug. I would need that suction machine enroute to Boston. It was small. I quickly shoved it into my pocket. Then I deftly untucked the blanket on the bed and wrapped Doah, who was wearing nothing but a diaper, in it. We were ready except for the half-dozen wires and electrodes attached to his body. With one smooth sweep of my hand, I disengaged all of them, setting off a half-dozen alarms simultaneously. With Doah in my arms, I slipped stealthily out of the room and bumped into the charge nurse, who was answering the alarms.

"What is going on?" she demanded to know.

"I am taking Doah with me," I replied briefly while looking for an escape route other than the elevator, which was now clearly not an option.

"You cannot do that. He has not been discharged by the doctor," she said, frowning and clearly tense.

"Certainly I can do that," I told her evenly although I had to struggle to maintain a calm tone. "He is my son. I can bring him here, and I can take him away from here."

"No, you can't," she insisted and then let the cat out of the bag. "The doctors are in court right now, getting custody of this child."

"Right," I said in the same steely, even tone. Lord knows how I was able to maintain the external calm with my heart pounding and adrenalin flooding my veins. "They are in court now, and I am here now. They may have custody in the future, but I have custody now. I am taking him with me." My eyes finally saw what I was looking for—a stairway exit at the end of the opposite hallway. I could reach it pretty quickly at a run.

"I'm calling security," she said, as she headed back to the nurses' station.

"Call whomever you want," I replied and sprinted to the doorway. I dashed down the stairs, all five flights, as if they were a hill of snow and I was on a sled. I don't remember actually stepping on even one of the stairs, but clearly I must have. Reaching the bottom, I ran as fast as I could to the car. All the intensive running-away practice I had had in my childhood and later in the Army now stood me in good stead. Still being in the US Army Reserve, running one weekend every month, had not hurt, either.

Thank goodness, the car was still there. Donnie had not yet been chased away by a meter maid. I opened the door and jumped in. Breathing heavily, I urged Donnie, "Go!"

We sped away, not home, but to the airport. I had earlier checked on the first flight out to Boston. It was on US Airways, and we had about an hour to wait. It was an hour of agony, wondering if custody would be granted in the interim, whether the security guards would figure out that we probably had gone to the airport, whether the police would be contacted, whether someone would think to check airline manifests. Finally, the plane was ready to board. I walked on with Doah, as if every day I stole my child from the hospital and flew with him to some other city.

On board, I relaxed. The stewardess told me that Doah was cute, and she spent a few minutes casually chatting with me. The flight from Renboro to Boston generally takes about 50 minutes. I had time to read the in-flight magazine and mentally prepare to meet my brothers. I had called Boston Children's. No beds were available until the next day, so Willie and Keith had promised to meet me at Logan Airport and take me home to Maine. We would spend the night on the farm and return in the morning when there would be room for Doah at the hospital. All was on track. All was calm.

All was calm, that is, until 30 minutes into the flight when the pilot announced that we were landing. Some of the passengers asked the stewardess what was going on and in what city we would be landing. "In Boston," she replied. "We just had a faster flight than usual because we have a medical emergency on board."

We landed, and the stewardess asked everyone to remain seated while they took care of a medical emergency. Then she approached me and said she would help me out. "I think you had better take care of your medical emergency first," I suggested, confused.

Now it was her turn to look confused. "We were told that you are the medical emergency," she said.

It turned out that Renboro Children's Hospital's security office did rather quickly figure out where we were and had contacted the airline right after we had taken off. They had frightened the pilot into double-timing to Boston by suggesting that Doah might stop breathing at any moment. The airline had made arrangements for my luggage to be retrieved immediately upon landing. They had also contacted Keith and Willie ("any party in the waiting area for the arrival of Elizabeth Mahlou"), lining up Keith and his car behind the ambulance that was waiting to transport us to Boston Children's where a bed had been miraculously found. Willie they had placed on the jetway so that he could talk me into taking Doah to the hospital should I not want to.

Literally only minutes later, Doah and I were in the ambulance, careening through downtown Boston with sirens shrieking and lights pulsating, with Keith and Willie in frantic pursuit. How fortunate that it was a weekday night when Boston streets are more lightly traveled!

We arrived at the hospital at the same time. The admissions personnel looked at Willie and Keith in the coveralls they had been wearing in the field and, confused, asked, "Are you two medical personnel?"

"Heck, no," answered Willie. "We're just farmers from down Maine."

Once Doah was in a bed on the ward, a resident appeared to take charge of him. "Renboro Children's Hospital has been in touch with us," he said, "and we have assigned Dr. Friedman to Doah."

"No, there is some mistake there," I responded, "Dr. Colodny will be his doctor."

"Dr. Colodny does not handle lower GI patients," the resident explained patiently.

"He used to," I informed the resident, "and I bet he has not forgotten how to do it. Look, I am really tired. It has been a longer and more exhausting day than you could possibly imagine. It is nearly midnight, and nothing is going to get solved in the dark of the night. I am going home with my brothers. I will sign papers, giving you permission to put Doah on a life machine should he stop breathing but to do nothing else. You talk to Dr. Colodny in the morning, and I will come back around noon to talk to him about Doah." I was certain that Dr. Colodny would take Doah as a patient although I had not been in touch with him. As the head of the urology division, Dr, Colodny had taken Noelle as his personal patient because she had some unique complications, and he liked challenges. Doah would also be a challenge for him, and I did not think he would turn down a challenge.

The next morning, toward noon, I returned to the ward and tracked down the resident. "Dr. Colodny agreed to take Doah," he said in a surprised, almost awed tone. "We have dismissed Dr. Friedman from the case."

"I thought he would," I responded. "I will be here round the clock so he can talk to me whenever it is convenient."

Dr. Colodny came and greeted me effusively. He agreed with my risk assessment and dismissed the idea of a fundoplication. He set Doah up on a diet regime that would ameliorate the worst aspects of the hiatal hernia, and he had his bed set up on an incline to help nature take over some of the cure. Given the tracheotomy, he had the ENT staff look at Doah. There was not much that they could do about the subglottic stenosis, but they did bring up his case at a regional medical conference that was taking place at the time, unfortunately with no resolution or additional insights. (I gave Bob's name to Doah's young, pretty, primary nurse. Bob turned out to be handsome, and the nurse and resident soon started dating.) A month later, Doah had gained four pounds. (In the month he was at Renboro Children's Hospital, he had lost a half-pound and was down to eight pounds at the age of six months.) Doah was released, but this time, he was being sent home with an apnea monitor, so we no longer had to worry whether or not he was breathing. There was a machine that would tell us. (Renboro Children's Hospital, when we had asked for a monitor, told us to tie bells to his shoes instead.)

Arriving back in Renboro, life returned to normal (for us). I continued teaching, taking Doah to my classes with me and placing him under the podium in his baby seat so that I could stop and suction out his trach tube whenever it became clogged. Doah still sported the tracheotomy tube that allowed him to breathe, staving off the death threatened by the subglottic stenosis. His care once again was coming from Renboro Hospital, the only local option, and the same dour prognosis persisted. Right before Christmas, I had a conversation with the chief of the ENT clinic that confirmed we would find no hope at Renboro.

"Now that we are back from Boston and Doah's general health is better, what can you tell me about a prognosis?" I asked.

"Look, you just don't get it, do you?" the doctor responded haughtily. "His prognosis is days, weeks if you are lucky. My best advice to you is to accept the inevitable and consider how you are going to handle his death and the days after his death."

Well, that was not an acceptable response. I looked at the doctor coldly, as I quickly dressed Doah, and said, "Neither you nor I can predict exactly what will happen in the long-term, but in the short-term I can very accurately predict that he will no longer be your patient." With that, I walked out.

I took Doah home, left him with Donnie, and returned to Renboro Hospital and Medical School. Flashing my graduate assistant identification card from the University of Renboro as if it were a medical school ID, I marched into the University of Renboro Medical School Library like an entire platoon about to take the next hill. Finding the ENT section of the library, I seized the latest volumes of the *Otorhinolarnygology Journal*. There I found my objective: Dr. Robin Cotton of Children's Hospital of Cincinnati had written several articles on subglottic and other forms of tracheal stenosis, and he described cases where the children had survived.

I called him and recited Doah's surgical records from memory. He said he thought he could take down the tracheotomy and reduce the stenosis were we to bring Doah to Cincinnati. Were we, an impoverished doctoral candidate and a forester-turned-art-school-student, trying to raise four children, two of whom had multiple birth defects, to bring Doah to Cincinnati after just having spent our last dollar to get him to Boston where the doctors had saved his life but could not repair his breathing?! It would cost more than $200, a sizable amount of money in the late 1970s, when my salary topped out at $800/month. Nonetheless, full of hope, I counted on getting Doah to Cincinnati. I did not know how that would happen, how we would get the Chihuahua of poverty from nipping at our heels long enough to get to Cincinnati and back, but I was confident it *would* happen.

A few days after my phone conversation with Dr. Cotton, I walked past the office of Liliya Vasilievna, a literature professor in the department where I was taking my doctoral studies. Liliya Vasilievna motioned for me to come in and shut the door. Then she handed me an envelope, saying "I heard from one of your fellow doctoral students that you have found a doctor in Cincinnati who might be able to help your son. Even by car, it will be an expensive trip for you. Here is $250 in cash. Pay me back when you can afford to do so and not before." (I did pay her back before she retired, which was at about the same time that I landed a supervisory job with the State Department.)

Getting to Cincinnati, however, was not going to be easy in spite of Liliya Vasilievna's loan. This was, after all, *my* life. While it has been full of blessings, very little about it has been easy. In this case, a week before we were to leave for Cincinnati, I fell down a flight of stairs and broke my back.

As my body crumpled against the cement at the bottom of the wooden staircase leading into our basement, a warm, grey ether stole up to me, beckoning me to follow. Oh, no, I thought. I cannot pass out. Doah is upstairs and may get a mucous plug. Shane is sitting on the porch stairs, and Noelle is in the back of the Pacer with no way to get out because her crutches are up front.

The only one who could have helped, 8-year-old Lizzie, had already gone to school. I had been getting 4-year-old Noelle and 3-year-old Shane ready to drop off at day care. Doah, of course, was coming to class with me.

I tried to stand up but could not, so I crawled back up the stairs. I could not stand up, either, to reach our wall phone, so I kept pulling at the dangling cord until finally the phone fell off the hook. Experiencing great difficulty in breathing, I nonetheless managed to get the ambulance to understand where I lived.

Then I crawled to the living room where Doah was in his baby seat on the couch and struggling to breathe through a mucus plug. An increasingly intensive blue hue was spreading across his ash-tinged pink face. I could not stand nor could I reach Doah. Frantic, I beat my hands against the couch, trying to create enough vibration to knock Doah off, but it was to no avail. Shane heard the commotion and came in.

"Shane," I said. "I have to reach Doah. See if you can get his seat off the couch." He would have been too heavy for Shane, but it was worth a try.

Shane scoped out the situation instantly. "I can suction him, Mommy. I know how to do it." Many nurses are uncomfortable suctioning trached children. How would Shane do it?

"Shane, it is a difficult thing to do, and the machine is on the wrong setting. I need the machine and Doah. Quickly!"

"I can't lift Doah," Shane replied, "but I can suction him. I can fix the machine. I can do it, Mommy, I can do it." With that, he flipped the machine onto the proper setting and suctioned Doah, whose skin color immediately returned to normal.

"Good boy, Shane," I said. "Now, go watch for the ambulance. I hurt my back. They will take me to the hospital." Shane went out on the porch and soon returned with the ambulance medics.

Our house (and life) must have seemed like a circus to the medics. They put me on a back board and prepared to transport me. "What about the little boy?" one asked, referring to Shane.

"He can stay with our neighbor," I answered. "He can show you where she lives. His sister can go with him. She is in the back of the car. The baby, though, has to go to the hospital with me."

The second medic went out to the car. I knew he had found Noelle when he called back to his partner, "Hey, Herb! This one has braces!" Yes, that was us: broken back, tracheotomy, long-leg braces—and more.

In spite of such an unpropitious start, Doah did end up in Dr. Cotton's care in Cincinnati. Dr. Cotton was able to stabilize Doah and take down his tracheotomy. Had Dr. Cotton or someone like him been at Renboro Children's Hospital, Doah's early life would have been much different!

While we were grateful that Doah's most serious problem was a thing of the past, we were angry that Renboro Children's Hospital could get away with such cavalier treatment. I thought about all the babies who had died during the winter of 1980—at least ten. During the winter of 1981, at least one more had died, and very likely there were others I did not know about. I thought about a ten-year-old trached boy whose parents had had no life because for ten years they took 12-hour daily shifts watching him. I thought, too, of the arrogance of the doctors in trying to take custody away from Donnie and me, writing in Doah's records that we were unfit parents, and thinking that parents have neither the right to decide on treatment nor information to contribute to a decision. The more I thought, the angrier I became. Something had to be done to stop such behavior.

I am the type who when faced with a problem meets it with direct and intense action. When Ma beat me, as soon as I was big enough, I beat her back. If I heard that someone had said or done something untrustworthy behind my back, I would call that person and ask. So, too, in this case, I chose to go to the perpetrators of the crime: the staff of Renboro Children's Hospital. We made an appointment with the hospital administrator. There we laid out our case. First, Doah could have died from any one of the mucus plugs or cardiac arrests. Suggesting that parents tie bells to his shoes was an inane way to tell them to monitor their trached children. Doah needed an apnea monitor, and we had obtained one from State College, Pennsylvania, thanks to the intercession of the Boston doctors. All children with breathing disorders should get them. Second, the doctors at Renboro Children's should not try to handle stenosis and related medical problems because they lacked experience in this area. Either they should refer the patients to Cincinnati, or they should bring someone from Cincinnati onto staff at Renboro.

Perhaps my expectations for Renboro Children's Hospital really were exceptionally high. A few years later when we moved to Washington, D.C., the chief of ENT at Children's National Medical Center told the resident not to let me leave until he had spoken to me. Actually, he did not want to speak to me. He wanted to "shake the hand of the mother who had found the only doctor in all of America who could have saved her child." He was, of course, referring to Dr. Cotton, who, it turns out, hailed from Canada, had moved to the USA only a few months before I tracked him down, and was, indeed, the only doctor in the USA capable of curing tracheal stenosis at the time. Were my research skills really that good, or did something else guide me in finding the articles by Dr. Cotton? And how was it that Dr. Cotton had recently moved to a part of the world where his skills were accessible to Doah?

Whether or not our demands were unrealistic, Renboro Children's Hospital fulfilled them. At first, the hospital administrator hedged. He called in the chief financial officer, who told us that our $40,000 medical bill (our post-insurance share) would be written off. We said we were not after money and that we would somehow find a way to pay the bill over time. What we wanted, instead, was changed practices. The hospital administrator would not make any commitment other than to consider our words, and we left feeling like we had just turned in a half-done homework assignment.

To our surprise, then, less than two months later our bill for the monthly rental payment on the apnea monitor came with a return address in Renboro. I physically went to the office to pay the bill. I was curious. The clerk told me that the office had opened recently because of the large number of new referrals from Renboro Children's Hospital!

Likewise, shortly thereafter, I received an excited phone call from the mother of the ten-year-old boy with the tracheotomy. "You won't believe this," she said, "but

Renboro Children's Hospital has a new ENT doctor on staff. He just came there from Cincinnati. He examined our son yesterday, and he thinks he can take down his tracheotomy." She started crying. They were happy tears: ten years of living in an emotional hell and a physical prison were about to end. I wondered how she would handle the immense change that she was about to experience.

Where did the strength come from to steal Doah? Of course, I had some doubts, but as with Noelle, any doubts were shoved away by a strong feeling of self-confidence, the source of which I did not question at that time. Of course, I felt trepidations, but they were deeply buried where they could not interfere with the task at hand: get Doah out of the hospital quickly and effectively. Was it the combat intelligence training, which was not without its own moments of pretend drama? Was it maternal instinct that overwhelms all other emotions even for animals in the wild? Was it anger personified?

Or was it something else, something that was seeded deep inside me, something that prompted me to go for broke in the home fights as a child and that fueled my striving to leave the burning house. Though I did not know it and would not have believed it at the time, could it be that God stepped into my life as a child and gave me courage—not lack of fear, for fear is informative and useful, but the ability to continue to the goal in the face of fear. People thought I was fearless, but I was not. Simply, fear never won because I was not fighting alone. This I felt implicitly although I could not have admitted, labeled, or adequately described what I felt at the time. It was just a simple, quiet, subterranean "knowing" that I was not alone.

# Fighting the Systems

The real difficulties of raising children with life-threatening and life-limiting handicaps are rarely those that others see. Yes, of course, dealing with three children in diapers was not easy, and yes, many medical appointments, the more than 30 surgeries of Noelle and eight surgeries of Doah, and the many arguments with the medical establishment were not easy. Yes, others could see that Doah was retarded and that Noelle was in braces and sometimes in a wheelchair (she had a habit of breaking her braces through attempts at wading in the ocean, accompanying Girl Scouts on hikes, and other unlikely activities for a paraplegic child, leaving her in a wheelchair temporarily while the braces were being mended). The more difficult problems, however, were related to day-to-day living, especially in dealing with others who thought that Noelle and Doah ought not to do everything that we, their parents, thought that they could do.

Lizzie, fortunately, was an easy child to raise. Aside from skipping first grade and seventh grade, she had no special needs. It was the other three who gave us cause to fight the special needs establishment—and quite an entrenched and self-congratulatory establishment it can be.

Noelle, for example, was required to attend Greenland Elementary School in Renboro, Pennsylvania, a public school to which she was bussed over our objections that she should be able to attend Frank Corwin Elementary School, the neighborhood school which Lizzie and Shane attended. Greenland prided itself on its contemporary approach to mainstreaming handicapped children. I suppose it all depends on what you mean by mainstreaming. When Noelle was in kindergarten at a private school, she climbed 55 stone stairs to get into the school. Her physical therapist, Andi Kush, helped her learn to do that. Also when she was in that kindergarten, she went roller-skating every Wednesday afternoon with her classmates at the next-door rink. Andi helped her learn to do that, too.

At Greenland, however, during recess, all the handicapped children were required to sit in wheelchairs near the school building while the other children played games or on play equipment on the playground. This was mainstreaming? I did not think so! I spoke to the principal about letting Noelle swing on the swings, slide down the slide if she could make it to the top in her braces, and play interactively with the other children. He looked at me, appalled, "She will get hurt!" he blurted out.

"Other children get hurt," I responded. "Why does she have less of a right to get hurt than they do? Their cuts and scrapes and falls teach them many things. Why does Noelle have less of a right to learn experientially than they do if she so chooses?"

"We have to be careful of lawsuits," he responded, possibly without thinking.

So, that was it! It had nothing to do with Noelle's needs or desires. It was all about protecting the school from a lawsuit. "I can take care of that," I told him, and I quickly wrote out a note: "Noelle has my permission to get hurt at recess."

He took the note, shaking his head. He was unconvinced, but I was adamant. "You have no worry about a lawsuit now," I told him. "I expect to see Noelle playing with the other children at recess. I will drive by occasionally unannounced during recess to make sure this is happening." I did, and it was. On one occasion, I saw Noelle swinging on a swing, being pushed by another child. On another occasion, I saw her playing kickball with a group of boys. She apparently had some Maine woman in her, too, even though she grew up far from the Maine shores.

For the rest of her days at Greenland, Noelle enjoyed real mainstreaming, not tokenism. However, when we moved to Virginia, the battle began anew. Noelle was initially forced into special education because of her physical disabilities: paraplegia, epilepsy, and hydrocephalus. Any one of them could have qualified her for special education. All of them ensured such a placement. We wanted her to be mainstreamed, and she herself wanted to be in the regular education classroom. Our refusal to send her to school until appropriately placed meant that the school had to take on the onerous burden of sending someone to my office every day to teach her while waiting on a placement decision. Every day I was immensely grateful to my State Department supervisor who, in those pre-enlightenment days, understood the needs of parents.

With the intercession of five psychologists, we eventually won the battle for Noelle to attend regular education at Tucker, our neighborhood school. The placement, however, was not fortuitous. The principal of Tucker delighted in telling new parents two things: (1) "we have the highest test scores in the county," and (2) "we have no handicapped children at this school." It was as if he thought that the first was the result of the second, but, of course, there is no cause-and-effect between being handicapped and test scores. Noelle always scored well on state tests.

Public Law 94-142 (known as the Individuals with Disabilities Act and also as the Education of All Handicapped Children Act) had just come into effect, giving handicapped children, at long last, human rights. PL 94-142 did not help Noelle at Tucker School, however. It was perhaps too new or the principal perhaps too clever in his behavior and too ensconced in the system. Noelle had been in school no more than three weeks when I dropped by, as usual, to pick her up after school. For some reason, the principal, his back to me, was standing at the door, looking out at the children on the playground. Noelle saw me and came in the door. The principal must have thought that she was coming in to wait in the classroom (an alternative to outdoor play for the after-school program) because had he thought I was standing there, waiting to pick her up, he never would have let the next words drop through his lips.

"Sweetie," he said, "I saw you with that group of kids just now. I know they are the popular group, but let me tell you something very important. It may look like you have friends right now. You may even like to think you are popular, too, but it's not true. It's just because you're new. These friendships won't last long. Most kids don't like to play with cripples."

I drew in my breath sharply, and he whirled around. Savvy man that he was, he did not hesitate or even look embarrassed but immediately said to me, "My word against yours!" I guess he had been down this path before and had won.

He was right. It was, indeed, his word against mine. More important, though, than disciplining him for those words and insisting that he provide equal rights for Noelle was the fact that his attitude would mean constant negative input for Noelle even if he never said another word. Noelle is quite intuitive by nature and would be able to discern his true attitude toward her. Donnie and I were unwilling to subject her to such negative input on a daily basis, so we gave up and asked for her placement to be re-considered. We would be willing to have her in special education for her remaining two elementary school years as long as she was able to get a quality education, equivalent to regular education.

The school district convened a hearing for Noelle's placement. Noelle, at the time was nine years old, old enough to make her own decisions on placement, in my mind. I had taught her much about the learning process, and we had discussed her own learning needs, as well as the pros and cons of a special education placement. The committee exhibited distress when I showed up with Noelle in tow and expressed its displeasure outright. The committee members did not prevail. Noelle attended the meeting, actively participated in the decision-making, and found the solution to a conundrum that appeared post-decision-taking. Since Noelle had the same physical condition at the time of the hearing that she had had upon entering the school district and had earlier been determined to be appropriately placed in regular education, some new handicapping condition had to be identified to meet the state law for moving her to special education. All kinds of labels and alternatives were tried, e.g. "other handicapping condition." However, nothing fit. Finally, Noelle held up a crutch and said," If you ask me, it's physical."

Everyone laughed at the insight of a child. The director of special education wrote to the state, explained the situation, and asked for a waiver to the identification of a new handicapping condition. All worked out fine for Noelle's move into special education.

About a year later, Congress held public hearings on the application and applicability of PL 94-142. One of the senators from Virginia (I forget which one it was now) came to one of the school auditoriums in Fairfax County to hear the experiences of parents, teachers, and administrators with PL 94-142. Noelle went, too. She was the very last speaker and had nearly fallen asleep by 10:00 p.m. when it finally became her turn to speak. She held the attention of all as she described in a child's voice and with a child's words her experiences in moving to Virginia: having to wait weeks to be enrolled in school when her able-bodied siblings were enrolled right away, the principal who called her a cripple, and the deficiencies she was finding in special education. She mentioned as well the requirement to be bussed out of the neighborhood and the subjugation to a system of labeling. "I am not a label," she stated in a vehement conclusion. "I am a person. I have a right to be a person." The last sentence was cited as the headline for an article about the meeting in the *Washington Post.*

Noelle's experiences in special education, in spite of the best intentions of the special education office, were not the equivalent of what they would have been had she been mainstreamed. Sometimes, she was simply forgotten, as in the case of the spelling bee. The principal automatically did not include special education children. When I made a fuss about that the next year, I was told that special education children are not included so as not to embarrass them. I insisted that they allow Noelle to participate. She won the school title. One myth of special education is that handicapped children cannot compete in anything with regular education children. Certainly, Noelle could not outrace them or climb higher than they could, but she could out-spell them, and having that skill validated went a long way toward building self-esteem.

At the same time, Noelle, like most hydrocephalic children, ran into problems with math. Shunts for many years were put through the part of the brain that "had no function," and then researchers determined that a function for that part of the brain really did exist: it processed the more advanced mathematical concepts. Here is where being in special education should have been a boon. It was, instead, a bane. The only way in which the special education teacher was willing to help Noelle was by breaking the pre-algebra concepts she was struggling with into smaller and smaller pieces—this for a student with a global learning style (i.e. one who learns through understanding the big picture and how it relates to the world at large). When Noelle's two months' of tears over being unable to handle graphs reached flood stage, we hired a retired college professor to tutor her for two weeks. He brought her newspaper articles with graphs, so that she could see how the graphs pictured information in another form. Being right-brained (metaphor- and picture-oriented), she quickly grasped what was going on. Then, he brought other articles with figures and statistics in them and had her develop her own graphs. After that, she was able to make and read graphs in context or out of context.

The time Noelle spent in special education gradually lowered her overall competence, most especially in mathematics. With six months left in Virginia before moving to California and having just moved on New Year's Day from Arlington to Aquia Harbor, south of Quantico, not knowing that within days I would receive a job offer I could not turn down in California, we put Noelle into home school, rather than go through the battle of special education versus regular education again. Shane, who had been in home school for four years and as an 11-year-old was already working in Euclidean geometry with a math professor from a local college, taught his older sister, concentrating on the subject that she would spend many more years wrestling with: math. When we reached California, Noelle tested at grade level. An 11-year-old had accomplished in six months what her specially trained teachers had failed to do in years. The most reasonable explanation: no one had told Shane that handicapped children cannot learn.

Shane was not only a gifted teacher, he was also a gifted learner. When he was barely three, he attended one day of nursery school at the Renboro University's School of Education laboratory school. At the end of the day, the nursery school director recommended that he begin first grade the next day since he had been reading for two years, understood a wide range of scientific principles at a high school level, had reached conservation of number seemingly at birth, and could add, subtract, multiply, divide, and handle money and fractions—all self-taught and we don't know how or when he learned these things. Those were joyful days. He would ride the bus 30 miles to and from the university with me while Donnie dropped off the other children at their various schools. Elderly people loved to talk to the cute, little blue-eyed blond who could hold his own in conversation, sometimes even making them drop their teeth in amazement, as on the day that he remarked that it was suddenly dark outside.

"Oh, sweetie," said the white-haired lady sitting next to him. "It sure is. Did you see the sun going down when we went across the bridge a little while ago?"

Shane looked at her with wide eyes. It was his turn to be amazed, his three-year-old linguistic system still interpreting everything literally. "Oh, no," he replied. "The sun did not go anywhere. We just turned away from it."

In short order, his linguistic legerdemain caught up to his scientific prowess, and going to school became more and more painful. He would run away from school, especially once we had moved to Virginia where he was a 7-year-old at the end of fourth grade. There, for 22 days in a row, he made himself vomit so he would be released from school by the nurse. The school district's diagnostic center determined that in math he was functioning at a pre-calculus level and that his science knowledge and literacy skills were not far behind. School programs could not accommodate him, we were told. Shane tried to help himself in vain. He would hand his school work back to his teacher, saying "No, thank you. I shall not be doing this homework tonight because I already know all of this. If you would be willing to give me something more challenging that would be worth the time I would spend on it, I would be glad to do it." Although Shane had identified both the problem and cure for his school-itis, the teacher labeled him saucy and was unwilling to adapt any of the coursework. When told to prepare a book report, he found all the books on the list to be inauthentic literature purposely prepared for children, i.e. the Dick and Jane books of fourth grade. Such books were another waste of time in his mind. He preferred reading the books on my bookshelf, where he found Faulkner's *As I Lay Dying* and fell in love with it. (I think his fondness for the book had something to do with the character of ten-year-old Jewel and his horse.) He thought that might make a better project for a book report than *George the Monkey Goes to the Zoo*. However, when he went to the front of the class to give his report, the teacher told him that Faulkner was not on the fourth grade reading list she had given him and therefore did not count. She gave him a 0 for a grade.

We found a self-paced school for Shane the following year where he completed one year of math every month and was able to read the more advanced literary works that he liked. He spent the first seven months after school at the Falls Church public library, then announced that I needed to find another place to pick him up after work because he had read every book in the library—including those in the "adult" section! Money became tight at about the same time: Noelle and Doah were back in the hospital for surgeries. So, Shane went into home schooling.

Since I was a college graduate, I was allowed by the State of Virginia to organize Shane's program myself. He would be tested at the end of each year to be certain that he stayed at grade level—in his case, four years ahead of his age peers. He did. We used the state standards for each grade. These requirements were not very demanding, so we enriched them, including such topics as the differences in conception of utopia and beauty between Socrates and Plato; the influence of Aristotle on Shakespeare; the role of history in shaping the works of Solzhenitsyn; the concept of history not as fact but as human/biased interpretation of events through the comparison of three US history textbooks (published in the North, South, and Europe); "lesser" authors such as Aeschylus, Lermontov, and Kafka; thinkers such as Kant; and subjects such as economics, dendrology, and philosophy. He acquired some German and Finnish at Concordia College summer camps and spent time with me in Helsinki and Moscow, where I was an exchange scholar during his elementary school years.

When Shane turned 11, my supervisor at the State Department offered him an unpaid internship. He spent a couple of afternoons a week teaching instructors and supervisors word-processing and desk-top publishing skills and working with the computer consultant there to establish interconnectivity between unlike computers during the days before cross-platform programs were available. Given his small size and young age, there were some interesting moments. The most interesting I did not witness. The story was related to me by the Director of External Relations.

"I realized today how used we have become to Shane working with us," Connie told me. "The Minister of Foreign Affairs of Finland came to visit, and during the tour, she saw Shane working on the computer with the director of the Spanish program. She asked me if we taught children here, and without thinking, I answered, 'No, the little boy is teaching the big man.' I did not realize how that sounded until I saw her face!"

While Donnie, Shane, and I managed Shane's giftedness all right between home schooling, community activities, and tutors from the college, there is something wrong in a country where children can possibly be too gifted to attend school. The financial burden on the parent to find a private school solution is often unmanageable, as it quickly became for us. The time burden is also difficult. I was fortunate in having understanding bosses, as well as bosses who found Shane's giftedness fascinating and wanted to foster his development. For parents without graduate degrees and scholarly interests, the cognitive burden also can be overwhelming. That part, for me, was pure joy, the reward that came from being able to mold Shane's education. At some point in his teenage years, given all his reading, one library at a time, Shane was able to begin to teach me many things, too.

Doah, being significantly retarded, was on the opposite end of the scholarly scale from Shane, but he, too, required our combat skills in the education arena. With Doah, usually I won. One example is the case in which I wanted him to be with one particular teacher (who happened to be the superintendent's wife) whose classes I had observed and found to be ideal for Doah. I had also talked to the teacher, and she was willing to take him. However, she worked at a school that was not on the bus route for Doah. We offered to transport him, but the superintendent was still adamant about Doah attending the school traditionally reserved for the multiply handicapped. It was an interesting conversation that we had with the superintendent and special education committee.

"I don't understand," I said. "If we are willing to transport him ourselves, there should be no problem with enrolling him. Is there perhaps something wrong with that teacher that you are unwilling to share with us?"

"Of course not," he replied quickly. (After all, the teacher was his wife.) "She is a fine teacher."

I was near the end of my patience and my time. Noelle had a medical appointment, and we needed to leave. I explained the time limitation and added, "It all is pretty simple, and since I have to run off to this doctor's appointment for Doah's sister, I will leave it entirely up to you. You can decide to enroll Doah in the class that we have requested, or you can decide to continue this discussion in court. Just let me know when you have decided which alternative you prefer." The committee decided that it would, indeed, be possible to enroll Doah in the superintendent's wife's class. Two years later, when she was transferred to a school in the same district but another city, Doah was transferred right along with her. It was a long transport for us, but it was worth it. Doah did very well in that class. While he did not learn to read at grade level, he did learn to read function words important to survival and mobility, and he developed reading concepts that would help him learn to read later when he was readier for a more rigorous approach to language.

# American Dream

Once Shura and Lev had visas in hand, the next steps in our plan were taken quickly. Within a couple of weeks, the promised airplane tickets appeared. Soon thereafter, I met a triumphant Lev and grinning Shura at the airport in San Francisco—they had finally touched American soil, and the dream had begun. Little did we know, though, that the nightmare was not yet over.

As we entered the house, all the children ran to greet Shura and introduce themselves. Noelle, who was a year older than Shura, had not had a chance to put on her braces when the hubbub started. So, she crawled to the doorway to greet him as he struggled up the stairs with legs that kept giving out.

When Shura saw Noelle, he looked up at me in surprise and asked, "Are people allowed to crawl in this house?"

"If they prefer, yes," I answered. Immediately he threw down his crutches and joined Noelle on the floor. After that, he would most frequently choose to crawl on his knees from room to room to take care of his various needs or wants.

After settling Shura and Lev into Lizzie's bedroom, Lizzie having graciously conceded to sleeping in Donnie's office for the time being, I examined Shura, a routine I had taken up with Noelle because paraplegic children often do not know that they have wounds since they do not feel them. Shura promptly showed me his gangrenous legs, and right away I went to work at clearing up the gangrene with that wonderful substance, betadine, which had helped Noelle out of many a nearly gangrenous pickle. Once I had shown Shura how to clean his wound with betadine and wrap it to keep it clean, he took over his own care.

Shura was a gangly lad. It was hard to tell how tall he was since he could not walk. However, not being able to walk did not hold him back. He never sat still. Once he had thrown down his crutches, he scooted all over the house, searching out activities, food, and playmates. He and Doah became great pals, and over time he also formed a strong liaison with Blaine, a child we had taken in several years earlier from a Salts barrio.

Now that Shura was in the United States, we needed to move quickly to secure medical care for him. If we had thought that getting him out of Siberia would be the most difficult part of his journey, we were mistaken. While Shura was becoming acquainted with Shane, Blaine, and Doah, Lev and I talked constantly about where we would find the money that the hospitals were demanding to have deposited upfront before admitting Shura for his needed surgeries. The prospects did not look good, but both of us were somehow confident that we would prevail.

We began in a traditional way: we contacted the media. The newspaper agreed to write a story about Shura. The interview was nicely done. The story was interesting. Almost no one contributed. The grapevine told us: "Not local, not compelling."

Following the appearance of the newspaper article, we found a television station to carry an interview with Shura and me, based on a showing of his art. We talked to a local bank president, and voilà, we were offered space in an upstairs room for the showing. The showing was open to the public. A few people came. The television interviewer was excellent. The television show was nicely done. The story was interesting. Again almost no one contributed. Once again, the grapevine told us: "Charity begins at home, not abroad."

I conferred with the various department heads at the Global Studies Institute. We needed something different, they suggested. Richard Pacman, our videographer, came up with a plan: a video. In the art book that he had published in Siberia, Shura had written short verses in Russian, English, and French. Rich had a musician friend write background music to go with Shura's fantasy pictures. Then, he found ten-year-old children who spoke these languages natively to read the verses as the music played in the background and the pictures appeared on the screen. The video was short and captivating. Just right for the preschool crowd. We began to sell copies of the video, along with copies of the book. Lev had brought several hundred copies of the book, and we reproduced dozens of copies of the videotape. We sold these items person-to-person both in California and in Washington, D.C. where Talia Gospod helped us. A few dollars began to tumble in. The Russian Orthodox Church in Felton was also selling books and videotapes. More dollars tumbled in. However, we were still desperately far from the amount of cash we needed to have and time was passing by far too quickly.

As luck would have it (or not have it, as it seemed at the time), I had to stop the desperate search for funding long enough to attend a conference of Russian professors in San Diego. I was a member of several committees, and the Global Studies

Institute had an information table that had to be manned. Lizzie, who was going to school at the University of California at San Diego had offered to help so that I had time to network with colleagues. I took copies of Shura's art book. Perhaps we could raise some additional funds, I thought. After all, the professors in attendance were interested in all things Russian.

The conference lasted three days, and on the third day a marvelous thing happened. A graduate student at the University of Virginia, Cindy Reginald, stopped to look at Shura's book and hear his story. "Have you thought of contacting John Kluge?" she asked.

"Who is John Kluge?" I responded. The graduate student explained that he was the third wealthiest American at the time. He was the founder of Metromedia, an internationally acclaimed and highly profitable telecommunications company that had branches in Russia. He had also once supported a British boy for brain tumor surgery in the United States. She promised to send me his address as soon as she returned home.

Sure enough, just a few days later, she sent me the address. I wrote a plaintive note, explaining the situation, and asking for any amount of help that could be given. To show the talent (and thereby, hopefully, the "worth" of Shura), I included a copy of the book and the videotape.

At about the same time, Shura and Lev learned about the Russian Orthodox Church in San Francisco. They felt that perhaps a trip to that church and a talk with the priest, Viktor Kotar, there would help. Since it certainly could not hurt, I drove them up there. We met with Rev. Kotar, who accepted a heaping helping of books and videotapes to be sold. (Both churches, the one in Felton and the one in San Francisco, would help to sell books and follow Shura's progress very closely for months to come.) While at the church, Shura and Lev stood at the icon of St. John the Wonderworker and asked St. John to intercede on Shura's behalf.

On the way back from San Francisco, we stopped at the post office, and I mailed my letter with Shura's book and videotape to John Kluge. What the heck? It was worth a try! Anything was worth a try. I had some hope because I was born an eternal optimist. Shura and Lev had some hope because they had their faith.

I had been chronicling our efforts on Shura's behalf weekly since the day that the Global Studies Institute set up the Shura Ivanovich Fund, months prior to his receiving a visa. The chronicle would last through all of Shura's surgeries and follow-up care and ultimately had a mailing list of over 100 interested individuals, as well as organizations that copied it for their members. So, this particular week we reported the trip to the Russian Orthodox Church and the hope it inspired.

Four days later, that hope reached fruition in the form of a phone call. The voice at the other end was pleasant and emanated a sense of competence.

"This is Julie Trudell," the voice said. "I am the coordinator of the spina bifida clinic at the University of Virginia Hospital in Charlottesville, Virginia. We have been contacted by John Kluge, who would like to sponsor Shura Ivanovich. I have in my hand two tickets if you will allow him to be treated here, all the doctors here have agreed to donate treatment, and the hospital has received a check for $500,000."

I called Lev from my office, where Julie had reached me. "Time to celebrate!" I told him. "When I come home tonight, we will go out to McDonald's."

I would have liked to have chosen a fancy restaurant, but money was very tight with Lev and Shura both living with us, as well as all the money spent on fund-raising activities, Shura's medical supplies, and Noelle's incontinent supplies. In any event, Lev and Shura had never been to McDonald's, and that would be interesting for them, I rationalized.

When I pulled up in the dooryard, Lev and Shura were waiting for me in excited anticipation. Lev was buttoned up in a suit, and Shura had on his Sunday best. Then I remembered. The only McDonald's that Russians knew about was in Moscow. As an American "restaurant," it was considered a chic place to eat, lines were typically four blocks long, and people dressed up to go there. Hmm. I explained, in vain, to Lev that the American version of McDonald's was low-key: a poor man's restaurant. He insisted on wearing his suit, so off we went to McDonald's, I in my work clothes and the two of them all gussied up. Once we reached McDonald's, Lev cast a glance at all the patrons in shorts and t-shirts, looked at me with a sheepish grin, and said, "Oh."

Overdressed or not, the celebration was as jubilant at McDonald's as it would have been at a fancy restaurant like the Chart House. Money, though, had to be conserved for the more important things in life—like paying for a hotel for Lev and Shura in Charlottesville. (I was not able to leave immediately with them because of work, but the fund set up by John Kluge allowed me to come in time for medical decision-making.)

The next day the trip to the airport was unexpectedly harrowing, as the road narrowed to one lane because of road work, then that lane became tied up from an accident. Lev, Shura, and I talked aimlessly about expectations in Virginia, all the time our minds nervously counting the escaping minutes. None of us expressed concern that we were about to miss perhaps the most important plane departure in any of our lives. We did not have to. The thoughts were so palpable that we could feel them without words. Finally, traffic broke free, and I raced to the airport, saying little more on the way. I was too busy watching out for the California Highway Patrol, noted for lurking in secretive hideouts along the curvy, wooded route. Afterward, I would remember the rapid peering into bushes along the roadside. Lev would remember my long hair whipping straight back from the air rushing through the partially open driver's seat window. Shura would remember pure panic: Was all for naught? Had he made it all the way to the United States to be wiped out on the roadside in a speeding car?

Shura's worries were misplaced. I drove up to United Airlines a full twenty minutes before plane departure, pushed Shura and Lev out the car door, and dropped their bags on the sidewalk. "Get ticketed," I told them. "I will be in as soon as I find a place to park."

I parked in short-term parking. Putting the parking ticket in the glove box, locking the car, and pocketing the keys, I flat-out ran to the ticket counter, assuming that I just might be able to catch up with Shura and Lev at the gate. As I ran up to the counter, there was no line: everyone was already boarding the plane. However, there stood Lev and Shura, patiently waiting for me. I had forgotten that they could not speak English! A baffled ticket agent expressed sincere gratitude at seeing me and helped us through the entire process efficiently. They walked onto the plane, and right behind them the crew closed the door. They had made it!

Lev and Shura arrived in Charlottesville without incident. Julie met them at the airport and checked them into the Howard Johnson's. It was near the campus and the hospital. This would be the last few days that Lev would be in the United States. He had to get back to Siberia and to the managing of his press.

When I finally arrived a couple of days later, having had to put things into order at home first, I, too, met Julie, who became an instant friend. She introduced us to doctor after doctor: urologists, neurologists, a neurosurgeon, a pediatrician, and an orthopedic surgeon. Given the gangrenous legs, there was no question about which of Shura's many treatments would be needed first: orthopedic surgery.

The meeting with the doctors took me back many years. The doctors on the orthopedic team huddled. They were many. We were three. What would they be talking about? What would they say? Decide? Do? One doctor passed out. Julie later told us that it was from the smell of Shura's gangrenous legs which were still in very bad shape in spite of the wondrous effects of betadine. Had they only seen the green-pus-covered mess that Shura had brought with him and had succeeded in clearing up considerably prior to going to Charlottesville, I wonder what they would have done—admitted him immediately to the hospital very likely, which would have made sense since he had had to be released from a hospital in order to get on the plane to America. The 3-4 weeks we had spent finding a financial sponsor could perhaps have taken his life, but Lev, Donnie, and I were all ignorant enough about the dangers of gangrene to set merrily about "curing" it ourselves and worrying not one iota about what *might* happen but trusting that something good *would* happen, as it did.

I could tell by looking at Shura's legs, that there might be a difficult decision ahead of him. There was.

Dr. Blanco approached us. The decision of the team was that both legs needed to be amputated. Bringing Shura to the United States for a double amputation was not the news I wanted to hear. "Is there no other way?" I asked. "There are always other possibilities. Perhaps antibiotics? All he has had access to until now has been betadine, and the legs look much better now."

Pain peered out from behind Dr. Blanco's eyes, then darted back behind them. "I'm sorry," he said, "I really am. If there were any alternative, I would try it. However, the gangrene has been in his body too long. If we don't remove the legs, he will die."

I suggested some quiet time for Lev, Shura, and me to discuss the situation. The doctors withdrew. Shura ultimately made the decision. He wanted to live. His semi-useless legs were of less importance to him than his life. After the surgery, Dr. Blanco would say something along the same lines to me. Feeling guilty that we had not been able to push the paperwork through the American Embassy in Moscow faster than we had, I asked Dr. Blanco whether he thought that he could have saved Shura's legs had we brought him to this country sooner.

"No," he said, "even a year ago I would not have been able to save both legs, but I might have been able to save one of them. However, that is the wrong way to look at this situation. By getting him here when you did, we were able to save his life."

Shura was bedded for his surgeries at the Kluge Rehabilitation Center at the University of Virginia Hospital. This center, it turned out, had been established some years earlier through the generosity of John Kluge, so his name was no mystery in Charlottesville. I had unknowingly contacted a philanthropist with a long-standing interest in the very medical area that plagued Shura and, as it also turned out, with an ex-wife who had a strong interest in art.

And herein lay a series of miracles, the first of which was how the letter got to John Kluge in the first place. That miracle we only found out later, when I mailed a thank you to Mr. Kluge following Shura's successful first surgery. That letter was re-turned to us as "no such address." We checked it out with the post office, and, indeed, we had been given erroneous information. There was no such zip code. Moreover, we learned from the hospital staff that John Kluge had not lived in Charlottesville for years. He lived in New York City. Nonetheless, the package and pleading letter had made it to him in record time. Within 96 hours of mailing the letter from California, the package had reached New York City (via Charlottesville) and a check for a half-million dollars had reached Charlottesville. I don't understand how it happened, but it did. At the time, I was very grateful for such good luck. Lev and Shura did not con-sider this to be luck; they were grateful to God and to St. John the Wonderworker.

God wasn't finished yet, though. Shura asked for a *moleibin* (prayer service) prior to his surgery. Talia Gospod arranged for it during a Tuesday evening service at St. John's Orthodox Church in Washington, D.C.

Due to the last-minute arrangements, the *moleibin* had not been announced in advance. Nonetheless, the service was well attended because it was the eve of a feast day. I am unsure now which feast day it was.

After the service, as is the tradition in Russian Orthodox Churches, everyone shared a potluck meal. Many people spoke to Shura and me about his situation, but one man in particular stood out. He kept looking our way, then finally stood up, came over, and held out his hand.

"Hi, I'm Max," he introduced himself simply with his first name, as I shook his hand. "I'm curious. Did you have any trouble getting a visa for Shura?"

Hearing that question, I let loose with our litany of troubles, as well as my opinion—and that of Dr. Uscinski—that consular officers apparently are required to undergo lobotomies before being posted to the U. S. Embassy in Moscow. Max listened politely and then informed us that he was one of the highest ranking people in the Department of Justice. His job was to oversee the INS, which controls the rules for visas, and therefore to oversee as well the consular officers at the American embassies worldwide.

"I'm not surprised that you had difficulties," he concluded. "The system is set up to prevent abuse, but sometimes it weeds out legitimate cases in the process. I know who you are now. Here is my card. I have written my home number on the back. Call me if you have any problems in the future."

On the way home from the *moleibin*, I told Talia about the meeting with Max. She had talked to him, too.

"I was surprised to see him there," she told us, "because he moved to Baltimore over a year ago and goes to church there now. He has not been in this church for months. He told me he was working late tonight, remembered that today was a holy day of obligation and therefore we would have an evening service, and decided to stop by on the way home."

How handy for us that Max stopped at the service on the one night that Shura was there for we would need his help. We called Max several months later when we ran into problems with one of the California offices that did not want to extend Shura's visa. Max took care of the problem in less than a day.

More interesting, however, is the fact that we never saw Max again. Neither did anyone at the church. It has been more than a decade, and the only time he has been in that church was on the one night when he could meet Shura.

Even with these marvelously unexplainable coincidences, clearly the Divine did not consider us to be in a state of surfeit. Once again, wonderful coincidence stepped into our lives in the person of Dr. Vladimir Kryzhanovsky. Volodya was a heart surgeon, visiting from the Ukraine. He heard about a young boy from Siberia, who did not speak English and would be undergoing a double amputation, and he appeared at the door of his hospital room. I met Volodya right before the surgery. Etched into my permanent memory is the view of him walking beside Shura's gurney into the room where Shura would be anaesthetized. As a guardian acting *in loco parentis* (Lev had had to return to Siberia before the surgery could be scheduled), I could not follow Shura into the pre-op room or into the operating room, but Volodya could go with him every step of the way—and did.

Later, Volodya inserted himself into the discussion of the kind of prostheses to prepare for Shura: not the cheapest but the best. Throughout Shura's recovery, he spent time with him, discussing Russian literature, the motherland, and those things that only Russian men talk about among themselves. Over the intervening years, Volodya has acted as friend, father, and fellow Slav to Shura. I cannot imagine what Shura's life would have been life without this doctor who seemed to have dropped from Heaven straight into Shura's hospital room.

A few days after Shura's surgery, I went to visit him at the hospital. I found him in a tree. He had refused all pain medication, saying that in Siberia all he ever got was morphine rather than real care and wanted no more of that. He had spent two days painting a fairy-tale-like picture that was later published. Then, he had moved outside to enjoy life.

Shura's post-surgery care would take months, not days. None of that was unusual. What was unusual, however, was that Julie turned out to be a former art teacher who immediately recognized Shura's talent. She contacted the Virginia Center for Creative Arts as a more humane place for Shura to recover while working on his art with professional artists. When the director told her that Shura was too young, she took samples of his art. He was accepted.

At the Center for Creative Arts, Shura was the youngest artist ever to be in residence. There he made the acquaintance not only of professional artists from across the USA, but also of the oldest artist ever to be in residence there who just happened to be there at the same time he was. And, of course, there was a local newspaper article on the interesting coincidence of the oldest artist and the youngest artist in the history of the center being in residence at the same time. (Shura's life at that time included routine interviews—in the beginning with reporters trying to help us raise money, then with hospital PR specialists interested in the donated care angle, and now with reporters intrigued by his artistic talent.)

Following this convalescent period, Shura returned to California. There he spent some time in San Diego, where Lizzie, Noelle, and now Blaine were attending college. The days of being in the sun and on the beach made an impression on him. Like so many visitors to California, he left in California that part of his heart that was not bound to Russia and Siberia.

Of course, follow-up care was needed. It always is with spina bifida individuals. So, Shura and I made periodic trips to the doctors' offices—by plane. After a few such trips, Julie made an offer. It was one that none of us could refuse but also one that would change our lives. Shura was about to receive a third mother.

"Why not let Shura move in with me?" she asked. "My son, Jonathan, is the same age, and I know how to care for spina bifida needs. And besides, I have spent twenty years as a nurse, instructing parents of spina bifida children how to take care of them, but I have never parented one myself. This would be a good experience for me." As a highly experienced parent of a spina bifida child, I was not sure that she knew what all she was volunteering for, but I accepted. So did Lara. Lev had met Julie and liked her very much. More important, all of us trusted her.

Today Shura says that he is luckiest boy in the world because he has three mothers. As for Julie, Lara, and I, we all became friends. Today Julie and I are as much like sisters as any blood sisters could be. After all, we have been American-mothering the same child for a long time now.

# Righting Wrongs

Cruelty does not always breed cruelty. Sometimes cruelty becomes so extreme that it breeds kindness in those who have been vividly shown where the lack of kindness leads. I wonder how much of Katrina's compassion was triggered in response to one of the cruelest moments I have ever experienced. When Katrina was four years old, we had a pet cat whom I loved but Ma despised, partly because it would bring her gifts of live mice, which it would lay in her lap, causing Ma to stand up and shriek. For a farmer to be afraid of mice seemed ironic, but she was, indeed, afraid of them. She would stand on a kitchen chair, as in the stereotypical cartoon, and shriek if she saw even the tiniest and friendliest mouse in the kitchen. So, the cat was not going to curry any favor with Ma. Nonetheless, the cat did not deserve its fate.

What was that fate? One day, as we children were playing in the yard and Ma was sitting on the porch stairs watching us, the cat unexpectedly jumped onto Katrina's back and frightened her. Whether or not the cat intended to hurt her was unclear to me, and I think it was also unclear to Katrina. However, for Ma, that was the "last straw." She grabbed the "vicious cat" by the nape of the neck and marched off Dad, demanding that he burn the poor creature hanging docilely from her hand. How could a cat be "vicious," I wondered, if it allowed you to pick it up so easily? In spite of my pleas and cries, the cat was handed over to Dad, who, unable to stand up to Ma's ire and worked into a lather himself from her fury, took it into the basement. Ma dragged us girls along to watch as Dad opened the furnace door, threw the cat onto the pile of wood being consumed by flames, and shut the door. The cat's piteous wailing, full of pain and terror, did not last long but was seared by flame into the life-long memories of three young girls. Over time, Ma has ensured the death of a number of cats: death by drowning, death by gunshot, death by whatever mechanism was handy at the moment. All were cruel, but death by fire was the cruelest.

I felt guilty that I could not save our pet that day. I have never forgotten its surprised, beseeching eyes as it sailed through the air onto the burning wood or its agonized screams as the flames consumed its life. Perhaps that is why as an adult I became very good at rescuing and taming feral cats, whether they be in the woods of Arroyo Seco, California or on the city streets of Amman, Jordan. In Amman, where feral cats were often atrociously abused by a population afraid of them, "Doktora Beth," cat rescuer, became well known to the local humane society.

Rescue operations did not end with cats. While some people's children bring home a stray animal, my children brought home stray kids. One became family.

Blaine had no family to speak of. His father had returned to Mexico when he was two years old, and his mother was a drug addict, living in a barrio. When, at the age of 14, he refused to drop out of school and run drugs for her, she kicked him out of the house. A well mannered boy, he found refuge that first night and every night for many years afterward in our house, becoming our fifth child. When he was 19, his mother was murdered in a drug deal, or at least, that was the consensus about the nature of her mysterious death. After her funeral, which he as the oldest son arranged, Blaine moved to San Diego to be with Lizzie, whom he eventually married, and Noelle. All three attended college there. With his enrollment in college, Blaine became the first in the barrio to break the cycle of poverty, drugs, and unemployment.

After Blaine came Ksenya. One day in 1994, as I was preparing for my next consult abroad—it was to be in Brazil if memory serves—I received a phone call from Moscow. It was Zina. This was a surprise. She had never before called me in the United States.

"How far do you live from the San Francisco airport?" she asked.

"About two hours' drive," I answered.

"Perfect!" came the response. "Ksenya is on the plane. She arrives in San Francisco in two hours. She is going to live with you now."

Here was new and interesting information. There was no time to get a handle on any of it, though, if there was not going to be a young Russian girl with no knowledge of English wandering confused around the San Francisco airport. I needed to leave immediately.

"I'll talk to you when I get back," I told Zina. "I need to leave now so that I can get Ksenya on time.

I found Ksenya walking around the airport with a forlorn look, anxiously scanning faces, hoping to remember the American face she had known in her pre-teen years. I did not recognize her immediately. She had grown. Her pigtailed flaxen hair had darkened and bushed into long, wild curls. From afar, I saw a look of recognition and relief cross Ksenya's face as she flew across the floor and flung her arms around my neck.

Some time later, Zina began to miss Ksenya. She managed to find the same American journalist in Moscow who had obtained the visa for Ksenya to sponsor her, and off she flew to San Francisco along the path taken by her daughter earlier, a reverse take on the tradition of a child following in a parent's footsteps. Within months of her arrival, Zina fell in love with an American mechanic, married him, and became a U. S. citizen. Now, she and Ksenya could live in the U. S. long-term legitimately.

After Ksenya and Zina (and Blaine and Shura), the rescuing continued. In 1999, we took in a young mother who found herself on the street while pregnant with her third child. When she became too sick from the pregnancy to work, her husband kicked her out of his home and his life. Vanessa moved in with her mother and, as soon as the baby was born, entered training to become a prison warden in the state penitentiary system. She finished the training successfully and was ordered to work at the high-security prison in Lonesome, California not far from where we were living at the time in Salts. She caught me online one day after having looked up America on Line subscribers living in the Salts area. She asked me about newspapers published in Salts and how to get copies. After a little questioning, I ascertained the major details of her life and learned that she was looking for an apartment so that she could begin her new assignment in Lonesome. I suggested that she get off line and call me on the phone. She did. We became acquainted, and a few weeks later she moved into our master bedroom suite, and we moved into rooms vacated by our children, all of whom had recently left the nest for college or work. After a few months, Vanessa brought the children from northern California where they were staying with their grandmother. It was refreshing to have three young children in the house again. The youngest, a three-year-old girl named Juanita, liked her new home very much. As white-bearded, portly Donnie sat at his computer, she crawled up his leg, patted his roly-poly belly, and stated with affirmation, "I want a Barbie." The next day I found her skipping around the living room, singing "I live with Santy Claus! I live with Santy Claus!"

When I think back on all the fighting we had to do for our children, certainly I feel the lingering frustrations and even, at times, anger. How unfair such a life was, at times, to them. Recently, though, their experiences—like my own—were put into graphic perspective. Waiting at the Fayetteville, North Carolina airport from where I was taking a flight to Atlanta were a number of young mothers with children, as well as grandparents with children. These children were not flying anywhere. They were awaiting the arrival of the next airplane, which was bringing the Special Forces soldiers back from combat in Afghanistan to their home base at Fort Bragg.

As I was inserting money into a soda machine, an eight-year-old with thick, curly red hair and a splash of freckles across his nose and cheeks ran up to me, unable to restrain his glee, "My daddy's coming home from Afghanistan!" Perhaps he was nine or ten, not eight. He could not stand still enough for me to assess anything about him except his unrepressed delight at the thought of seeing his father.

"When is your daddy coming?" I asked him,

"Really soon!" he responded. Then he danced off and sidled up to another passenger in the gate area to announce his good news.

I carried my soda to a seat by the window and sat down. Two seats to my left a brown-eyed, blond toddler was standing on a seat with his nose plastered to the window. As a plane passed by, the toddler looked up at a gaunt gentleman beside him.

"It's Daddy, Grandpa," he said.

"No, that's not Daddy's plane. Not yet. Be patient. It will come."

I looked over at the gaunt gentleman who was speaking and asked, "Are you waiting for someone from Afghanistan?"

"Yes," the man replied proudly and with a tinge of relief in his voice. "My son."

Just then another plane landed. The man pointed it out to his grandson, "Look! There is Daddy. It won't be long now. They're taxiing."

The boy looked up at his grandfather in confusion. "It's not a taxi, Grandpa," he pronounced solemnly. "It's a plane."

I left them alone to prepare to meet father and son, happy in the knowledge that their relative was returning. Others sent to Afghanistan and other wars have not been as lucky.

Just scratch the surface, I thought. It is a thought I have often had over the past three decades of raising handicapped children. When you think you have a hard lot, all you have to do is scratch the surface of someone else's life, and yours suddenly looks not bad at all. There are those who would say that God gives each person no more than he or she is capable of bearing, but I don't think God gives us burdens at all. In my experience, the burdens come from the workings of nature, our own ineptness, and the sometimes ill-intentioned behavior of others. God steps in and provides the support when our load becomes an overload. Breaking points differ, though, for one person's load is another person's overload. That is what Eliana and I learned three decades ago.

When my children were little, Eliana's were, too. Like my children, hers had serious medical problems. Her older son was born with Immune Deficiency Syndrome. He was the first "bubble baby" to be raised outside a bubble, mainly because Eliana is a force to be reckoned with. She was unwilling to let him be put into a bubble. Whenever I thought my problems were bad, I would call Eliana, who had been my best friend in college. We ended up living only 30 miles apart for a while when our children were small. I was at Renboro University, and Eliana was working for an insurance company in White Spring. Eliana and I would compare notes. Somehow she always thought that my load was worse; after all, I had two children with problems. I always thought her load was worse; after all, her son, Paul, had a much smaller chance of survival than did Doah and Noelle although for a while Doah had been given no chance at all of living, something that I, like Eliana, was just not willing to accept.

Eliana had another difficulty, one that I did not. She was Jewish, and her husband was Catholic. Donnie and I, being agnostic (he) and atheistic (I), never had to deal with familial religious dissent on top of the strain that birth defects put on a marriage and family. Eliana and Bob had few problems in the early years of their marriage: she went to synagogue on Fridays and he went to mass on Sundays. Then came the kids and the struggle as to choice of religion in which to raise them. Judaism being matrilineal and Eliana being matriarchal, Eliana won. The children were raised Jewish, and Donnie, the children, and I had a wonderful time at their bar mitzvah and bas mitzvah.

Eliana and I continued to be very close friends while our children were growing up, and I think that helped us both in many ways. One of the things that Donnie and I worried about in the early years was appointing a guardian for our children. In the event that something should happen to us, we wanted a guardian who would raise them similarly to how we would raise them, who would fight for them, and who would teach them to fight for themselves. We certainly did not want Ma raising them, and Donnie's mother was too old and would have been unable to cope with all the medical problems. Eliana was a perfect choice. She was young, and she was used to handling children with birth defects. She agreed. Of course, she would—for the same reason that I agreed to take in Shura.

Eliana, in spite of her robust ability to handle nearly any crisis sent her way, had a limit to her emotional resilience. She found that limit in the summer of 1982. She and Bob had taken their children, Paul and Mavis, to Philadelphia, Eliana's home city, to find a good oncologist for Bob. The ones in Renboro had declared that treating Bob for cancer that came from being exposed to Agent Orange during his military assignment in Vietnam was useless. The cancer was too advanced when the doctors found it. As usual, Eliana was not willing to accept such a prognosis. She packed up Bob and the children, took a leave of absence from work, and drove eight hours to Philadelphia to meet with doctors she trusted. The doctors there, as Eliana suspected, were able to coax Bob's cancer in remission, and Eliana made plans to return to White Spring in a few weels. That was when she received the urgent call from the pediatrician. Mavis, the healthy child, apparently was showing signs of juvenile diabetes, based on tests done right before the family left for Philadelphia. With her usual enthusiasm substantially subdued, Eliana immediately returned to White Spring with a still-ailing Bob, daily medicine for Paul, and concerns about Mavis. Ah, it would be so good to be home after eight weeks away! As she drove up to their house, however, something seemed wrong. Something *was* wrong. The back door was swinging on its hinges. Eliana walked in cautiously. No one was there. The place was empty—very empty. The house had been ransacked. Nearly every personal possession she cared about was gone.

Eliana did not cry that day. She was too stunned. She did not cry the next day, either. Instead, she did some research and found out who was considered the best psychologist in the White Spring area and made an emergency appointment.

At the psychologist's office, Eliana laid out her whole story. I imagine that took some time! When she finished, the psychologist was silent for quite a while. Then he quietly said, "I'm sorry. I will not charge you for a visit because I do not have any good answers for you. If I were in your place, I would just go have myself a nice little nervous breakdown. I think you have earned it."

Eliana started to laugh. She laughed all the way home. She never did end up crying over the lost possessions; she just rebuilt her house and life. Bob is still alive. Paul outgrew his lack of immunity around age 12. Mavis never developed juvenile diabetes; it was a false alarm. Now, though, any time I feel that I have an overload, I think of Eliana and the entitlement to a "nice little nervous breakdown," and I laugh like Eliana did. Once again, a divine intervention in an unlikely source—a psychologist without an answer—had given both of us a mechanism for handling our lives when they went into overload. The knowledge that the best psychologist in White Spring had given a free prescription for a nervous breakdown was enough to lift our spirits. Neither of us ever filled that prescription.

## Just Helping

On one bright, cold winter day, I dragged my sled three houses down the street to our neighbor's teton-shaped hill, where all the children in our area of town gathered to race down to the mostly untraveled country road below on sleds, cardboard, or whatever else was available. I pulled my sled up the hill, waving to the other children in the neighborhood but mainly concentrating on the anticipated thrill of the ride.

Sledding can be a community sport, and it was precisely that on Lenin Hills behind the University of Moscow where Lizzie and her American friend Sarah, daughter of an American diplomat, shared Sarah's cherry-colored, round, plastic, American sled that immediately drew to them the attention of the Soviet children who had never seen such an object in their lives, their *sanki* being oblong and wooden with metal runners. Soon a Russian girl piled onto the cherry disk with Lizzie, and they sailed down the hill amid shrieks and giggles that bonded the American and the Russian in a moment of joy in a moment of time. Then it was Sarah's turn to spin down the moderate slope with a Russian boy. The communal play lasted for a couple of hours, during which the *lingua franca* was laughter.

The scene on our neighbor's hill 30 years earlier, however, was significantly different. We were a community of children in the sense that we all knew each other, but our sport was an individual one. We did not share adrenaline-spurred shrieks of fun but rather we quietly felt the thrill that defined the fun of downhill sledding.

That afternoon as I was pulling my one-person wooden sled up the hill a third time, I noticed a young boy, clad all in white and definitely not adequately covered for the sub-zero temperature that rosied our noses as they protruded from the scarves wrapped around our necks and faces and tucked into the hoods on our coats. I puzzled over the boy in white only momentarily as I mounted the hill and then the sled and began my third downhill run toward the road. Suddenly, about half-way down the hill, the boy in white, blended into the surrounding snow in my visual field, began moving across the path over which my sled was about to speed.

"Get out of the way!" I yelled. I was as much annoyed at his being in my path as I was afraid of hurting him. What he did, I do not know. I briefly caught his sad look as I zipped past.

The memory is old and the details lodged in the mind of an 8-year-old whose perception of the world had moments of extremism. Therefore, I will not insist that every detail was precisely as I remember it today. What I do remember precisely, however, was being shaken by my own unkind words. I hurried home, towing my sled and a bundle of regret and concern. Somebody had to help the boy in white. He was wandering through the New Hampshire cold with no coat! He would freeze on the hill—or anywhere else in our neighborhood. He seemed oblivious to his surroundings and to the cold. He must be poor, indeed, I thought. We did not have much when we were children, but we always had warm clothes and were always bundled up, displaying a "cared for" look.

"Ma," I called as I dropped the rope of the sled and ran into the house. "There is a boy on the hill without a coat. He is going to freeze! We have to help him!"

"Well, let's go," she said. I could not point him out through our window, so we set off for the hill. By the time we got there a few minutes later, however, he was nowhere to be found. We looked farther afield, but we saw no lad in white. Ma asked some of the other children, but none remembered seeing him. I was at a loss to explain to Ma why he was not there, but she was not angry this time.

In spite of her inability to love her children in an altruistic manner, whenever someone in the greater community needed help, Ma was always jolly on the spot. Those two seemingly mutually exclusive attitudes—cruelty to her children and kindness to the community—made it difficult for us children to understand Ma. It also made it difficult for the community to understand our reaction to Ma for the community's experience of her has always been positive. Indeed, when it came to community affairs, my life experiences have been involved positivism.

One of those positive experiences of childhood under Ma's wing taught all of us children pro-activity and responsibility for others. When I entered first grade at our local two-story wooden school, Ma pronounced it a fire hazard and death trap. There was only one staircase, and anyone caught upstairs in a fire would be too high from the ground to jump to safety. So, Ma bundled all of us children, at that time four of us, in heavy coats, hats that came to our shoulders, scarves that covered our faces so completely that we could barely breathe, thick homemade mittens, woolen pants under woolen skirts, and woolen leggings covered by wool socks and heavy boots. Then off we marched with her. Willie, equally swaddled in layers of wool, lay in the hand-pushed sleigh that served as a baby carriage in snow-covered New England of those days. At door after door, we knocked, and Ma would explain the dangers of a fire starting in the school house. Person after person would sign her petition for a sprinkler system at the school. We met every person who lived in our town, or so it seemed. Several weeks later, Gram came to babysit us, and Ma went to the school board meeting. A few weeks after that, the school had a sprinkler system. Through example, Ma taught us activism—and perhaps more than a little pugilism.

As for the boy in white, I never saw him again in the neighborhood. My friends insisted that he never was there, that he was a figment of my imagination that had frozen in the cold and was hallucinating snow images. Not a boy in white but a boy of snow. Still, I can see him today as clearly as I saw him on the hill so long ago. Today, I wonder if he was not there to teach me a lesson in kindness, in neighborly love—and to reveal perhaps why Ma may, indeed, live in grace, in spite of all her earlier cruelty and self-absorption. Perhaps God was using her, too? If God could use an atheist, then perhaps a believer with a temper might also be a potential instrument.

My intuitive sensing of Ma's latent generosity is likely why, seeing the boy in white, I immediately ran home to Ma for help. To people in need, Ma would always extend a helping hand, sometimes offering the hands of us, her children, as well. She even managed to scrape together pennies to make donations to charities that she felt strongly about. We had food from the farm. We made our own clothes from the left-over scraps of wool that my grandparents brought home from the textile mill where they, and later I, worked. During the cold New England winters, we had wood for the stove, cut from the forest on our land. We had light, if necessary, from inexpensive kerosene lamps. On those things, we could survive. Beyond survival, Dad and Ma made interesting choices in resource management. Bills might be paid in dribbles, but Dad always bought books and Ma always gave to charities. Somehow, in spite of all the whippings and our fierce declarations to grow up and be entirely different from our parents, we all incorporated these two good things into our adult lives: to cherish books and to gain joy from helping others.

Somehow in the contours of my life, the lives of my siblings, and the actions of my parents, God used an abusive parent to teach us to love one another and to love our neighbors as ourselves. God's incredible wisdom in this is breathtaking for learning to love clearly contributed to our sense of self-worth and our ability to mature into a viable adulthood, for the most part not crippled by the rages of childhood. God's incredible power to use an abusive parent gives validity to the suppositions of the author of the *Cloud of Unknowing*: God, the Almighty, can do anything. Using people like Ma and me is proof, to me, of God's omniscience and love.

A great Jesuit thinker, Teilhard de Chardin, saw our work in the world as carrying on the work of creation. He wrote: "We may perhaps imagine that creation was finished long ago. But that would be quite wrong. It continues still more magnificently, and at the highest levels of the world. . . . We serve to complete it, even by the humblest work of our hands."

While it is possible that Ma was simply born with helping genes, it is more likely that she unconsciously followed a model set by her parents. Pop, for all his unsavory sexual love for little girls, had an altruistic love for his fellow man. As the saying goes, he would give anyone the shirt off his back—and did so on more than one occasion. Gram was equally altruistic when it came to helping others.

During the Great Depression, Gram and Pop were living on a farm down Maine, i.e. in the rural north where the rivers flow downhill in a northeasterly direction (hence, the expressions "down East" for the coastal areas and "down Maine" for the far north) into the Atlantic Ocean. Although they had limited money, they had enough food to share with many. So, they took in a number of down-and-out men as hired hands to help with the sowing, hoeing, and harvesting in exchange for a place to sleep and food to eat. What most of these men probably figured out with time is that Gram and Pop did not really need their help. The one handyman they had started with was really enough, but they always found work (or, more likely, manufactured it) in order not only to give charity to those in need but to help them feel that it was not charity but payment for services so that they would feel better about asking and accepting.

Seeing this respect and kindness toward others surely had an impact on Gram's and Pop's four children. All of them are kind to others from what I have observed. If only Ma could have been kind to her own children, as well!

Extending a helping hand has never been difficult for me. Accepting help, however, was something I had to learn. My New England rugged individualism experienced self-worth in giving but weakness in receiving. Raising handicapped children taught me that accepting help when it is needed is also a form of giving for others, too, enjoy the satisfaction that comes from just helping.

As we struggled to keep Doah alive during those two challenging years of 1979-1981, helpers sprang up all around us Good from bad? Indeed!

One of my professors was asthmatic. He would look at Doah and say, "I can empathize with him."

My undergraduate students came to know more about my life than students usually do, but why not? A year after Doah was able to have his tracheotomy removed, one of my students who had been in one of the classes that Doah "attended" regularly asked for a recommendation for graduate school. She wanted to become a social worker and help people who are trying to lead professional lives while raising special needs children; watching Doah and me had prompted this decision.

One of my advisees took Noelle to an all-day party one weekend to give Donnie and me some time alone with the other children. Noelle had fun, and we had am much needed respite from the multiple-times-a-day catheterization and range-of-motion exercises.

Wherever we turned, people wanted to help us. Noelle and Doah brought out the best in people back then, just as they always have and still do.

The most remarkable thing, though, is that all through the difficult years of living with handicapped and seriously ill children, I never doubted that things would turn out well. Through each medical intervention we undertook, some ineradicable hope maintained my confidence that this was just the next step to making everything better. I always trusted that there would be a *deus ex machina*, and there always was.

## Ma & Dad

If we had any doubt that Ma and Dad could not live without each other or that at least Ma could not live without Dad, the night spent on the stairs, waiting to be burned alive unless Dad made it home before 5:00, was ample proof. And, of course, there were all those new babies that kept arriving year after year.

Personally, I do not recall ever seeing the two of them fight with each other although Katrina, a lighter sleeper, claims to have heard some arguments. Publicly, Dad's word ruled. Ma was beastly toward us but obeisant toward Dad. She bore many children because Dad wanted a large family even though he could not afford one. Ma did not work because Dad wanted her at home. My parents displayed their affection openly and often. We children may have felt unloved, but I knew what marital love was from watching our parents together.

Ma and Dad met in the little town of East Gloucester. Dad had moved there after the war. What brought Dad to East Gloucester from Londonderry, I don't know and probably never will. Nonetheless, there he was, age 35, running a radio repair shop on one of the dozen short streets that comprise East Gloucester when Ma was 21 and living in the house on Cochise Avenue to which we would all eventually move.

One day Dad saw a pretty but voluptuous young woman walking past his radio shop. Unable to resist an impulse, he flipped to a song in a stack of records of popular music that he was methodically playing one at a time through a gramophone that sent music spilling into the street outside the radio shop.

"She's too fat, she's too fat for me!" blared the words from the song.

That was too much for Ma. She marched into the radio shop to demand that the record be turned off. There she encountered Dad. The rest is our history.

I am probably not the right person to tell Ma's story. How does one get inside the mind of someone who thinks abusing you is the equivalent of good parenting, citing God as support, or fairly tell the story of someone who has hurt you?

Danielle is convinced that Ma is a *bona fide* narcissist, perhaps made so by all the spoiling in her youth. A narcissist has no concept of consequences; neither does a child have a concept of consequence. Ma may have entered adulthood as both child and narcissist, and that was almost a deadly combination—for us.

Ma was not all bad. She taught us to write thank-you notes, to be polite, to be grateful for others' help. She taught us literacy and math skills, involved Dad in teaching us physics, and, until the money ran out completely, hired a piano tutor. These lessons were balancing forces for while they may have been taught in accompaniment to the switching of a forsythia branch, the lessons themselves developed attitudes and skills that ultimately contributed toward our saving ourselves.

Nonetheless, we never viewed Ma as a mother, only as a master. That is the way it was until we became adults ourselves, began raising children, learned more about human psychology, and deliberately worked not to continue the cycle of abuse. Once, as an adult, I watched a two-year-old on a plane cuddle with his mother. It reminded me of an experience I had as a 9-year-old who wondered about affection. I wondered how it felt. I wondered who deserved it. I wondered why some parents hugged their children. So, I figured I would see what would happen if I laid my head against Ma. We were sitting in the car, side by side, and there was a moment when it was possible to show a brief slice of affection. I should have known what would have happened. Whack! "Get off me! What's wrong with you? Sit up straight!"

There were times in later, adult years that Ma would attempt a hug. She had, indeed, mellowed. However, the patterns were set, and the instincts were strong. At her very touch, I would recoil. That reaction was not something I could prevent.

At an age before most people can even contemplate "the other," I had developed a psychological understanding of Ma. She did not have a personality type suited to raising children, I concluded. However, in those days, raising children is what women did, and not being able to achieve excellence in her school subjects or popularity on the playground, Ma saw her own children as her means to glory. And so, the woman who should never have had any children was always pregnant with yet another stone in her Mother's Ring, another jewel to display in the community—and more fuel for the rage that burned within her.

While I may have spent some time, even as a child, reflecting on Ma, I have never known her to engage in self-reflection. Like a child, she has always been hostage to emotions. She still is.

During WWII, Dad distinguished himself by expertise in radio theory, working on figuring out how captured German radios worked. I loved his story about how his rapid promotion was questioned by a superior officer, who proceeded to quiz him on radio theory, using the Army's most current manual—which Dad had written!

In fact, I loved all of Dad's stories, and he loved telling them to me, sitting on the backyard side of the small hill on which our house stood. I would listen raptly to recitations of family genealogy, from the family that came to the United States on the

Mayflower to our descendency (descendency is very much the right word!) from the Adams family of presidential fame to the Native American great-grandmother who had added local blood to immigrant blood. I laughed at the stories he told of how he got into trouble as a child, especially the time that he had built his own radio at the age of 12 and tuned into the local FBI frequency, in reaction to which the FBI showed up at the door and confiscated the thing while Grandma shook in fear.

Following his marriage to Ma, Dad's repair business became a sideline as the needs of a growing family forced him back into the shoe shops. Dad would help people for free or forgive their debts if they could not pay. I remember spending 45 minutes to get to one lady's house. She said that she could not even get a picture on her television set. When we arrived at the lady's house, she showed us her completely dark screen. Dad looked at the television briefly, walked around to the back, picked up a cord from the floor, and plugged it in. Immediately her television was working. Dad refused to charge her anything, not even for gas. Gas he needed desperately. We found that out when we ran out of it at the top of a hill a few miles from town and had to hitchhike to a gas station. Still, he said, it was not ethical to ask someone to pay for a mistake. He had not done any real work. Perhaps this kind of ethics, which I learned from Dad, has contributed to my years of fighting the poverty dragon. .

Like me, Dad loved reading in the apple orchard. I remember him to this day sitting in his wooden chair, his thin legs covered to the ankle by green workmen's pants, holding a book shaded by apple branches, and lost in reverie. An intellectual lifestyle was his unreachable star. In the end, he died bitter, ill with pneumonia and sick from seeing Danielle and me getting married the same year, assuming that we would become housewives and throw away our education (neither of us did), and from seeing Katrina drop out of school to earn money for tuition, assuming the work world would keep her, like him, away from the world of books forever (it did not). I suppose there is a lesson in this: do not let the plot development predispose you to guess the end of a story because you might well guess wrong.

Dad, for all his intellectualism, would never realize his dream even to graduate from high school. He took correspondence courses and got As in all of them, but he had too many children needing attention, a wife in a near-permanent rage, and a double workload with farming and shoe-cutting. He never found the time to finish before the hospital mistake that took his life at the age of 58. However, he had already passed his educational aspirations along to his children. It was they, not he, whom he wanted to see graduate from college. Even high school graduation was a special moment for him. When I garnered the highest scholarship award, he stood up excitedly to take my picture, then promptly missed the chair and sat on the floor. His pride in us, unlike Ma's sick pride of wanting us always to "bring honor" to her, was a healthy pride. It was likely this pride that kept me chasing those unreachable stars.

Katrina does not share this image of Dad. While at Ohio State University, she worked summers in a local factory for her next round of tuition payments and was thus forced to live at home again. It was during these periods that she found herself estranged from Dad. That was a situation that I did not understand because Dad was the gentler of our two parents. It was only later that I realized that he and I shared an intuitive-thinking personality that made it easier for me to learn from him.

Learning was the crux of our relationship. Dad taught me Latin during my third-grade summer. On weekends, he showed me how to develop negatives in a dark-room. Year-round during my elementary school years, he assigned me readings from an encyclopedia of radio and television theory. I was great at theory, but it was Katrina who provided the better help at television repair. She was less likely to depart into fantasy and much more likely through practical application to find the cause of failure of a non-functioning television set. Still, it was the theory that intrigued Dad, just as it intrigued me. So, he always gravitated toward me more because of the traits we shared. What Katrina wanted from him was physical and emotional support—attendance at school events, assistance with transportation—and he found that boring and, later, as he grew weaker, did not have the energy to provide either.

Quite ironically, it was Katrina who was with Dad when he died. For many years, she did not tell me about that experience. After Don and Danielle's wedding, Dad fell ill with pneumonia and ended up in the hospital. He seemed to recover while there, but suddenly on January 23, 1973, he had a heart attack and died.

The heart attack should never have happened. Later investigation showed that the wrong medication had been put into his IV. Ma never sued. She needed the hospital's services for the little girls and feared that a lawsuit would close off access to the only hospital in the area. So, she was left without a breadwinner, without a job, with five children in need of care and support, and no money.

Dad's heart attack lasted long enough that he recognized that he was dying. One can only imagine what emotions he was feeling, but one thing he did say, and that would leave a negative legacy that could never be remedied. Taking his last breath, he looked at Katrina, the only person with him at the time, and said, "Why could it not have been Beth here with me at this moment?"

These were words that he probably did not give much thought to, considering how fleeting the moment must have been. Yes, I had been the one who spent more time than anyone else with him; I was the one with the same personality type; I was the one who had studied whatever he had put in front of me; and I was the one who as a high school student had spent hours in debate with him as he developed my critical thinking and argumentation skills. So, it makes sense that he probably did want to have me there, too. Nonetheless, one short sentence left Katrina with an eternal sense of not being wanted.

Perhaps I am being too lenient with the memory of Dad, considering that all my siblings view him differently—as an effete parent, distanced from his children, one who played favorites with the two who shared his intellectual temperament (Willie and me). My siblings sensed in him a viciousness that did not depend only upon provocation from Ma. They assumed that, being 14 years the elder and idolized by Ma, he could have stepped in and stopped her but chose not to do so.

I differed both in opinion and in experience with Dad. I was the oldest. I knew Dad the most intimately. His love for books became my love for books. His love of intellectual challenge became my life of intellectual challenge. His strong sense of ethics became my strong sense of ethics. In the same way that Katrina felt compassion for Ma, I felt compassion for Dad.

Over time, I saw him allow his hope for his own education to be dashed by the need to bring in money for a family that grew larger every year. I saw him start to live his goals only through his children, who, sadly, at the moment of his death, had not yet consummated their educational programs. I saw him beaten down by a sense of failure at life, especially when Ma insisted he give up his beloved radio repair business. I do not remember him as anything but exhausted from my teen years on as he worked both on the farm and also in the shoe shops.

I saw him frustrated by his inability to protect his children (sometimes I think he preferred not to know how much Ma beat us in his absence) and by his shame at those times that he, too, beat us. I saw him give up a year at a time, a failure at a time. Sadly, the man who in my childhood refused to choose between his child and a wife demanding that he make such a choice eventually chose no life at all. His death as the result of mistaken medication in the hospital was simply fulfillment of a death he assumed would come soon, anyway. Six months earlier, he dreamed that he would die in less than a year in a hospital in the presence of three of his children. Ma would not be there. Ma had an identical dream the same night. Immediately, Dad had increased his insurance coverage sufficiently to pay off the farm mortgage and any hospital bills and had asked Donnie and me to be the guardians of my two preschool sisters should something happen to both Ma and him. Whether it came from personal disappointments, years of exposure to the rage gene, failure to reach even one star, a dream that predicted his death, or a combination of all these things is hard to tell. What was clear, though, is that at the age of 58, Dad gave up living.

I think it was a matter of Ma's rage winning out. Over time, Dad slowly but steadily withdrew from his children, an emotional distancing that my siblings are today still unwilling to overlook. He went to the shoe factory and spent the days swinging a heavy machine to cut leather into the various parts of shoes, drove nearly twenty miles home to the farm, and then sat down with us to supper.

Suppers brought further reason for him to give up. Ma would bring a leather strap to every meal. The strap was for hitting whichever child did not clean his or her plate. We became adept at sneaking food we did not like to the cats or into the hollow metal legs of the table (which, after time, started to smell so bad that the table had to be replaced—no one thought to think of checking the table legs for rotting food and none of us was going to tip off our parents.) After listening to Ma scream at one child or another or reach out and belt one child or another, Dad would stand up, his plate still nearly full, declare that he was not hungry, and retire to the living room, like his father before him who slept off hours of depression on a couch. Except for those times that he got irretrievably drawn into it, conflict made Dad ill.

We live not in a world of black and white, where people are either good or bad, but in one of grey. My parents really were not monsters. They were people who made bad choices that they subsequently tried to justify, allowed their emotions to rule their reason, and committed egregious mistakes, the responsibility for which they sidestepped. In this process, they came close to destroying their children.

Although most of the good that Ma and Dad did was reserved for others, inside the burning house, there were indeed interludes of peace. Music was one of them. At times, Dad would play the violin for us. At other times, he would sit us all down in front of the gramophone and later in front of the record player to listen to classical music. His love for classical music prompted my learning to play Liszt, Chopin, and Beethoven on the piano, and to this day, playing classical music soothes me.

Moreover, in spite of all the times she called us worthless, Ma was fiercely proud and protective of us. When she was not busy hurting us, she was busy attending school events, helping us with homework, teaching us to sew, and serving as 4-H leader. Danielle insists that Ma's contradictory nature was hubris and not pride, self-absorption and not maternal protection since Ma always clearly considered us merely reflections of herself. Nonetheless, Ma's public pride and fierce protective-ness helped in small part to heal the wounds she inflicted on me in her moments of private rage.

For the truly bad things that Ma and Dad did, I have forgiven them. Perhaps it is that forgiveness that compels me to describe them as grey, not as black.

Looking back, I can understand the origins of my atheism. We were raised in a vortex of religion, ritual, rage, and reckless hubris that nearly carnaged the 8-pack and spewed me out of a church where I had found no evidence of anything divine. This happens where religion replaces faith and ritual takes the place of relationship with God.

# Healing

After moving in with Julie, the spina bifida clinic director at the University of Virginia Hospital, Shura's medical care, like the caissons of Army fame, kept rolling along until we came to an expected hill. At the very first examination, Dr. Joshua, the neurosurgeon, noticed the external sac into which a portion of Shura's spina protruded, typically the first indication an obstetrician has that he or she has just delivered a baby with spina bifida. In the United States, the sac is incised and that area of the body repaired at birth. Shura, however, had escaped this surgery, and now Dr. Joshua was eager to schedule a date for the surgery. Certain that this was not the best route to take, I had earlier asked him to wait until the more urgent matter of double amputation of Shura's legs was accomplished, and he had agreed.

The day came, though, when Shura was doing well with his prostheses, and the neurosurgeon reinserted himself into our lives. Dr. Joshua, considered to be among the top neurosurgeons in the United States, had stood by patiently, waiting for Shura to heal from his orthopedic surgeries. Now he stood at the ready, scalpel in hand.

Concerned that the proposed surgery, by realigning the spine and cutting off the escape route of spinal fluid from the brain, might actually cause hydrocephalus to develop, something from which Shura does not, luckily, suffer, I suggested that Shura say "no" to the surgery. Shura decided to follow my advice and turn down the opportunity for more cutting. Dr. Joshua, however, continued to brandish the scalpel. Something needed to be done! It was time for a trip to nearby Washington, D.C. to see Dr. Uscinski. So I made a phone call.

Dr Uscinski enjoyed every bit as much fame in the neurosurgery world as Dr. Joshua, but he always kept his scalpel on the tray, not in his hand. He used it only when there were no alternatives. He also had copies of Shura's Siberian medical records and x-rays from the days that we worked together to bring Shura to the United States.

"Come here to D.C.," he said. "We'll talk about it over lunch."

So I came. Dr. Uscinski met me for lunch at the university cafeteria. There I described Dr. Joshua's insistence on surgery. Dr. Uscinski agreed with me: a stabilized condition was best left untouched.

"What do you need my opinion for?" he asked. "You have it all figured out." Oh, but I did need his opinion. So often when I had things all figured out, one medical figure or another would tell me with decisive knowingness I was wrong, sometimes from purely selfish motives. Then, not being educated in the medical arts, I sometimes became unsure of myself. Dr. Uscinski was an incredible blessing and ultimately made a better world for both Noelle and Shura. He listened. He explained. He taught. He trusted. Most important, he cared, and he helped. In this case, he suggested I bring Shura and Julie to Washington for an examination and discussion.

When Julie, Shura, and I arrived at the hospital, we had Dr. Uscinski paged. He came to see us and impressed Julie, who knew him only by his stature in the world of neurosurgery, with his great physical stature and great warmth, both of which were dramatically demonstrated when he lifted me into the air in a huge hug. Dr. Uscinski examined Shura, came to the same conclusion that he had reached from looking at the x-rays, and sent us off, armed with good advice and the conviction to leave well enough alone.

"Tell Jonathan Joshua," he said, "that he is a great neurosurgeon, and I have much respect for him. He is, however, not infallible, and this time he is simply wrong."

We returned to Virginia and canceled any further discussion of surgical intervention. Shura has never had that surgery. Shura has never needed that surgery.

Once Shura's health was established as stable and enduring, he wanted to go back to Siberia to see his friends and family and especially to show the members of the little, wooden Russian Orthodox church nestled on the wooded steppe among the birch and *kedr* trees that protected it from the typical winter onslaught of *meteli* and *metelitsy* (big and little blizzards) how their prayers for him had been answered. That is how I ended up standing in front of the congregation of the Siberian church that Easter morning.

What I have related above is the story of Shura in America that I told to them that day. It did not matter to them that the story was told by an atheist for they saw all the miracles that had been orchestrated by God directly as well as through those who, like me, were unaware of their use as God's instrument to bring a dying child into vibrant adulthood. It may have been such instances as these that prompted the author of the anonymous missal, *The Book of Privy Counseling*, to write "I am convinced that God in his great goodness will continue to act as he wishes in those he chooses that in the end his goodness may be seen for what it is, to the astonishment of all the world."

The unexplainable coincidences spread beyond Shura to enrich the lives of all who had participated in his story—a story that could be a modern-day parable, except that it was very real and brought many people face-to-face with God. Not me, though. Not then.

# II

# *Grace*

"You've got to be kidding!" I said, staring at my dinner partner in total disbelief.

"No," she said softly. "I mean it. It is your turn to say grace."

"You don't ask an atheist to say grace!" I retorted, frustrated and nonplussed.

"I did," she said, again softly. "And I'm not going to eat until you do."

Well, this could be a long, hungry evening, I thought. I shook my head in amazement at her self-assurance. To describe Jean would probably reveal identities that are best left private. So, for now I will refrain. I will mention only her soft, insistent voice, urging me to pray.

"Look," I answered. "I simply cannot. Just go ahead and eat. Please."

"No," Jean shook her head. "I am not going to eat without grace being said, and it is your turn. Just try!"

"You say it," I insisted.

Again she shook his head. "It is your turn." So this was the outcome of my courteously having agreed to let her say grace at the last two meals we had had together!

"I don't want to!" That pugilism of mine was about to strike.

"We all have to do things we don't want to." She just was not going to give up!

"I don't know how!"

"Well, just say whatever comes into your head."

She seemed quite serious about not eating until I said something, but I had no idea what to say and no desire to say anything. Here I was again, in a situation akin to the one I experienced in the Siberian Orthodox Church 11 years earlier. Nothing had changed in my beliefs. I was as confirmed an atheist as ever. Only now I was hungry, and I had a stubborn dinner partner with strong beliefs that were quite different from mine. One of us had to budge, but I was completely at a loss in a spiritual environment—and pretty defiant about spirituality being forced upon me.

In fact, when I thought about the word *grace* or even the concept of grace, the story of my Aunt Grace's experience at an annual community baked bean dinner in East Gloucester many years ago will not leave my mind. Aunt Grace worked in the kitchen and served the tables. With the entire town showing up, as usual, the serving crew was quite busy getting everyone seated and served. Shorthanded, the crew heaved a sigh of relief when all the beans were on all the tables, and all the people were sitting behind their plates. They went into the kitchen to catch their breath.

About then, one of the local pastors stood up. "Let us all say grace," he intoned in a voice that carried beyond the door of the kitchen. Not all the words were clear behind the closed door, but my exhausted Aunt Grace did hear the word *grace* and thought she was being paged. Annoyed at what she thought was yet another request, Aunt Grace jumped out into the dining room where all were suddenly looking right at her since the pastor was standing in front of the room near the kitchen door.

"What the heck do you want now?" she asked impatiently of the startled crowd. No one in East Gloucester who attended that baked bean supper does not remember Aunt Grace's question. So, every time I heard the word *grace*, I thought of Aunt Grace. As a result, I could not take grace seriously. Especially not like Jean did.

Jean was a social acquaintance of mine, and we had been working evenings on a community project. This was the third time that we had worked until after 8:00 on this particular project. After the first late-night session, we had decided to get a quick bite to eat together before going home. That had now become a habit if three times in a row can be considered a habit.

I did not know Jean well. We lived in different towns, she on the ocean and I a bit inland in San Ignatio. We did not spend much time together, except for this project. So, I was neither surprised nor not surprised at our first supper when Jean announced that she would like to say grace. I explained to her that I was an atheist but she was welcome to indulge her beliefs. I waited patiently while she said grace—aloud.

The second time was a repeat of the first, except that we were in a different restaurant and Jean already knew that I was an atheist. Once again I patiently waited while Jean said grace. She thought she was saying grace for both of us. I thought I was being remarkably tolerant in putting up with such nonsense.

Now, it was our third repast, and Jean had announced that it was "my" turn to say grace. Right! At first, I thought she was joking. Then I realized she wasn't. Months later, I asked her why she had behaved in this way, and she said she did not know, that she had never intended to do that, that she had fully intended to say grace herself, but other words, the announcement that it was my turn to say grace, quite to her own surprise, tumbled out of her mouth instead.

Well, I was not about to be bullied into saying grace. Having said what she had said, apparently not by her own intent, she was not about to say grace, either. So, there we sat, silently. What was I to do?

# Prayer

At the thought of prayer, my mind shifted instantly to childhood and to the last time I had been "required" to pray. I was 8 or 9 years old, and we were still living in the small New Hampshire village where we lived prior to moving to the farm in Maine. There was a huge forest fire outside of town that had roared out of control and was breathing heavily on our little village. All the volunteer firemen had raced to the perimeter to try to put out the fire before the houses in town burst into flames-from its hot breath. The other townsmen, those who were not firefighters, had gathered together at the firehouse to see how they might help. The women and children were left at home to pray for the safety of the village.

Ma had hurried us out of bed and down to the enclosed front entryway where she had lined us up on a long couch. That way we could run out the door should the house catch on fire. At least, that was what she said. It did not seem like a very good plan to me at the time. If all the houses were on fire, where would we go? Would the street really be any safer? Thoughts of an early demise were whirling through my head and, I suppose, through the heads of my siblings.

"Pray, damn you, pray." Ma's words, accompanied by the swish-slap, swish-slap of a fly swatter she had seized on our march to the front entry, helped me focus on her. I looked at her but did nothing. My demeanor did not indicate that I was praying. Actually, I was thinking something along the lines that I had said to Danielle earlier about her pigtail: Ma's approach to fire was dumb.

"Pray now, damn you!" She repeated. "Pray hard!" Swish-slap! Swish-slap!

There was an angry rhythm to the fly swatter's swishing. My siblings were quietly praying. Perhaps they were only feigning, but it did not matter. As far as Ma was concerned, they were complying. To Ma, compliance was everything. To me, noncompliance in what I considered to be dumb situations was everything.

"Are you praying?" Swish-slap! Swish-slap! Ma's full attention was on me now.

Even at that young an age, I was already an audacious atheist. As such, I angrily ventured that firemen with retardant might be more expedient than prayer. Swish-slap! Swish-slap! Swish-slap! Swish-slap! Then, blood! Oh, oh! The sight of blood always infuriated Ma. How dare we bleed! This time was no different. Fly-swatting instantly changed to kicking. Kick! Kick! Kick! Kick! Kick! Kick! Kick! And then: welcome oblivion!

I don't remember what happened next. It is not likely I remained unconscious for long, but I may well have subsequently fallen asleep. I have always had an unusual reaction to both great stress and great pain: I deliberately ignore it, separating my mind from the physical (or mental) pain so well that I fall asleep. Perhaps Ma grew tired of switching and kicking me. Perhaps she chose another's hide to brand with her swatter. I do not recall. All I remember is that time passed, and, as I was becoming slowly aware of my surroundings, Ma was telling us that there was no need to pray any more. The fire danger had passed. Ma's fire, too, had diminished. "Go to your room now," she said to me. "And don't ever let me see your face again unless you learn to obey me!"

Never! I thought. Never would I obey! I had to maintain my self-respect, and doing something that I did not believe in was an affront to my self-respect. In spite of Ma's most draconian measures, obedience was not something that came naturally to me. Instead of inspiring me to be obedient through abusive punishment after abusive punishment, Ma had choked any hope for obedience out of me.

She also killed any respect for prayer. It would be years before I would think of prayer as anything except formulaic words muttered at best through nearly closed lips in response to an external threat: a fly swatter, a switch, parental anger, pastoral anger. I never thought about God as part of prayer since I never thought God existed. Only recently have I come to see prayer as more than formulaic and ritualistic, as even more than petition, rather as a giving back of love, "the adoration of the one whose being is necessary," as Ibn Sina writes in "Kitab el-najat" in *366 Readings from Islam* (tr. Robert van der Weyer).

My mind moved forward to my experiences as a young mother. Doah at the time was sporting a tracheotomy. I had researched the complications of raising a child with a tracheotomy, and there seemed to be limited ways to avoid the ever-present danger of infections in a trachea open to the environment through a plastic tube that not only let in air for breathing but also germs for multiplying. Usually the pediatrician's antibiotic prescriptions killed the infected green goo oozing from the tube, and life would return to normal after a week or two of worry and constant monitoring. One time, however, the antibiotic did not work. After the traditional ten days of medication, the infection was no better. If anything, it was worse. Near the end of the ten-day period, Doah had developed severe tracheitis. Rather than making an appointment for the ENT clinic, which usually meant a wait of 1-2 weeks, we decided to take Doah into the emergency room. We had found that while he might be triaged with a lower priority, he at least would be seen the same day if we brought him there.

In this case, we had apparently underestimated the severity of the tracheitis. He was triaged with the highest priority, and the chief of ENT nearly instantly appeared at our side. He very briefly examined Doah. Then, in a forthright non-bedside manner, he turned to us and said, "I don't know if he will live."

Before we even had a chance to react to those words, he scooped Doah up in his arms and headed toward the staircase. "Get me a third-floor operating room stat. I don't care what you have to do. Just make it happen!" He called these words over his shoulders to the head nurse in the ER as he ran out the door.

We watched as he took the stairs two at a time. Then, not knowing what else to do, we headed for the surgical waiting room, a place where we had previously spent many hours.

We were to spend many hours there this time, too. Five, to be precise. For five hours, we had no idea of the significance of Doah's breathing problems. For five hours, we could only guess whether or not the surgery was going well. Five hours can be a long time when one is waiting to learn whether a child has lived or died.

Waiting is not my forte, and the dominant feeling was one of impatience. After years of inundation with overwhelming medical challenges, my initial reaction was always to determine what I needed to do to get past the next hurdle. Other emotions were put in abeyance—sometimes for years. Emotions were a luxury I felt I could not afford when my children's lives were at stake. In life and death situations, I did not panic but felt an immense sense of calm, as I did now—along with impatience.

I looked around the waiting room. There were other parents like us, waiting to hear the results of a child's surgery. Some of the surgeries were routine. We had been through those, and the waiting was typically boring. Obviously, one mother was in that situation. She was reading one of the magazines left there to occupy parents' time while waiting. She was so involved in her reading that she did not notice anyone else. Hmm, I thought. An easy surgery. The emotions associated with iffy surgeries interfere with such kinds of self-distraction.

One couple was crying. Yeah, I thought, I understand. I've been there. There are times I would have liked to cry, too, but I had been taught not to be spleeny. Any crying I did was not for the public and not on the outside. It was only on the inside.

Another couple sat motionless. I could tell from their demeanor that their child was in serious condition, perhaps as serious a condition as Doah's. As I watched, they began praying. Like that's going to help! I thought.

What helped me was doing things. I needed to make arrangements for that day's classes, so I went to the phone and called Pat, the teaching fellow supervisor. I was supposed to lead a class discussion on teaching methods during the next hour. "I can teach my 3:00 Advanced Russian class this afternoon," I told her, "but this morning I would like to stay at the hospital in case someone needs me during the surgery. Would you be willing to let me lead our methods discussion next week instead?" Of course, she agreed.

I returned to the waiting room. The praying couple was still praying, the crying couple still crying, and the reading lady still reading. Another couple had entered and was wandering around the room in a daze. They stopped to look out the window. I approached them and asked about their child, partly from my habit of wanting to help, partly because I had learned that parents can learn much from other parents, and partly because talking helps the time march past with greater vigor. It turned out that their child was having a tracheotomy. I shared Doah's history with them and gave them my phone number so that after the surgery they could contact me and perhaps join other parents at a meeting of the Western Pennsylvania Apnea Association. Tracheotomies do not take very long, and soon the doctor appeared to tell the couple that their child had passed through the surgery without complications.

The reading lady had finished her article, and I approached her next. I don't remember what surgery her child was having, just that, indeed, it was something relatively simple. Through the nearly 30 surgeries endured by Noelle and Doah that I have waited out in waiting rooms, I have met parent after parent and learned about one kind of surgery after another kind of surgery, adding each time to my informal medical education. Over the years, all the waiting rooms and parents have blurred together. Only a few instances, like this one, do I remember more distinctly. When a doctor seizes your child in his arms and runs from the room, telling you that he does not know whether the child will live and yelling to the nurse to get him an operating room stat, one remembers the waiting.

The child of the crying couple was having heart surgery—upside-down heart is what the doctors said. They held out little hope, and the parents were sad but reconciled to the loss of their child. Reconciled? I would not know how to reconcile myself to something like that. I have always tilted at the windmill. The fact that the windmill always finally moved somehow never surprised me.

My complete faith in the moving of the windmill, though, did little to help me understand the praying couple. I don't know what their child's problem was because I did not approach them. Well, they have found the crutch that they want. That is what I thought at the time. Let them pray. It would not comfort me, but it seemed to comfort them. I considered them deluded, while thinking of my trust in Life, Serendipity, Hope against Hope, Chance, Luck, and a half-dozen other labels I used back then as perfectly normal.

Part of my unwillingness even to consider the possibility of divine intervention was our family's intermittent exposure to do-gooders and evangelizers who truly had no idea of what our lives were like and who assumed that somehow they could tell God what to do and God would do it. I found their arrogance off-putting. One instance, in particular, comes to me vividly even today.

In 1982, Noelle was six years old, ambulating with braces and crutches. She was happily swinging through a grocery store, shopping with me, when we were approached by four women in their late twenties or early thirties—about my own age at the time. They introduced themselves by name, asked Noelle her name, and told us that they were visiting town for some kind of evangelical gathering. They seemed pleasant enough, and I was not surprised that they had stopped to speak to us because Noelle with her wispy blonde hair, color-crayon blue eyes, eyelashes curling up to her eyebrows, freckles, and dimples often attracted people's attention. (Of, of course, there were also the braces and crutches that caused her to stand out, as well.)

Apparently, the ladies watched us after that because as soon as we had checked out and walked out the door into the parking lot with our grocery cart, they approached us again. I thought they were going to offer to help put our groceries in the car, but they did not. Instead, they entered into a conversation that others had broached with me before and would broach again in the future.

"May we speak to you for a minute?" the older of the four asked.

"Sure," I said somewhat cautiously, suspecting what was to come. "About what?"

"About Noelle. Actually, we would like to pray for her."

"Well, that's kind of you," I answered. "Sure. Keep her in your prayers. That will be fine."

"No, we mean now," one of the other ladies interjected.

"Here? In the parking lot?" I asked, a little incredulously.

"Yes." She turned to Noelle. "You would like to be able to walk, wouldn't you?"

"Okay, guys," I responded. "We have to leave. It was nice meeting you, but this conversation is over."

They blocked my way and began a (thankfully short) prayer, asking God to heal Noelle immediately. Then, ignoring me, they smiled at Noelle and said, "We will pray for you again tonight. Rejoice, Noelle, and have faith! Tomorrow you will be walking without your braces and crutches."

These ignorant people would never know that their prayers were ineffective. They may well have returned to their homes, assuming that they had done some marvelously good deed for Noelle, firmly believing that she would, indeed, be walking the next day. They, like others we have encountered in various guises and on various missions, never stayed around to see the real results of their "caring."

All the way home, Noelle bubbled with excitement. The prospect of walking was not one she had ever considered before. She could hardly fall asleep that evening even though I explained as cogently as I could that her inability to walk came from a broken X chromosome, something that cannot be healed the way a broken leg can be or even the way paraplegia from a car accident can sometimes be now that doctors are beginning to have some success in repairing spinal cord injuries. Noelle's paraplegia was not a result of an injury. It was a matter of gene encoding. Her genes, located on that broken chromosome, were encoded for not-walking, just as her eye color was encoded for blue. Praying for her to walk would be like praying for her eye color to change to brown. The people she had met clearly did not understand this.

The next day came. Immediately upon waking up, Noelle, full of faith in the words of the four ladies who had prayed for her, tried to stand and fell in a heap on the floor, sobbing. This was only the second time she ever displayed any sense of self-pity.

The first time was when two-year-old Shane began walking. Shane was a late walker. In fact, he did not begin walking until he was more than two years old. He would scoot around the house on his bottom, crab-like, following big sister Noelle, whose crab-walk was her only means of locomotion at the time. Crab-walking, with one hand on each ankle and a pull-to motion, was also Shane's only means of locomotion until the day he started going to a day care center. Obviously, he could have walked much earlier because within minutes of arriving at the center and being put with the other two-year-olds, all of whom were walking, he stood up and took his first steps. When he came home that evening, pulled himself up on the arm of the couch, and began cruising along the length of it, with one hand on the cushion, three-year-old Noelle panicked.

"No, no, Nanie," she exclaimed. "Sit down. Sit down. Nanie get hurt!"

Shane did not sit down as he would have in the past at these words. Rather, he cruised to the end of the couch and took a step by himself toward me. I held out my arms, and he walked into them. Noelle began to sob.

"What's wrong?" I asked her.

"Nanie walks," she said.

I tried to cheer her up by reminding her that she would have braces in a few days. Then she would be able to start walking, too.

"I don't want braces," she declared emphatically. "I want legs that work, like Nanie's." There was little to be said at that moment.

Three years later, watching Noelle once again dissolve into tears, I became very angry. My anger was not directed at God. I did not believe God existed. Rather, it was directed in heavy doses at the do-gooders who had promised her a miracle. I vowed to keep Noelle away from everyone who might want to pray for her. (I did not keep that vow very well, however. Once I found out that church schools often have the best educational programs, I enrolled Noelle in one of them for her first four years of education. Moreover, in spite of my best efforts to convince her otherwise through discussions, reasoning, and reading materials, she developed a strong belief in God at a very young age.)

Could God have healed Noelle? Could God have stepped in and changed the laws of nature for one person? I have no doubt that God could have, but why would God choose to do this? Why would God choose to exchange a life that worked, albeit with hardships, for an easier one that might not work at all. Noelle, like Doah and like me, has been used as an instrument on a number of occasions. She has inspired students to go into health occupations, doctors to broaden their concepts of what handicapped children can be expected to do, brace makers to think about making sturdier braces, principals to mainstream handicapped children, older adults to accept gracefully frailties to which they were not accustomed in younger days, exclusionary ethnic groups to include previously spurned individuals with disabilities, and more. Her life works at the level that it needs to work. If you were a farmer with a dozen sprinklers for irrigation, one of which had a bent nozzle that made the pulsation of water irregular but at the same time splashed it out in greater abundance than did the other sprinklers, reaching more barren ground, would you replace it with a physically perfect sprinkler?

Why then should God make everyone's life perfect? What is there to be learned from that? We learn more from our imperfections and struggles than we do from our successes. That is one reason why gifted students may not be as successful in life as those with what Sternberg in *The Triarchic Mind* calls "street smarts." That is why I have always been happiest when my students were making mistakes. They were learning, and in this way—through trial and error, through seeing their own mistakes, through the struggle that leads to greater perfection—they ultimately developed the habits and skills they have needed for success in their professions and in life.

Perhaps God lets infirmity be so that the able-bodied and able-minded can learn compassion and develop the desire to help others. Socrates' concept of utopia, as described by Plato in *The Republic*, advocated putting to death any person born with a handicap in order to ensure a perfect society. Such a society, however, would not inspire compassion and would not therefore be truly utopic but rather selfish and complacent.

Perhaps God lets infirmity be so that the infirm can develop a character that allows them to accept the help of others with gratitude and grace. Accepting help from others can sometimes be very difficult, especially among the citizens of a nation that places a high value on independence. Few people understand the joy that they bring to someone else by letting someone else help them. In this way, mutual helping is going on: physical help to the infirm person and emotional help to the able-bodied.

For certain, many people, including Shura, have been helped as a result of Noelle not receiving a miracle. Miracles were created all around her for others who needed them. Perhaps it might be considered unfair that she would be an instrument for betterment and not experience the betterment herself. I don't think so. As an instrument myself, I know the chronic happiness that develops as a result of being divinely used. Noelle does, too, for she is also chronically happy. Happiness is not simply a gift that is bestowed upon us. Nor can we chase and catch happiness. Rather, we must stop chasing after it and let happiness catch us. After all, happiness is what gushes up from becoming a living gift. Happiness comes from living a good life.

There is a clear difference between an easy life and a good life. Neither Noelle nor the rest of our family has had an easy life, but God granted us all a good life. Rabbi Rami Shapiro described the wonder of what God let stands in our lives in a pithy poem about the value of passing through the valley of the shadow of death if God is by your side.

> *May we discover through pain and torment*
> *The strength to live with grace and humor.*
> *May we discover through doubt and anguish*
> *The strength to live with dignity and holiness.*
> *May we discover through suffering and fear*
> *The strength to move toward healing.*
> *May it come to pass that we be restored to health and to vigor.*
> *May Life grant us wellness of body, spirit, and mind.*
> *And if this cannot be so, may we find in this transformation and passage*
> *Moments of meaning, opportunities for love,*
> *And the deep and gracious calm that comes*
> *When we allow ourselves to move on.*

What the do-gooders did not understand was the value of an imperfect life. In looking for perfection, they overlooked the profundities, grace, humor, strength, love, and even joy that derive not only from learning to cope with imperfection but also from discovering the advantages of it. They thought that they, in their search for perfection and in their sense of their own perfection, could cure Noelle. What they did not realize was that she might have cured them of their feelings of superiority, of their egocentric judgment of what is good and what is not, and of their misunderstanding of what is truly important for a good life had they only listened rather than talked, had they only attempted to learn rather than attempted to teach. What they did not realize is that Noelle is perfect as she is.

# A Season in the Land of the Wandering Jews

Ironically, I spent the last two of my 40 years of being in a spiritual wilderness in the same geographical wilderness around which Moses led the Israelites for 40 years. Between the undergraduate and graduate campuses near and in Amman, Jordan, where I was working as chief academic officer and dean and to which I commuted daily, lay Mount Nebo, from where Moses glimpsed the Promised Land.

On a clear day, one can still see the Promised Land from Mount Nebo, just as on a clear day Bethlehem can be glimpsed on the distant horizon by a viewer standing on the hills of Jerasch or living in the western outskirts of Amman. Otherwise a nondescript mountain of moderate elevation, Mount Nebo enjoys today a stream of visitors to the mosaic-floored church that has been built atop it. Among the visitors have been people of renown, including the late Pope John Paul II. Sometimes it is difficult to imagine Moses standing alone on the top of the mountain, given today's activity there, including the artisans, selling their wares at the bottom. Still, if one comes before or after the crowds or closes one's ears to them, one can see past the stunted, water-starved trees into the verdant valley beyond and imagine the emotions of Moses, climbing up out of the sandy desert that lay to the South and East and seeing an expanse of green to the West. I took visitors to Mount Nebo often. It was only a few minutes from where I lived.

Between Mount Nebo and the border of Israel lies the Jordan River. The site where John the Baptist baptized Jesus occasionally has some water but often is mostly sand. Lebanon and Israel divert the water for the needs of their inhabitants before it can flow all the way to the Dead Sea. As a result, the Dead Sea is shrinking. The Dead Sea, called the Salt Sea and the Sea of Arabah in the *Bible*, has been known by a wide variety of names, including Bahr Lut, Lake of Sodom and Gomorrah, Lake of Lot, and Stinking Lake. The Crusaders often called it Devil's Sea. Ten times as saline as the oceans and twice as saline as Utah's Great Salt Lake, the Dead Sea is somewhat unique in that being the lowest point on earth (1300 feet below sea level) means that the water does not drain from the lake but is evaporated. Every day seven million tons of water evaporate, leaving behind rich minerals. The sea itself has long been considered to have medicinal value, especially for disorders of the skin, and people come from all over the world to bathe in it. As I found out, swimming is not possible: because of the 35% salinity, one can only bounce on the surface like a bobbing ball.

For me, the Dead Sea also played a medicinal role. When I first visited the Dead Sea shortly after arriving in Jordan, I had recently had two biopsies, both skin related. During one of my consultations abroad—I don't remember just where—I had discovered two oddly sized and oddly colored spots, one on my arm and one on my back. For a while, I had ignored them. They had caused me no pain. Then, friends had found out about them and had urged me to see an oncologist. They were, in fact, not going to let me get away with ignoring their advice.

Julie set me up with Dr. Switzer, one of the leading oncologists in the United States. He was on the staff at the University of Virginia Hospital. So, my fate was sealed. Biopsies were needed. The excision without painkiller was painful, but thankfully, the diagnosis was "benign." The spot on my arm, however, a dermatofibroma, continued to be a problem in that it bled every day. Over time, I had become used to being plagued by blood spots on my clothing, so I thought little about it when I jumped into the Dead Sea for the first time. After perhaps an hour of bobbing about, I lay down on the sand under the sun and fell asleep. Waking up an hour later, I found myself totally encrusted in salt. Itching from the salt had awakened me. I stood up and walked over to the fresh-water spigots that have been placed on the beach a distance from shore to wash off the minerals and salts. As water splashed down my arm, removing the baked-on mineral crust, salt was not the only thing to wash away. The dermatofibroma had completely disappeared. It has not returned to this day.

A colleague recently commented to me that perhaps the healing was a result of the strength of my faith. It was not. I had no faith at the time. Where God had played a role, though, was through opening the door to the Holy Land at a time when I needed to be there to prepare for the Presence I was to meet later and closing that door when I was ready for the Presence and needed to come back to the USA to meet faith head-on. I would indeed end up with a faith that would be palpably visible to my friends and colleagues and so that later comment about the reason for the disappearance of the dermatofibroma was not without cause. At the Dead Sea, however, what cured my dermatofibroma were the wondrous minerals, salts, and oils.

Living in the Holy Land—spending a week in a tent with a Bedouin family, standing on Mount Nebo and seeing the Promised Land as Moses had centuries earlier, becoming so familiar with the excavations of Jerash (Gerasa of *New Testament* fame) that I was able to give tours to visitors—had an interesting affect on me as an atheist. While it did not bring me overtly closer to God, it did give me a sense of belonging to something greater than myself. This sense was not unique to me. Many visitors to Jordan have told me the same thing.

As I looked out from our third floor window where we lived in the Om Othaineh district near Sixth Circle in Amman, I could see all seven hills on which the city was built. Covered exclusively with white stone buildings, as city law required, they helped me understand something very important, something that Americans talk about a good deal: my place in this universe. Jordan is a timeless land. The traditional composition of many of the buildings speaks to an ancient past. The modern architectural style of the new buildings speaks to the future. Yet, they are all held together by a white stone present. Where I belonged was clear. The past was gone in some ways but in other ways embedded in a present that would give rise to the future. My place was here and now. There is a great comfort in knowing one's place, and "here and now" is about as perfect a combination of reality and dream as one can get.

In the United States, praying outside of church is private. In Jordan, praying outside of the mosque is as often as not public. Five times a day, the call to prayers sounds throughout the country. The first call would wake me at 5:00 in the morning. With each call, people would obediently lay their prayer rugs on the floor and bow in prayer. Well, actually, the pictures of prostrate Muslims are misleading. Their prayers are more involved than that. They stand, then bow in prostration, then stand again, then bow again, over and over, repeating standard prayers while standing and making requests while bowing.

Because prayer in Jordan and other Middle Eastern countries is more public than in the West, if a prayer room is not available, people will pray wherever they happen to be. At first, this public display of praying seemed odd to me. After a while, though, even though I had no religious beliefs, I found that I was taking prayer time for others into consideration in any planning I did as an academic administrator. For example, my office, the office of an atheist, was often used by my female work-study student for prayer times because of lack of prayer-room facilities for women at the male-dominated university. Further, I kept a prayer rug in my office and several at home in case visitors needed them.

Beyond the daily prayers, religion, particularly Islamic practices, infuses life in Jordan. Chief among these is the observation of Ramadan. Ramadan is not only a religious holiday. It is also a national holiday, and fasting is enforced in public places. In Bahrain, those who break the fasting law can be jailed. In Jordan, the law is less restrictive, but there is little opportunity to break the law: all fast food chains and restaurants are closed from sun-up to sun-down during Ramadan. So, I observed Ramadan, and I respected the rights of individuals who needed or wanted to pray five times a day. I even enforced the holy day (Friday) when the university's foreign head honchos wanted to make more money by offering classes or make-up classes on Friday. I supported their right in an academic environment to talk about spiritual matters if they wanted—that is the way in the Middle East and I was not about to turn the university into something other than one compatible with the cultural climate in which it was located.

I even used allusions to Allah in speaking Arabic because one simply cannot omit "Allah" from the Arabic language. There is no "thank goodness" expression, for example. One can only say "thank God." There is no way to say "bless you" without saying "God bless you." "Praise the Lord" is the typical phrase used to indicate surprise at something marvelously wonderful that has just occurred, and the future tense always contains the phrase *inshaallah (God willing)*. Neither the Arabic language nor Arab culture exists apart from God—even for the atheists within the culture, as I found out from the one atheist friend I had. (Finding atheists in that part of the world is difficult. In fact, generally, when asked about one's ethnicity, the two possibilities to check off on any document are Muslim and Christian. All Westerners are considered Christian. As an atheist, I found this to be an awkward appellation for myself.)

My support of Islamic traditions confused my colleagues and students who knew I was an atheist. The course in ethics (social philosophy) that I was drawn into teaching when the assigned professor failed to show up confused them even more. They wondered about my own ethical system, which they found to be well established but could not understand why. "How can you be ethical," they asked me, "if you do not fear God's punishment for bad conduct?"

Ah, in answering that question I would have to explore the core and the outcroppings of the entire field of social philosophy. The simple answer is that atheists can exhibit moral and ethical behavior. Most do. The complex answer is that interpretation of behavior depends on how one defines the words *ethical* and *moral*, and those definitions, in turn, really depend on an underlying belief system, although not necessarily a belief in a Supreme Being.

Such questions were the essence of the social philosophy course, and I enjoyed teaching that course far more than I ever anticipated. My students learned not only to examine life and the precepts of the various philosophies that have shaped social behavior and values over the centuries but also, and perhaps even more important, to examine their own lives. "The unexamined life," according to Socrates, "is not worth living."

Through reflection about their own belief systems, observation of their own behaviors, and argumentation about right and wrong, these students were doing precisely what Socrates advocated: critically examining their own lives. My goal was to develop the students' critical thinking skills. It never entered my head, being an atheist, to influence their religious beliefs one way or another. Rather, I wanted them to recognize what they believed, know where it came from, and understand how it influenced their behavior, thinking, friendships, and values.

In ironic contrast to my efforts to get the Muslim youth of Jordan to examine their lives, I never examined my own life and my own beliefs. As an atheist, I accepted that nature sometimes was chaotic, that people's behaviors were influenced by their own belief systems, and that societies generally were formed and managed by people acting within those belief systems and not in any way through divine intercession. I accepted, without question, the traditional practices of the cultures in which I found myself working, living, or studying.

My ability to understand, accept, and fit into the culture allowed me to help the new American professors (about a dozen of them) who had been recruited to teach various subjects at the university. Most of them spoke no Arabic and were therefore dependent on me for help beyond their lack of knowledge of the culture. Helping came naturally and enjoyably. Disentangling sticky situations challenged my analytic inclinations. The opportunity to intertwine two cultures amicably inspired my creative ones. Seeing Americans thrive among Jordanians and Jordanians improve their educational approaches based on successes I borrowed from yet other cultures and shared with our institution as well as with the public educational system brought a sense of fulfillment. So did helping professors from the West and the East for the problems were greater than just those of blending. The university administration back in the United States had only one concern: money. People did not matter to them so I had to make them matter in Jordan. That required much work on my part to improve both working conditions and salaries. I was not surprised, then, that visitors and permanent faculty were grateful. What I learned only later, however, was that many called me "God's agent in Jordan"—until they found out that I was an atheist. Some were not able to accept my atheism. They felt that I just did not know that I was "God's agent."

I met Dr. Omar Imady, United Nations Program Officer, Syrian poet, and, later, professor of political science, near the beginning of my tenure in Jordan. He had an international air about him and quickly became my dearest friend, confidant, and, ultimately, team-teaching partner when we taught a writing course together for upper-level undergraduate students at the university. The product of that collaboration was a book, the collection of short stories by our faculty and students that we subsequently published.

We collaborated on other things as well. We applied for a grant to build an Arab-American Center at the university. Unfortunately we did not receive it. We applied for a different grant. Unfortunately, we did not receive that, either. Undismayed, we put to work the lesson I had learned from winning the seventh-grade science fair: it is not what you have that counts but what you do with it. Using artifacts from our own homes, we decorated three rooms with American and Middle Eastern flags and posters: a video room replete with videotapes on the Middle East and the USA, a library of books on cultural topics, and an entry room with traditional Middle Eastern carpets. What fun we had turning what was essentially storage space into a cultural experience for students by raiding our own homes and those of our friends!

Yet another area in which we collaborated was a project to bring contemporary teaching approaches to the English Language Center. To help Dr. Omar learn contemporary second-language teaching methods, such as content-based instruction, I had him teach beginning-level Arabic to me and one of the professors from the USA in an Arabic-only classroom. Lesson 1 focused on the geography of Jordan, Lesson 2 on the history of Damascus, and Lesson 3 on the differences between Islam, Christianity, and Judaism. These were all topics he might teach in his various content classes for Arabic-speaking students studying geography, history, or comparative religion. Doing it in a second-language classroom gave adult students adult content for their classrooms and hastened their journey to full foreign-language proficiency. Once Dr. Omar saw how content-based instruction could shape the teaching of Arabic, he could do the same in the ESL classes with which he helped out, thanks to excellent English from an American mother and a Ph.D. from the University of Pennsylvania.

When I was asked to go to Bahrain as acting dean, essentially shuttling back and forth between Bahrain and Jordan, I learned that the Bahrain campus was seriously out of compliance with accreditation standards. I immediately brought a few faculty from Jordan to assist me with the Bahrain programs. Among these was Dr. Omar.

If all Dr. Omar and I had done was to pursue professional success, I would not likely have fallen into the grip of the cosmic nutcracker. Mornings before heading to teach his classes, Dr. Omar would drop into my office to talk about work, his poetry, and especially cats. He was captivated by my quest to rescue as many cats as possible from the streets of Amman where they were often hurt. He felt that God takes special care of people who rescue cats.

Evenings Donnie and I often joined Dr. Omar and his wife, Inas, for lamb chops at Farujna, a restaurant in Swefieh within walking distance from our apartment in Om Othaineh, an establishment that was popular with the native Ammanites and where, as the theme song of the television show *Cheers* says, "everyone knows your name." Sometimes we would enjoy pizza at an Italian restaurant in Rabia, where the upper crust of Jordan society lived. Our conversations almost always revolved around spiritual matters. Dr. Omar would tell us about how his mentor Al-Bani, a cleric at the Grand Mosque in Damascus, worried about the welfare of Syrian cats. He also told us many Sufi stories. Dr. Omar not only never understood my atheism, but he also never believed that I was an atheist at heart, just in mind. We would debate his convictions, but his convictions never changed. I was the one ultimately to change, but not until after we had parted.

I suppose some would say that Dr. Omar was sent to be a part of my life. The poem that he wrote about me and sent to me after I left Jordan put some of our discussions into a larger perspective. It also gave me some things to continue thinking about—things that Dr. Omar had said or implied in many of our conversations, such as his conviction that my heart knew God but my head did not. Perhaps he was influenced by the words of the Prophet Mohammed: "When your good deed pleases you, and your evil deed grieves you, you are a believer." Certainly, I have always instinctively known the difference between good and evil and have always been drawn to the good. In fact, I have always assumed that everyone knows the difference and prefers the good. I nearly always act as if that is the case, with repeating disappointments because there are, indeed, many instances of evil in the world. In his poem, Dr. Omar succinctly described his convictions about me:

> *From your Muslim humanist –*
>
> *I'm trying to start a blog*
> *http://Dr. Omar.com/Personal/BLOG/BLOG.htm*
> *But a blog is, in essence, a journal, a record of inner thoughts and*
> *    feelings... I stare at the screen and nothing comes out.*
> *Perhaps I should write about a woman I once knew...*
> *A woman who would inspire me to write and smile and return home*
> *    feeling energetic.*
> *Perhaps I should write about a woman who emphatically insisted she*
> *    did NOT believe, while never failing to leave those she encountered*
> *    flowing with faith.*
> *Perhaps I should write about cats and honesty and someone who al-*
> *    ways tried to do what is right no matter what...*
> *But I left the screen empty, save for a photo...*
> *Perhaps I need to see her again soon...*
>
> O

The words, "who emphatically insisted she did NOT believe while never failing to leave those she encountered flowing with faith," had haunted me for the four months that stretched between my receipt of Dr. Omar's email and the pizza dinner with Jean. At dinner with Jean, the issue of faith was about to rise to a higher plane. She was expecting me to say grace.

# In the Presence

And so there Jean and I sat in front of a small, square, wooden table with a red-and-white checkered tablecloth pulled across it diagonally. Nearly alone in this nondescript pizza kitchen with nondescript, about-to-be shared, and quickly-growing-cold pizza pies sitting on the table between us, we simply stared at each other. Who would win the battle of the stares? I waited for her to give in, to say grace herself or just start eating, but that did not happen. Finally, I was the one to give in. What harm could saying grace do? What result could it have beyond getting me to the dinner that I was hungry for?

Grace? I searched in my mind for the right words. I searched for *any* words. It had been five decades since I had even uttered a child's grace and then it had been a meaningless, memorized formula, forced from unwilling lips.

Blessing. You have to say something about blessing, I figured.

"If You truly exist, bless this food, and bless us with Your presence," I said in a half-muttered, unbelieving tone with just a tad of annoyed taunting.

Bless us with Your presence. Vacuous words. Or so, I thought. They rolled off the tip of my tongue meaninglessly.

There! I had said them. I hoped it satisfied Jean's needs. Good, I thought. That is over. At least, now we can eat.

I picked up a piece of pizza. We must have been hungry when we ordered. Two medium pizzas steamed in front of us: a vegetarian pizza and a deluxe combination of meats and vegetables. That was a lot of pizza, but after a long day and evening of work, I was quite ready to ingest a sizable portion of the meal in front of us.

Then it happened. Presence we had! Strong presence. We both felt it. It was if we were encompassed by a diaphanous entity, gentle in love and firm in persistence. I was immediately and completely disoriented. Not only were we surrounded by Presence, but also something had entered inside me, down to the cellular level, filling me with an expanding sense of life beyond myself. Fr. Thomas Dubay in *The Fire Within* describes infused prayer (contemplative prayer) as a divine invasion, but this Presence was not merely an invasion, it was a divine occupation. I breathed with difficulty. I thought only randomly.

I don't remember any of our conversation that evening so consumed was I by this Presence. Nor does Jean. I do not remember if I ate a lot or a little. I do remember the restaurant closing seemingly too early and a strongly perceived need to continue talking. We ambled around the peninsula, talking as aimlessly as we walked. Jean seemed not to want to leave the Presence, and I wanted not to be left alone with it. Neither of us talked *to* the Presence, which now seems like a lost opportunity of grand proportions but at the time was unthinkable. We both clearly but unspokenly acknowledged the Presence, and we certainly have discussed it much since. Then, though. it was as if we had brought our conversation into a new universe, continuing discursively to comment on topics at hand while meandering down a path that we noticed only peripherally and avoiding paying attention to an environment so unreal as to defy processing, let alone understanding, by our mere human minds.

Jean and I stopped beside the ocean, sat on the beach, and talked for perhaps an hour. Incomplete sentences. Incomplete thoughts. Still caught in the diaphanous Presence. The evening was coming to a close, and we both needed to return home in order to catch some sleep before going to work the next day. Were it not for that, we might have spent the entire night on the sand.

Driving home, I felt disoriented. I was still disoriented the next morning upon awakening. In fact, I remained disoriented for two weeks. The Presence simply would not leave me. I felt like I was caught in a cosmic nutcracker. "I won't crack," I swore to myself and said the same thing on several occasions to Jean. "I am like a Brazil nut. My shell is strong and hard."

The strong shell of my Maine woman's pugilism and my natural, long-standing defiance had hardened even more during years of protecting myself from abusive adults as a child and from abusive health-care providers and other so-called "helpers" as an adult. All my life I had fought: bureaucracy, schools, doctors, you name it. I had built an impermeable shell around any vulnerability.

That seemed not to matter. The Presence kept gently squeezing the Brazil nut in the cosmic nutcracker tighter and tighter, ever so gently, ever so persistently.

My immediate response was to flood Jean's email box with a lot of Biblical references that I analyzed in my own way—negatively. She did not respond to any of my arguments against God. She did not even read them in detail. Later, she told me that it was as if I were throwing an electronic temper tantrum.

I suppose I was. The more the cosmic nutcracker squeezed me, the more I thrashed about in its pincers, fighting back. I never considered the hopelessness of this fight because I had not read the poem of Jelaluddin Rumi, an Afghani Sufi and the first whirling dervish:

> *Don't forget the nut, being so proud of the shell,*
> *The body has its inward ways,*
> *The five senses. They crack open,*
> *And the Friend [God] is revealed.*

I was not about to crack open for I was indeed proud of my shell. Like Francis Thompson, I "fled" the "hound of heaven" "down the nights and down the days" of the next two weeks. I thought I had already escaped God in "the arches of the years" and in the "labyrinthine ways of my own mind." I was comfortable in my atheism. To now find a divine "hound" at my heels, doggedly pulling at my coattails, slinking into the recesses of my consciousness, and woofing into the warp of my sleep unnerved me.

Sensing a Presence that I could not deny, I became angry. I was angry that I could not free myself from the nutcracker. I was angry that this Presence occupied my every thought. When I found that I could not flee the "hound" at my coattails, I turned, like a trapped animal, and fought. That is, after all, what I knew how to do best. I fought, as usual, not from fear but from anger. In my anger, I argued with and questioned this Presence—and even blamed It.

Never before had I questioned why I bore children with birth defects. Since I did not consider that there might be a God whom one could expect to intervene, I just accepted the fact that Donnie and I did not have the most felicitous combination of genes and for that reason 50% of our children suffered from multiple defects. My question, when confronted first with Noelle's birth defects, then Doah's, was not "Why?" but "What do we need to do to keep them healthy and prepare them to lead worthwhile lives?"

Only now, with this Presence occupying my thinking space day and night, did the errant thought finally come to me, "Why?" If a deity existed, then I could accept these birth defects and the myriad other tribulations that we had experienced with some degree of equanimity only if that deity were effete. But I knew from teaching social philosophy that the fearsome God of the Jews, the loving God of the Christians, and the almighty albeit gracious and merciful God of the Muslims was anything but effete. Bewildered and hostile, I wanted answers, and I demanded an explanation. I did not conduct a trial and find God guilty as did the Jewish leadership at Auschwitz during the Holocaust of WWII. No, my response was much simpler. I asked God why.

*Job!* Read the *Book of Job*. More than a thought but less than a voice, the words slammed into my consciousness. Still entranced by a surreal sense of a divine Presence fully occupying all my faculties and even directing my thinking, I accepted these quietly compelling words at face value as an answer to my demand to know why bad things had happened to my family, people whom I considered to be essentially good, even moral. Not only did I surprise myself by accepting these words, but also I reacted to them instinctively, without examination of what I was doing or why, so strong was the Presence in and around me.

While the response to my asking why took less than a minute in coming, the answer took days to understand. From my childhood Sunday School classes, I knew that Job was somewhere in the *Old Testament*, but I did not even have a Bible. In this case, as in so many other cases where I have needed general research, the Internet rescued me.

I found the *Book of Job* and read it. Ah, the patience of Job! That is an expression everyone knows. I did not think, though, that the message I was supposed to be getting had anything to do with patience. After all, how does patience explain why children might be born with handicaps?

So, I read the *Book of Job* again. I read about all the torments and testing, about how Job remained faithful through all the tests. I did not think that was the message I was supposed to be getting, either. That, too, did not explain why children would be born with handicaps. My children were not torments. They were delights.

So, I read *The Book of Job* a third time, paying attention to how Job's friends exhorted him to turn his back on God, but instead he turned his back on their advice. This, too, did not seem to be the message I was supposed to be getting for I neither blamed God nor believed in God at the time of my children's births.

The reading of *Job* was becoming rather frustrating, and I began to think I would need the proverbial patience of Job to ferret out whatever meaning I was supposed to be getting from it. Nonetheless, I read the *Book of Job* a fourth time and began to feel much empathy for him, especially in the loss of his children. I noted well that I had been spared such pain even in the case of Doah whom doctors refused to believe would live. An understanding was beginning to emerge but not one that I could articulate. Just one more time and perhaps I would understand!

I read the *Book of Job* a fifth time, and then I finally got it. It was not the concept of patience that I needed to understand, nor was it a test whose requirements I needed to meet. No, it was the concept of unconditional love that I needed to develop. No matter what was taken from Job or what he had to endure, he continued to love God. That, I think, is a message that is not often preached. More frequently preached is a panoply of "benefits" of coming to Church, being holy (whatever that means), and exercising patience. I don't need to be promised wealth in order to give to God. I don't need to be promised the avoidance of eternal damnation in order to obey God. Nor do I need fear of reprisal to walk along the path that God has laid out. I don't even need to be promised salvation in order to love God. I do all of these things because I want to not because I have to or fear the consequences of not doing them. Love for God is not a selfish love, looking for something we can get from it. It is an unselfish love, like God's love for us, full of desire to give back to God by modifying our behavior to be worthy of God's love, serving as God's instrument for good, and being open to whatever it is that God would have us do.

What the message of *Job* says to me is that God's presence in our lives and what happens to us and those we care about are separate things. God does not create problems for us. (*Job* 34:10 says "Far be it from God to do evil, from the Almighty to do wrong.") Rather, God has promised us to be with us if we allow it. What happens to us, on the other hand, is often a result of free will with which God is determined not to interfere although sometimes God does intervene. Love of God must be unrelated to what happens to us, and our love of God must be as unconditional as is God's love for us. It took five decades, but I do finally get it. What happens in life—the bad things and the good things—cannot be conditions for whether or not we love God. They are tangential. These things generally come from our own misguided actions allowed by free will, the free will of others that encroaches upon us, the sometimes infelicitous combination of genes as people marry into various gene pools (i.e. the free run of nature), and even perhaps, as in the case of Job, from the interference of Evil. Just as God's love for us is unconditional, not depending on whether or not we are always "good" (an impossibility, anyway), so, too, our love for God must be free of conditions. I understood that God was not to blame for any of the bad things that happened to Job or to me, but God has been omnipotent at turning the bad, once it happened, into good.

The reading of *Job* took care of my question as to why there could be a God and my children might be born with birth defects, why God might not want to intervene, or why it might be better to allow the birth defects to occur. My children's lives are not defined by their birth defects but by what they do with their lives, how they help others, and what they contribute to the world. It is defined not by what they *cannot* do but rather by what they *can* do and *do* do.

There was one more thing, though, one that seems to be overlooked frequently: God protected Job. It did not seem that way to Job because Job was not in on the agreement that God had made with Satan. Satan could take things away from Job and then, later, God even allowed Satan to torment Job physically. Job, however, was never in danger of dying. His life was always in God's hands and protected by God, as so many times have been my life and the lives of my children even when I, like Job, could not see that anything good at all was transpiring.

The *Book of Job* was not all the reading I would be encouraged to do. I was still in the two-week nutcracker period. I was still fighting the Presence, not wanting to believe that God really existed. My mind, memory, and previous reading provided me with many rationalizations of my long-time acceptance of atheism. That is when

I was encouraged to read about Solomon and his mistakes. Neither believing nor disbelieving, feeling more trapped than entranced, I felt a growing need to follow these promptings that were clearly leading me somewhere. It was odd that I would obey a voice that my atheist mind would declare did not exist. Yet, listen I did, and obey I did. I was living neither in this world nor another world but in some dimension in between.

On a conscious level, the direction was one in which I did not want to go. Perhaps I was afraid of learning that the Presence was truly real because of what that would mean for the rest of my life. Nonetheless, the intellectual curiosity that had taken me from rural Maine farm girl to international educational advisor propelled me to pursue any new information that came my way, and this information was both new and personalized. As such, the promptings were compelling. I did not want to listen, but I could not help listening. After all, these were answers to the "big" questions of life. They were answers to the kinds of questions I had raised in my philosophy class. For that reason, I found them seductive. Had I not been seduced by intellectual curiosity, however, I would still have found myself following the clues on the treasure hunt placed before me for I was truly helpless during that early period of divine occupation.

The reference to Solomon turned out to be more enigmatic and challenging to hunt down than was Job's life. I quickly found out that there is no Book of Solomon, so I read what seemed to come closest: *The Song of Songs* by Solomon. I was surprised to find such lyrical, sensual poetry in the Bible. I had not remembered *that* from childhood! Obviously, though, these pre-sonnet love songs were not the message I was supposed to be seeking.

Then, I remembered something about the wisdom of Solomon and how he determined who the true mother of a child was by suggesting that the child be divided in half between the two mothers who each claimed it to be her own. Thanks to the search feature of the Internet, I was able to locate the passage about Solomon's wisdom quickly, but the content of the passage did nothing to enlighten me.

So, I returned to the Internet, this time searching for the life of Solomon. There I found the message. Tucked away in *Ecclesiastes* was a description of Solomon's life that in many ways paralleled mine, especially the part about supercilious intelligence. How often Ma had said to me, "You are too smart for your own good." In this particular case, she was probably right. King Solomon had rejected God and worshipped false gods. That hit home. I did not worship traditional false gods, but what is atheism if it is not an adherence to a belief system? It just happens to be a non-theistic belief system. Here was a guy, then, not unlike me, who had been given wisdom (more than I have, for sure, but I have been given some academic ability, at least) who then parlayed that gift into avid materialism and turned away from God. Hmm. That got me thinking. I read *Ecclesiastes* many times. I still read it. I saw myself in Solomon: someone who thought that I had all the right answers. The danger of intellectual arrogance—that was one message I got from *Ecclesiastes*.

There was more, though. Qoheleth, the assumed author, in attributing words to Solomon, talked about chasing the wind:

> *With all my wisdom I tried to understand everything that happens here on earth. And God has made this so hard for us humans to do... everything is just as senseless as chasing the wind...Then I decided to find out all I could about wisdom and foolishness. Soon I realized that this too was as senseless as chasing the wind. Then I thought about everything I had done, including the hard work, and it was simply chasing the wind."*

So much became understandable through those words. All my efforts put into the work of the world were as evanescent as the wind, dashing through valleys and tiptoeing around mountain tops! I had gone from a barefoot farm girl to tailored-suit advisor of ministers of education and theory-brandishing author of seminal works in my field, but I had never deliberately listened to the voice of God. I had brushed aside any input God might have tried to give me. Instead, I had developed my own view of the world and my own sense of the meaning of life, based on what? The fragments of life I had seen as I chased the wind up the mountains and down the valleys? I had multiple degrees, yet I knew nothing. Chasing the wind is what I had been doing for more than fifty years. I chased the wind from one job to another, each more exciting than the last but none as fulfilling as one minute in the Presence. I chased the wind from one hemisphere to another, in 17 languages, and through 23 countries. Nowhere did I find the peace that the Presence brings just walking on the mission grounds or standing quietly in the mission cemetery where thousands of native Americans who helped build Old Mission San Ignatio now rest in peace.

*Ecclesiastes* overflowed with messages for me. It still does. Perhaps the most important one, "to everything there is a season," warned me that my period of atheism was drawing to a close. That warning caused me to thrash about agitatedly in the pincers of the cosmic nutcracker. I very much wanted my period of atheism to endure a lifetime, not just a season.

The messages in *Ecclesiastes* have drawn me back to that book more often than to any other. Taken to heart, the messages in *Ecclesiastes* made me very susceptible to two events (modern-day miracles) that happened at the end of my nutcracker period.

## Spoiled by God

My great atheistic trust in things always turning out well likely emanated from the many times that they did turn out well. Although I would never have admitted, or even recognized, God's presence in my life, what, other than divine protection, could have saved me from permanent disfigurement, psychological dysfunction, repressed spirit, life-impairing injury, or other harm as a child? As an adult, when jobs evaporated, new opportunities instantly arose. When something dangerous happened, a safety net immediately enveloped us. When money was urgently needed and none was to be had, just precisely the right amount appeared unprompted. We had only to wait and rarely for long. As Dr. Omar has contended, God has always spoiled me. Part of that spoiling has to do with God always protecting me.

Were I to have had any doubt about my safety in the Middle East, one incident in 2004 would have dispelled it. But I had no doubt. Somehow, I just felt secure. "Protected" would have been the better word had I given any thought at the time to the possibility of divine involvement in our lives.

During the 2004 incident, I had traveled on university business to Lebanon (a trip that subsequently put me on the "search her on every leg of every trip," i.e. "randomly selected for search," list at airports worldwide). One morning in Beirut I started down a ghetto-looking street, devoid of vegetation or people, wondering if I had somehow misunderstood the instructions that the hotel clerk had given me in French. (French and Arabic are the two commonly used languages in Lebanon. Of these, I chose to speak French. My mastery of French was greater than my capacity to communicate in Arabic, and I certainly looked more European than Arab although when I donned *hijab*—a headscarf—I could surprisingly pass for a Middle Easterner in looks.)

The stone buildings stood stoically silent as if on guard, comrades of mixed color and size, humbly displaying the wounds of past wars for any accidental passerby. Some had chipped corners and broken stairs. Most were bullet-ridden.

As I walked down the street, a man suddenly appeared. Where had he come from? He looked directly at me and called out to me.

"You are not from Beirut, are you?" he asked in excellent English although his countenance was definitely Arab. He then commented, "You look Western."

"I am a Westerner," I answered cautiously, careful not to mention my American heritage. In the Middle East, I was always honest but never candid. If, in any given situation, I could pass for European or, as more often happened, a Russian, I did so. It was safer, given the war in Iraq and highly emotional reactions to Americans in the Middle East in general.

In response to my admission, the man replied, "In that case, you don't want to be walking down this street. It would not be safe for you. Where are you trying to go?"

I crossed the street to where he was standing so that we did not have to continue to shout. He waited patiently, without moving. Coming up to him, I explained that I was looking for an ATM. He directed me to another street. I thanked him and walked away. I thought he had remained at the spot where we had spoken, but as I was passing through the intersection only seconds later, I saw that the spot was empty. How fortunate, I thought at the time, that he was in the right place at the right time to protect me. Fortunate? Or protected?

In his poem about me, Dr. Omar had written, "someone who always tried to do what is right no matter what. " No matter what" means whether or not one is harmed physically, emotionally, or financially. I have always said that if a leader is going to be able to do a good job of supporting the people who work for him or her, that leader must be willing to put his or her job on the line. One must be willing to lose one's job for the greater good. Otherwise, it is not possible to be a really good leader. I have told that to many managers whom I have trained or mentored. Few have listened, but those who have listened have turned out to be among the best managers I have met.

I have put my job on the line on several occasions for employees. When you put your job on the line, you have to be ready to lose it. I usually called the bluff of those who were causing harm to my employees (or intended to). However, in Jordan, as a probable result of the cumulative effect of supporting the faculty in both Jordan and Bahrain and a poorly timed phone call from the United States with an unexpected potential job offer, I did lose my job. Without warning.

Dr. Omar was both surprised and depressed over that particular event. He was depressed because he did not want me to leave, and, indeed, I did not want to leave, either. Our evening discussions and friendship had become very important to me. He was surprised because he always thought God would somehow protect me. God always has.

God was protecting me in the Holy Land, too. Dr. Omar, others, and I were only looking at the surface things: the contract cancellation, the parting. We were not looking at the things that were unseen, as Paul and Timothy admonish the Corinthians: "While we look not at the things which are seen, but at the things which are not seen: for the things which are seen are temporal; but the things which are not seen are eternal" (2 Corinthians 4:18). We had seen the temporal physical displacement and decried it. We had not seen the eternal spiritual change that the temporal physical displacement would occasion to occur. God clearly wanted me to return to California, where the cosmic nutcracker was lying in wait. Within a few weeks of losing my job in Jordan, I had a job offer in hand in California for a better position than the one that had just been taken from me.

At first, though, it did not seem like God was watching out for me at all in Jordan in the fall of 2005 although that hardly mattered since at the time I did not believe in God. I opened one door after another, and they were all immediately slammed shut. A dean who offered me a job in Jordan returned to faculty ranks unexpectedly. A university position in UAE turned out to pay too little although the originally advertised pay would have been sufficient. Consults dried up. An enterprise I tried to develop never got off the ground although I have since been able to establish some of the same activities in Jordan, working from California. No, it seemed that God was not going to help me stay in Jordan.

I have a clearer understanding now. God had a different plan for me from the one I wanted for myself and from the one that many others who were finding job after job for me wanted me to have. God was not going to let me stay in Jordan because the cosmic nutcracker was waiting for me in California. No wonder all of the jobs in Jordan fell through.

When I returned to California, I found an instant happiness with my new job and my new colleagues. I wonder if that happiness naturally emanated from immediately finding a home in San Ignatio—which happened rapidly and surprisingly. I drove by the home where I now live an hour after the owner had posted the for-rent sign. It would appear that the Lord's plan for me was now securely in place. *Psalm 128* comes to mind: "Happy is everyone who fears the Lord, who walks in his ways. You shall eat the fruit of the labor of your hands; you shall be happy, and it shall go well with you."

The words of Donnie Kingsley also come to mind: "There are two freedoms: the false where a man is free to do what he likes, and the true where a man is free to do what he ought." Or perhaps more appropriately worded, "...free to choose to follow God's will."

A very special kind of being spoiled is being rescued. Rescue I often needed because going where the brave dare not go was not without its disconcerting moments. I have been abandoned in more than one country when plans for pick-up fell through. Always, though, an unexpected rescuer appeared, sometimes in the most unforgettable way.

On one flight to Sao Paolo, Brazil, I sat beside a young businessman named Eddie Parreiras from Campinas, a town about an hour outside Sao Paolo and ironically the town to which I was headed. When I arrived, the embassy escort was nowhere to be seen. A call to the embassy's weekend duty officer brought no elucidation or assistance. I would have to get to Campinas on my own, figure out what hotel I was supposed to be at, and track down the director of the institute I was supposed to be helping—all on a Sunday afternoon and with no contact information. I had only the office phone number of the embassy officer responsible for my trip—and Eddie's home phone. A little reconnaissance at the airport turned up a bus service to Campinas. Upon arrival, I called Eddie, who was surprised to hear from me so soon but gamely picked me up at the bus station and brought me to his home for dinner with his wife and daughter, where I spent a more delightful evening than I would have spent alone at a hotel. Later in the evening, we checked in the yellow pages for the information number at the institute where I would be working the next day, called there, and got the home phone of the director from the recording. Once we reached the director, everything was back on course.

Going where the brave dare not go—my *modus operandi* during my international consulting days—was also not without moments of danger and the need for divine protection. Being mugged in Moscow and Amman and even in quiet Urbana, Illinois where I was tazered by a purse snatcher made that evident. Fortunately, in all cases, I was not harmed and had almost no money in my purse—four cents is all the Illinois purse snatcher earned for his efforts. On the positive side, my traumatic experiences earned me a glimpse at police stations and police processes in Russia and Jordan—cross-cultural information I would not otherwise have learned. Interestingly, the small-town Illinois police were far less successful at tracking down the perpetrator, let alone getting my things back, than were the Moscow *militsiya* (police force) in a city of 13 million.

Worse than being mugged, though, where the attackers want only your money, is being stalked, where those nearly stepping on your heels could be after your life. Lizzie and I experienced this in Arlington, Virginia one Saturday as we were walking home from the metro station. Three strapping and obviously stoned men walking behind us on a suburban street temporarily devoid of pedestrians began marching in step and chanting in unison, "You're going to die." Continuing to walk at the same pace we had used from the metro station, I gave no indication to Lizzie that I was concerned about the stalkers behind us who were very rapidly drawing nearer. At the same time, my mind was casting about for a safe ending to our situation. Fortunately, on the next block I recognized the home of a man whom I did not know but who always waved to me as I walked in the mornings to the metro station. Trusting that he would help us, I pushed open the gate, saying to Lizzie, "Ah, here we are!"

We walked up to the door and rang the bell. The three stoned men leaned against a tree, watching. No one was home! Becoming as calm as the ocean on a windless day (my typical reaction to dangerous situations), I quickly conceived another ruse.

"Right!" I said to Lizzie, hopefully loudly enough for the three not-so-well-intentioned musketeers to hear. "He said he would be working on his bicycle in the back."

Lizzie and I walked around to the back of the house, as our trio of stalkers watched. Once we were out of sight, I turned to Lizzie and whispered urgently, "Run!" We scampered home along the back alleys, like rabbits running from hunters.

Recalling this incident, I have to wonder how an 11-year-old had the presence of mind and spirit to show no concern as three burly and unruly men threatened to kill us at every step they took. As for me, I had some extra adrenaline coursing through my veins, but I never believed that we would be killed. I felt protected, but at the time I would not have been willing to put a name to the source of protection. Perhaps an explanation of what really happened that Saturday afternoon can be found in the *Book of Privy Counseling*, where the author was likely speaking about someone like a Good Samaritan:

> *...[any such individual]...will certainly be protected from the onslaught of his enemies within and without, by the gracious goodness of God himself. He need not marshall his own defenses, for with faithfulness befitting his goodness, God will unfailingly protect those who, absorbed in the business of his love, have forgotten concern for themselves. Yet is it surprising that they are so wonderfully secure?*

During the stalking, I felt very little fear. What I felt instead was a surreal tranquility that let me take advantage of our fortuitous coming upon a known house and the knowledge of the back alleys. At some deep level, I must have known that we were protected.

Ironically, the event of greatest risk, in my mind, was allowing God into the life of an atheist. That, initially, was frightening indeed. It changed my image of myself, and that changed my behavior. At last, though, I understood the source of my pervasive sense of protection.

# Konstantin of Kaluga

One day not long ago, as winter was settling in throughout the countries of the Northern Hemisphere, Donnie received an unusual note, which he passed to me.

"This does not look like a typical scam," he wrote in the forwarding. "What do you make of it?"

The note came from one Konstantin Mikhailyuk, who lived in Kaluga, Russia. It read as follows:

> My name is Konstantin. I'm student and I live with my mother in city Kaluga, Russia. My mother cannot see and she receive a very small pension which is not enough even for medications and food. I work very hard to be able to buy the necessities for my mother, but my salary is very small, cause my studies still not finished.
>
> Due to deep crisis authorities stopped gas supply in our district and we cannot heat our home anymore, because our home-heater works with gas. I don't know what to do, because the weather will be very cold in the next months and the temperature outside can be lower than minus 45 degrees Celsius, as it was in the last winter.
>
> I am very afraid that the temperature inside our home can be very cold and we will not be able to survive. I don't know what I can do in this situation. I found several e-mail addresses and thanks to the free internet possibility in our local library I decided to appeal to you. If you have any old sleeping bag, warm blanket, portable stove, warm clothes and shoes, electric water-boiler, canned and dried food, vitamins, medicines from cold, any hygiene-products, I will be very grateful to you if you could urgently send.
>
> If you think that it would be better or easier for you to help with some money, please write me back and I will give you details for sending it safely if you agree. This way to help is very good because in this case I will be able to buy a portable stove and heat our home during the winter. I hope to hear from you very soon. I also hope very much that this hard situation will get better very soon.

There was nothing in the note that would make me think it was anything other than the real McCoy. Winters in Kaluga are, indeed, cold. Pensioners do, indeed, receive insufficient income for normal living expenses. Handicapped individuals do, for certain, have difficulty finding work. Student stipends are, for sure, miserly if they are received at all.

I was not entirely without suspicion, however. So, I wrote to Konstantin and asked him how he had managed to find Donnie's email address.

Konstantin's answer came in two days, and it was plausible. He wrote that in desperation he had searched the Internet at the public library and put together a mailing list of people associated with Slavic studies in Europe and the United States. He had found Donnie's email address from the masthead of an international newsletter that I edit and Donnie typesets.

Konstantin had passed the test. All of this matched reality as I knew it. So, I asked him to check out the cost of a stove, and if it were within reason, I would send him the money by Western Union. He agreed.

A few days passed before I received the answer from Konstantin. In the interim, I told some friends and colleagues about Konstantin's situation, and they began donating blankets not only for Konstantin and his mother but also to help out neighbors and other students in similar circumstances. My living room began to fill with blankets on hold for a mailing address from Kaluga.

When I received the response from Konstantin, he apologized for the delay. He explained that he had access to the Internet only from the public library, which was far from his house, so he went there only once or twice a week. He reported that he could get a stove for 120 Euros. I did the conversion into dollars: $181. That was manageable. I emailed him that I would wire him the money and write to him once it had been sent.

The amount of money needed by Konstantin became even more manageable fifteen minutes after I sent him the e-note, promising him the money. After finishing reading email for the day, I opened the mail from the post office. Among the letters was an order for books from the small press that Donnie and I manage. The order came from the University of Mississippi library. This was an odd time of year for a university library to be ordering, I noted in passing. I sent the order to the printer for printing and drop-shipping. As I calculated the printing and shipping costs, I noticed with considerable surprise that the difference between cost and income (i.e. our profit margin) was exactly $181. Sending this money to Konstantin, then, seemed something I was destined to do.

A friend of mine questioned whether or not this could be a scam, but I was convinced that it was the real McCoy. After all, the order matched the amount of money needed for the stove. It wasn't as if I was spending money from my paycheck. This was "found" money. No, this was clearly the right thing to do.

So, Donnie and I drove to a nearby city, there being no Western Union office in San Ignatio. I wired the money to Konstantin and upon return home informed him via email, asking for a DHL address for sending the collection of blankets that had now taken over our living room. Then we went off to a local pizzeria to celebrate my grandson's birthday.

That evening, when I was working on the computer, I was prompted to do an Internet search for Konstantin. It was rather strange to be prompted to check out Konstantin after the fact. I certainly did not expect his name to pop up in Google, but it did—dozens of times. Some of the websites that talked about Konstantin Mikhailyuk were in English. Some were in Russian. One German site from Berlin, called "Den Brief aus Russland" ("The Letter from Russia"), tracked Konstantin's activity from 1999 through the current year. Every year, the details changed. Sometimes they contradicted each other. Some years Konstantin stated that his mother was receiving too small a pension. In other years, he said that she could not receive a pension. Sometimes he had a brother; sometimes he did not. His role changed, too, from spokesperson for a group of workers to student. What did not change was his age, which advanced one year for each year that passed. Today he is 26. The other consistency was his location: Kaluga.

I learned that in 1999 a group of workers from Kaluga, Konstantin among them, made the same plea, nearly word for word, that Donnie had received. The group of workers had received the help they needed, and they thanked the donors. Konstantin alone saw spamhandling as a good way to make money and has annually defrauded many people, so many that the Russian postal service has made him declare himself a business and has even sued him for postal fraud.

Appalled, I sat in silence for some time. What had gone wrong? Had God suddenly become untrustworthy? Was I too quick to trust? Everything had fallen into place so cleanly, especially the cost of the stove being the exact amount of profit on the book order. Was that purely coincidence?

I did not understand. By now, I had recognized and admitted God's role in my life and had begun to depend on God routinely for guidance. Had God looked the other way briefly? Had I been deliberately misled? In either case, I could not understand why I had been prompted to check out Konstantin only *after* sending him the money. Had I moved ahead on my own too quickly? Had I made the mistake described in the prayer of Canada's Royal Military College: "let me constantly re-member that all my actions are in vain unless they are guided by your hand?" Was God's hand not in this transaction?

I finally concluded that God's will had flowed through me much easier when I was an unaware atheist. As a believer, I try to help and end up second-guessing God, unintentionally blocking God's access to me.

I called Western Union. Konstantin, it turned out, had not yet picked up the money. I explained the situation to Western Union. The representative asked if I would give permission to turn the case over to the FBI and the California State At-torney's office. These offices would investigate the situation. If they found Konstan-tin to be guilty of using Western Union to conduct a scam, they would shut down his access to Western Union permanently. In the interim, Western Union promised to return all of the money to me, including the remittal fee, and gave me a confirmation number for picking up the funds.

Three weeks passed before I found time to go to the city and get my money back. When I gave my name and presented my confirmation number to the lady working the Western Union booth at the K-Mart Store, I did not expect to be told anything other than "Here is your refund." That is not what I heard, however.

The clerk called up the appropriate screen and then stared at it for a few min-utes. "Is there a problem?" I asked.

"No," she responded. "However, there is a very strange note in here. It says that this person to whom you tried to send the money is a scammer. No money can be transferred to him or to his mother from any Western Union office in the world. Did you know this? If anyone tries, the system will block entry of the information. As for returning your money to you, I am supposed to ask for your original receipt."

That was no problem. I had brought the receipt. Hearing that Konstantin was now on an official scam list, I felt better about having been scammed. Now no one else anywhere in the world would be scammed through his request for money via Western Union. That note dramatically reduces his ability to defraud people since there are few other international wire transfer firms. Perhaps I had been wrong in my assessment that God was looking the other way. Someone who had defrauded hundreds of people a year for seven years had just had his business significantly curtailed. At the same time, I got every penny of my money back. I began to think that this might have been God's plan all along. Had I not responded as I did and been seemingly put at risk for a short period of time, Konstantin would still be flagrantly scamming people. God, it seems, protects the foolish and thwarts the bad.

## Keeping My Promise

A couple of months before the experience with Konstantin and immediately following the evening of saying grace, I had been spending two full weeks living under divine occupation as described on previous pages. Two weeks of unsuccessfully fighting to free myself from a diaphanous, felt and heard but unseen Presence took their toll on my endurance and strength. So, I came to a full stop. I had found myself in what T. S. Eliot in "Four Quartets" called "the still point of the turning world."

During that time, my ever-skeptical mind asked, "Did the recently discovered vMat gene (the so-called 'God gene') that scientists claim hardwires the brain to believe in God get turned on inside my head?" "Were chemicals released when I said that grace?" "Was my thalmic center activated?" I yearned for a scientific explanation that would account for this feeling of possession, one that would negate what seemed to be the obvious, but unscientific, answer. Yet all the time a small voice kept whispering, "Does it matter what mechanism God uses to encourage prodigal children to come home?"

As for the God-gene, its recent discovery may simply be an uncovering of a piece of God's clever planning. The gene appears to be described in *Jeremiah 24:7*. "I will give them a heart to know me, that I am the Lord. They will be my people, and I will be their God, for they will return to me with all their heart."

The constant pressure from the cosmic nutcracker was causing this Brazil nut to begin to crack, or perhaps more appropriately expressed, to begin to open. As firmly as I tried to hold onto the sides of the shell and keep it closed, there seemed to be nothing I could do to prevent its opening.

The nutcracker was union with God. I figured that out much later after reading books on contemplative prayer by the mystics and especially by Thomas Dubay (e.g., *Seeking Spiritual Direction*). It was God's amazing gift to an atheist and something for which believers yearn for years. That God has gifted me with this form of intimate communication, in which I and the physical world around me dissolve into a non-physical Presence that I can no more describe than could people before me, overwhelmed me then and still overwhelms me.

During my cosmic nutcracker period, I wanted to keep a constant connection with the physical world. I did not want union. I wanted separation! In fact, I did not want to believe that any of this was happening, but ultimately I had to face the fact that God was just not going to go away.

So, in the spirit of the best defense being a strong offense, I took a small leap of faith—small, because, after all, with the Presence with me all the time, it did not take much faith to admit it existed. It just took some faith to admit that this Presence might, indeed, be God.

My acknowledgment of God's presence in the world and long-term in my life was ultimately the result of the Presence not releasing me from the cosmic nutcracker until I had reexamined my life and reached different conclusions about why certain things had happened. I have never had to take a Kierkegaardian leap of faith for I was presented with what seemed like empirical evidence. So, I responded via the opened channel of communication with two requests.

The first request came from frustration. For nearly three months I had been trying to help the wife of one our employees find a job. She and her children had been living more than two hours away for nearly a year, and this was taking a toll on the family, especially the teenage children. She had applied to our division but did not have a sufficient background to be hired into any of the units in my organization although we kept her application on file in our personnel office just in case. I had networked with colleagues in appropriate fields in the local community. All were sympathetic. None had jobs to offer at the moment. It looked pretty hopeless. So, I ventured a prayer, this time a real one, not one forced on me, albeit one that initially contained as much doubt as hope: "I give up. I cannot help this employee's wife, Janie. If You really exist, please help her."

While I was at it, I thought, I might as well make a second request. Another employee had used up nearly all her sick leave because of a recurrent illness that she seemed unable to conquer. This had been going on for nearly six months, with an obvious negative effect on her work. So I added a couple of lines to my please-find-Janie-a-job prayer, "And, if you will heal Janet, I will go to church every week." I have no idea what prompted me to make that promise. It came out of the blue, totally unpremeditated or even contemplated. As soon as I said those words aloud, however, I felt somewhat nervous. One should not bargain with God, I thought. That seemed like a hubristic and dangerous thing to do, so I added "Never mind. I will go to church without any conditions and trust You to heal my colleague."

After making the requests, I remember feeling that my life was about to change in uncontrollable ways. Somehow I *expected* those requests to be honored. Answered requests of this type, though, would mean only one thing: God exists. If God exists, then my atheistic interpretation of life was founded on philosophical quicksand, an uncomfortable place to be, for sure.

When I arrived at work that morning after my two prayer requests to the Presence, I opened my email as I typically do at the beginning of each work day. As usual, there were more than 200 notes to read. Most of them were about deadlines, logistics, requests for meetings or consultations, or general announcements. One, however, was different. It came from a special projects director who worked in another division. "One of my managers, Robert Shaw," he wrote, "served as an external member of a hiring committee for your division recently and noticed the resume of Janie Lane among the candidates. Robert tells me that Janie's background does not fit any of your operations but she has precisely what we need for a position that just opened in our production shop. Would you release her application to us?"

I was stunned. I read the note again. There was no doubt any more in my mind of God's reality. The answer to my very first prayer of petition had come in less than 30 minutes. Like St. Thomas, I did not want to believe. Like St. Thomas, I had to believe. If I had not been sitting at my computer in an office where I could be heard, the words of St. Thomas might have burst forth in a joyous cry, "My Lord and my God!" This being the 20th century and both the act and the people being considerably less significant than that of the first century, the words only trembled on my lips as I contemplated how the awesomeness of this intervention from God was going to change my life.

Two days and one interview later, Janie had been offered the job and had accepted it. I had arrived at the end of an amazing two-week period. It started with just a little water washed over a stone, a short grace forced out of me. That trickle was followed by soft, gentle water that for two weeks never let the stone dry out in reminiscence of the words spoken to Abba (Father) John in the fifth century. Abba John, a Persian and one of the Desert Fathers (early Christian monks living in the Egyptian desert) had gone to see Abba Poemen, a shepherd renowned for his wisdom, who told him, among other things,

> *"The nature of water is soft, and the nature of stone is hard; but if a bottle is hung above the stone, allowing the water to fall down drop by drop, it wears away the stone. So it is with the Word of God: it is soft and our heart is hard, but the man who hears the Word of God often opens his heart to the fear [awe] of God."*

Water on stone. A cosmic nutcracker's constant pressure against the hard shell of a Brazil nut. Divine occupation. Whatever image is used does not matter. The cumulative effect was overwhelming. With the answer to the prayer for Janie, awe replaced my resistance. Then along came absolute confidence in the Presence. I knew that since Janie had found work, Janet, my sick colleague, would get well. So, I had a promise to keep.

That is how I began going to church. That is how I started believing. That is how I started trusting and obeying. As I promised, I just trusted that my colleague would be healed. One miracle had taken place immediately. The other was certain to come, I firmly believed. It did. From the day that I said the prayer for her health until nearly eight months later, when she took a new job, Janet had perfect attendance.

I have mostly kept my promise to God. I have only once gone more than a week without attending mass. Sometimes, because my job requires much road and air travel, occasionally internationally, it is difficult to keep that promise, but I do keep it. Recently, for example, I did some work in Ohio that ran into the weekend. The staff offered to entertain me in any way I desired—theater tickets, museum, and dinner, whatever I would like to do Saturday evening. Since I was flying on Sunday, there was only one possibility for Saturday night entertainment: I asked them to find me a church or chapel that was celebrating vespers. They did—and they came with me to mass. I have sometimes attended Sunday morning mass at airport chapels. Perhaps I am too literal about keeping the promise I made, given the complexities of my work life. When I begin to think that way, though, I remember that God did not seem to consider how complicated it might be to heal Janet. God did the part I asked for, so I do the part I offered to do. *Ecclesiastes*, however, does come to mind again: "Don't talk before you think or make promises to God without thinking them through." Now I find that verse! I also found the following one that keeps me looking for those chapels throughout the country: "Don't be slow to keep your promises to God. It's better not to make a promise at all than to make one and not keep it." Yes, I know that Isaiah tells us that God "is generous in forgiveness" (*Isaiah* 55:7). Nonetheless, a promise made is a promise that should be kept.

Entering the church the first time, however, was difficult. The question of where to go never came up. When I made the promise, the image of Old Mission San Ignatio, located just two blocks down the street from my house, popped into my head unbidden. I had no idea what denomination Old Mission San Ignatio was, but whatever the denomination was, it would become mine. God had chosen for me.

The weekend after I made my promise to God, I walked up to the doors of Old Mission San Ignatio for Saturday vespers. The doors were closed, and people were singing. I was two minutes late. I walked over to a bench in the garden outside the church and sat down. I knew I should go in, but I had no idea what I would find inside. If I was not yet ready to enter the church confidently as a believer, I was certainly not ready to enter it late.

Near me in the garden was a family: mother, father, three children. Tourists, I thought. They were taking pictures of the roses. Suddenly, they grouped together, looked directly at me for a moment, and headed toward the church. It was as if they had been sent to show me that it is permitted to walk in late. They opened the door and entered. The mother in the group turned and held the door open for me although I was quite a distance away. After a moment's hesitation, I followed her through it.

The family boldly marched down the middle aisle of the 3-aisle church, knelt beside an empty pew, crossed themselves, and sat down. I stood tentatively at the door, searching for an inconspicuous seat. Noticing that I was standing beside an unoccupied pew against the back wall of the church, I slinked into it and sat cautiously upright. Next to the door—an easy escape if needed, I thought! The words of the person reading something at the distant front of the church barely made their way to my ears. With the murmur of these half-heard words in my head, I looked around the church uneasily. I felt like an interloper at best, an imposter at worst. What was I doing here? I recognized no faces, but I did recognize my feelings. It was as if I had suddenly found myself alone in a foreign country with no cultural preparation and no understanding of the language. (For that reason, these days when I notice a new face at church, I try to find out who the person is and, if that person is truly new, I try to figure out how to make the person feel comfortable.)

No one on my first day noticed me or my uneasiness. They were all intent on reciting, singing, standing, sitting, kneeling in an order that made no particular sense to me. I did understand the most important thing: the church was Catholic. "God, what are you thinking?" I wondered. "You want me at a Catholic church?"

I should have known that the mission was Catholic. After all, it was a California *mission*, and missions were established by Catholic friars from Mexico. That the thought had never entered my head only serves to underscore how naïve I was about religion and its formularizations at that time.

Catholic liturgy was alien to me. Thanks to my experience with Shura, however, I could follow the service where there were similarities between Russian Orthodox practices and Catholic ones although, ironically, I had no idea what words were used in English. I knew the liturgy in Russian.

Many different faiths in many languages and countries have intersected my life. As a child, exactly 40 years earlier, I had given my sermon extolling atheism and had been consequently expelled from a Protestant church. I had designated a Jew as legal guardian for my children, and I had learned something of the Jewish faith as a result. The Russian Orthodox tolerated me because I had rescued one of their own. At one point while living in the Middle East, I had roomed with an Iranian of the Baha'i faith, and I had taught moral philosophy to Buddhists. With the latter, I would enter into religious discussions from the point of view of philosophical systems. Most recently, I had been spiritually reared by Muslim believers. Except for cradle-Catholic friends, with whom I never discussed religion, nowhere in the mix were Catholics!

In fact, I had been to weddings and other religious celebrations for friends who were Jewish, Muslim, Mormon (at least, the portion of weddings that non-Mormons are allowed to attend), Eastern Christian, Protestant, Greek Orthodox, Coptic, and Russian Orthodox. Never, oddly enough, had I been to any Roman Catholic celebrations or ceremonies. Had I misunderstood?

Suddenly, I felt the Presence very strongly. God *did* want me in this church. God was here, and that comforted me. For the first time, I welcomed God's presence. The cosmic nutcracker could be put away. I was no longer interested in fighting the inevitable. How ironic! The church did not bring me to God. God brought me to the church.

Old Mission San Ignatio, it turned out, was founded by the Franciscan Order. I looked up information about the Franciscan Order and immediately understood that St. Francis's philosophy contained the concepts and feelings that had always been in the depths of my heart and at the center of my subconscious mind. How did God know? How could God pull me out of Jordan and plunk me down two blocks away from the church with the most fitting philosophy of all for me? Omniscience! Never again will I question God's omniscience or wonder if God really understands me. Clearly, God understands, God cares, and God orchestrates. I had serendipitously found a house in a town I loved, and then I had serendipitously found a church, which I loved once I gathered the courage to step over the threshold. This was not serendipity in action. This was an act of Serendipity.

I did not question the reason for the choice of Catholicism at the time, but I have thought about it a lot since. Eventually, I figured out why God would want me in a Catholic church, at least, why I think God might want me there. I have been a leader most, if not all, of my life—with the 8-pack, at school, in the Army, in my profession. The Roman Catholic Church was one place where I could learn to be a follower. If I can follow God while being a leader in earthly pursuits, I can be an even more useful instrument. And then there is that fight-first ego that needs to be put to rest, a topic commonly encountered in Catholic literature.

Old Mission San Ignatio is a compellingly beautiful and compellingly simple church, the perfect place to learn how to put ego aside and simply follow God. The mission's white adobe walls are adorned in places with small, simple, pastel-colored, floral designs and pictures from the Stations of the Cross. The red alcoves behind the altar contain statues of saints. The uneven tile-brick floor and wooden ceiling remind parishioners of all those who have communed with the Lord before them in the sanctuary of the church. One side door opens onto an olive grove that serves as cemetery to 3500 Indians, the original inhbitants of the area who provided most of the labor to build the mission. The other side door opens onto a rose garden.

For many weeks, I sat in that same pew, at the very rear of the church, right beside the back door. I have since moved a little closer to the front, about one-seventh of the way from the back door. There is a part of me that still feels unworthy to be there at all, given five decades of atheism. In fact, there are times at Old Mission San Ignatio that I have found myself trembling, especially when drawing close to the altar. It is not fear. It is awe of the power that God has to touch those who have come to worship. It is awe that God would want to touch someone so difficult, someone so hesitant to come farther forward than the fifth pew from the back. It is awe mixed with large portions of love and gratitude that God would care about one Brazil nut. Brazil nuts, I have often thought, are not worth the effort it takes to crack them. God apparently thought differently.

The liturgy gradually became understandable and then automatic. Early on, though, I realized that if Old Mission San Ignatio was where God wanted me to keep my promise, I needed to become educated about Catholicism. So, I began attending the Rite of Christian Initiation of Adults (RCIA) classes. Thanks to Father Barry, who led the classes, and Marie Cosgrove, who assisted, the puzzle pieces of my life and of Life began to lock themselves into a picture I could accept. (Complete understanding is yet, if ever, to come—in words from *Ecclesiastes*, such understanding is beyond the capacity of even the wisest human being.) In re-assessing my life and God's role in it, I realized that framing my life has been a series of miracles, beginning long before Shura's story and continuing to the present moment. Now that I have finally recognized the Source of miracles, I simply expect them.

## The Territory beyond SPLAT!

I could relate to Konstantin's letter. Perhaps that is why I was so quick to respond to it—and to believe him. Not simply because I grew up in a frozen land, both physically and emotionally, but also because I grew up poor. Especially because my life, like the one he described in his e-note, has been a series of splats.

When I think about my life, a Pfeiffer cartoon from the 1980s comes to mind. In this cartoon, a young girl approaches a wise old man and asks, "Whither?"

He points with his cane: "Thither." The young girl walks in the direction the old man has pointed and suddenly runs into **splat!**

Disheveled, she returns to the wise man and asks again, "Whither?"

Again he points: "Thither." Again she runs into **splat!**

Barely crawling, she approaches him a third time and again asks, "Whither?"

Again he points in the same direction: "Thither."

"No," she cries, "not thither!"

"There is but one thither," he replies, "and it's a mile past **splat!**"

Thither would become increasingly difficult for us to reach. Thither was always a mile past **splat!** We bumped into **splat!** often. For every **splat!**, however, there was a seeming miracle that gave us the strength to continue on toward thither.

After returning to California, I truly thought that we were now on the other side of **splat!** We certainly seemed to be enjoying thither in our small house in San Ignatio. Sitting on the stoop one sunny day in August 2006, absorbing the sun's warm rays, I felt God's Presence soaking into every crevice of my mind and body the way that this whole town feels, to visitors, to be drenched in prayer, the way Doah with the innocence exuded only by the mentally challenged announced to me while visiting one weekend, "God here." So this was thither?

Not at all! We learned in October that we were still on the border of **splat!** That information arrived innocuously enough in an e-note from our tax accountant.

Donnie returned from Jordan in late August, six months after I had already taken up my new work. His later return occasioned the need to delay filing our 2005 income taxes. The IRS had granted us an extension of the deadline to file from April to October because Donnie himself and our records were still in Jordan in April. As soon as Donnie returned, we immediately sent all the 2005 information forward to our tax accountant, confident that we owed no taxes since all our income had been earned abroad. Were we really living in thither that would likely have been the case. Unfortunately, we were still at the border of **splat!** According to our accountant, we owed $11,000 in taxes.

The IRS agreed that a portion of our Jordanian income was taxable. That was confirmed by a bill of $11,000, due immediately. Ha! Fat chance in ___! We had just finished moving, and while the majority of our moving expenses had been covered by my new employer, many unanticipated expenses had not been covered, e.g., the need to transport four cats back to the United States and Donnie having to survive four months in Jordan past the end of his contract when my new employer experienced a budget freeze that delayed Donnie's move-out. Complicating matters, of course, was the loss of our safety valve of $14,000 when the University of San Francisco Hospital emptied Shane's bank account where he had been stashing it for us. Yes, indeed, we were only at the border of **splat!** and had not yet set foot into thither. The bottom line was that there was no bottom line. All our income had dissipated or been used to cover moving expenses. Now, Uncle Sam wanted $11,000!

Our tax accountant was able to get us a six-week delay, no more. Six weeks to find a spare $11,000 while finishing moving from overseas back to the United States and trying to set up housekeeping, a major one-time expense in itself, turned out to be too great a task for my overwhelmed brain. So, I did what I have always done but with a new twist. I left it up to God, but this time I asked God for help because this time I knew Who had been helping all along.

My trust was so complete that I asked only once. Then I put the problem out of my mind, continuing on happily with my daily life, confident that some unique response would come before the end of the six-week period. It did.

A few days after asking God for help, I received a letter in the mail from Indiana University, where I had worked five years earlier. My job there was another story of God stepping in to help me when I did not even know that I needed help.

While conducting seminars in Turkmenistan, I was asked by a friend if my resume could be used by Indiana University in a grant proposal to show the kind of person they might hire for director of a new center for Turkic and related languages should the Department of Education award the university a grant for such a center. I agreed, and since I was in Turkmenistan, a place to which it was very difficult for an American at the time to receive a visa, I wrote to the professor in charge of the grant and asked if he would like me to bring back newspapers, books, and other useful language-learning materials from that country. Of course, he did. A few months later, when I was doing some short-term research in Illinois, I sent an e-note to the IU professor, arranging for a time when I could drop off the materials. Indiana University was only two hours away. I was happy to hear in reply that the grant had been received and the university was in the process of building a center. The materials would come in handy.

I drove to the university, arriving at the appointed time only to find out that I was an hour late because Illinois and Indiana are on different times during part of the year. I felt a little bad because I had made arrangements to meet for lunch, and now the professor would have been waiting for a full hour for me. Still, it was just the two of us, so thinking that these things happen, I made my way to the faculty dining facility to hand over the materials and chow down on whatever was left from lunch, being hungry after my two-hour drive. The professor met me outside the door to the dining room, as planned, and led me, with a smile, into the dining room and over to a large table of university faculty and administrators whom he had gathered together for lunch with me. Now, I did feel bad about not knowing about the difference in time zones. As I sat beside the assistant dean, munching on left-over dribblings from the various buffet buckets, she welcomed me to the university faculty. Not to the faculty dining room, but to the faculty. Several other faculty members followed suit. I made non-committal noises in response and concentrated on my food. Something was clearly amiss.

After lunch, I cornered the professor and the dean. "Excuse me," I said. "Do you think I am planning to work here?"

"Yes," responded the professor, "as director of the center. We got the money for it, and you have been accepted as director."

"But I never applied for the job!" I countered.

Now they were confused. "But your friend gave us your resume. We thought that you had agreed to become the director if we received the grant."

Oh, my! Here was a new wrinkle. This was the first time I had received a job for which I had never applied. The university was highly respected. Had I been looking for a job, it would have been a good one to land. However, I had already worked out a deal with an institution I shall call California University for reasons that will become clear. My role there was to set up a language center for a sphere of studies, into which I had been trying to push the profession as a whole for some time. I had even helped California University apply for thousands of dollars in grant money, which they did receive. I had already been named as director of that center. How could I be director of two centers, one in California and one in Indiana?

"We need to talk," I said. "Where can we go?"

We walked over to a university building, intended to house the new center. They laid out their situation. They had no other leads on directors with the kind of background I had—native speaker of English, fluent in several languages, degree in applied linguistics, language program management experience, knowledge of the cultures of several of the countries included in the center, and significant amounts of time spent working in three of those countries. My background was a unique combination of training and experience that perfectly fit their needs. I wracked my brain trying to find a duplicate of me, but I could not. There were people more knowledgeable about countries where Turkic languages are spoken but without my linguistics training and language program management experience. There were people with better linguistics training but without knowledge of the geographical area or language program management experience. Unfortunately, there were few individuals at all with greater language program management experience. Stuck! Ethically, I felt that I owed something to the university. True, it was clearly a miscommunication back at the beginning of the grant process, but now unless the university came up with an alternative, they would lose the grant. The biggest problem was timing. The grant was to begin nearly immediately.

I left. I had a consult in Washington the following week. I promised to think about the situation and try to come up with an out-of-the-box solution.

I did. After talking with my new supervisor at California University, I worked out a schedule for the first six months of my position in which I would spend two weeks a month in California and two weeks in Indiana.

A grateful IU team applied themselves with great assiduity to finding a replacement for me. Over the six months I worked at Indiana University, I assisted them in founding the center, conducted extensive faculty development, and devised the templates for the first two textbooks to be published by the center. The work interested me, and I enjoyed passing along my experience to others. I enjoyed the faculty, as well, and I was introduced to even more new languages and cultures, one of which became important when I took over my current position, since part of my job now focuses on that area.

In contrast, the position at California University turned out to be a bumpy ride. While I spent the two weeks a month there that my contract required and did get the center rolling, my relationship with my supervisor resembled a roller coaster ride. While supporting all my efforts and even evincing pride in my work to others, she failed to complete the paperwork to pay me. Whenever I brought up the matter, she would blame the payroll office. Finally, I talked to someone at the payroll office and learned that my supervisor was the stumbling block. Four months passed without a cent. I increased the pressure on my supervisor, and she called Donnie, asking him to help me be patient.

Donnie responded, "I cannot help you. I have lived with Beth for more than 30 years. I can tell you that she will do anything for you as long as you don't make her mad. When she's mad, you're in trouble. I can also tell you that you *have* made her mad. Good luck!"

Another two months elapsed before I was paid. Right before I finally received that check, I tendered my resignation and returned to full-time consulting, including founding a national organization to promote the issues to which I was dedicated and for which I had helped establish the California University Center (which, amazingly, became an enduring part of the new organization). Fortunately, Indiana University, which had by then found a replacement director for me, had established my payroll account quickly and had paid me faithfully. So, I had been able to survive and to jet between the two states on a regular basis, thanks to the salary paid to me on a consistent basis by Indiana University. Had that unplanned job not fallen into my lap, I would have been in serious financial trouble that fall and winter.

Reading the return address on the letter from Indiana University brought the details of the dilemma-turned-to-delight of my past flooding into the present. Now I could recognize God's hand in the ironic situation where I received a job I had not applied for and which I later turned out to need because the job I had negotiated myself did not pay me for nearly half a year.

The letter in my hand concerned my retirement fund. I had such a small retirement fund with the university that I had actually forgotten about it. Fortunately, the university had not. According to the letter, all individuals no longer on payroll needed either to take out the retirement funds or roll them over into a retirement fund external to the university. I called the fund, and the amount available for take-out, minus (of course) taxes, gave me 50% of what I needed for the IRS. God had rescued me yet one more time.

The other 50% owed, I was certain, would show up before the end of the six-week period. God had never before left me hanging at half-mast. Sure enough, a week later, a quarterly summary from another retirement fund at another institution, where I worked years earlier, arrived in the mail. I had put that particular fund out of mind because it had taken a big loss years ago. According to the recent statement, though, it still had most of the dollars that had been invested from my pay checks tucked away in it, earning a penny here and there in interest. Those dollars would cover another 40% of what was owed. I called the fund. A very kind gentleman agreed to close my account and send me those much-needed dollars. He could not give me a precise amount but thought it would be close to the amount in the current quarterly summary that I had received in the mail. He explained that I would have to wait for the stock market results at the end of the day, which would determine the precise amount to be disbursed. I would receive whatever the fund was worth at that time, most likely the amount he had just cited to me.

We were close! Clearly, we would not be trapped in **splat!** forever or married to the IRS for eternity. The remaining 10% would show up somehow. If necessary, I could eke it out of my salary or borrow it from someone.

As it turned out, there was no need to worry about the remaining 10%. The stock market leaped upward over the next few hours. Donnie said he thought it might have been due to the release of iPods on that day—some of our stock was in technology. On January 11, we received considerably more than we expected. The amount allowed us to pay off the IRS debt in full on the 12th, the last day of our extension. It also paid our tax accountant's bill in full. Moreover, like the bread and fishes that kept multiplying, after paying all those with their hand held out, we found an additional $400 in our basket. What to do with that? The answer was obvious. That was God's money, so I found a way to return it to God.

Perhaps we will never reach thither. Perhaps we will always live in **splat!** or make it only to the border. Truly, it does not matter. Just as God feeds the ravens and arrays the lilies of the field, so, too, God will take care of our needs. Of that, there can be no doubt. God has demonstrated a willingness and ability to do that again and again. The dual jobs, the $11K for the IRS, and all those other times—protection from all kinds of threats, *deus ex machina* solutions to medical problems, and long-term solutions to educational difficulties—provide all the proof needed to remain securely, comfortably, and safely in **splat!** if that is where God wants us to be.

When we received Konstantin's letter, Donnie and I thought about the cold and difficult life of people in the new Russia, the cold and difficult life of the people of Russia of all times, of our difficult life. We thought about **splat!**. We responded to Konstantin because we wanted to help.

Help was something I was called upon, surprisingly, for Jean not long after my nutcracker period. The need to help Jean unnerved me at first. I had depended upon her insights and guidance up until that point. Now she needed me, and I was not sure that I was ready. There was, however, no choice. I had to be ready.

Jean handily worked in my building, so she often dropped by after work, and we would grab a bite to eat, talk, or do something together. One evening, as I was working late, Jean burst into my office, eyes large and frightened. "Beth," she exclaimed. "I think the Evil One is after me!"

I had never heard Jean or anyone else mention evil in those terms before, so I was taken aback at first. "What do you mean?" I asked.

"I suddenly feel estranged from God," she replied. "I feel like I am being pushed to do things that I would not normally do and that God would not want me to do."

"Such as what?" I asked. She would not tell. She said that she was ashamed of the urges. I understood that they were related to selfish acts, wantonness, cavalier treatment of family members, and other characteristics that just were not Jean's. We prayed together, and she left in a calmer state.

This one session, however, was not to be the end. She came by nearly every evening, and we prayed. Always for the same thing: to bring Jean back to where she had been spiritually, to eliminate this negative influence, to be in compliance with God's will. Although it seems that I am unceasingly praying, given my history and idiosyncrasy, when I petition God for specific help, I usually ask only once, assuming that God heard and trusting God to respond in the way that is best for the situation or person about whom I am praying. With Jean, though, it was different. It seemed that just as soon as Jean leaped over one hurdle, another was placed in front of her. Just as soon as one prayer seemed to have been answered, the need for another prayer appeared. Just as soon as her faith reared its head, it was stomped into the dust again by something she kept referring to as evil. I even saw her do things that I found incomprehensible. Those acts were not in keeping with Jean's character as I knew it to be.

I began praying for her every day, for hours. I also read St. John of the Cross's *Dark Night of the Soul*. It seemed to speak to some of what Jean was experiencing, but not all. I thought that if she read the book, it might help. Although Jean seemed lost and desperate and to a point depressed, she was unwilling to read the book. She felt that it would make her feel more, not less, trapped.

I, too, became desperate. At one point, I recall marching around the mission grounds and declaring that I would not pray about anything else until God brought sunshine to end the darkness that Jean was enduring. In all, I spent more than 20 hours in petition for Jean.

In the midst of all this petitioning, one not-so-fine evening, feeling unjustifiably overconfident, I offered to take on Jean's trials myself, and the Presence departed from me. No matter how much I tried to communicate, I could not feel the presence of God. I felt lost and alone. I had not realized how much God had become an every-minute part of my life. Irony of ironies, I desperately wanted back the Presence that I had earlier tried so hard to evade. "Where are you?" I asked again and again that evening. I received no answer.

When I awoke the next morning, the Presence was back. Thank God! From that brief disappearance of the Presence, I understood that this was akin to what Jean was experiencing. Now I know how terribly depressing that experience can be. I also understood that what got me through that night was faith without spirituality. Clearly, God had been spoiling me, granting me spirituality, not forcing me to walk in faith alone. Since that experience, I have often wondered if I am capable of living by faith alone.

I knew at the time that I did not want to have to try. "Please, God, don't do that again!" I implored. "I don't like it when I cannot feel Your presence." If the purpose of the dark night of the soul, as St. John of the Cross has suggested, is to create great longing for God, I can attest to its effectiveness after just a few hours.

Having emerged into daylight after two weeks of darkness, Jean told me that 18 years earlier, she had met someone she thought was her guardian angel. Among other things that person had said to her was the following: "Someday you may experience temptation and trial. Should that ever happen to you, I hope that you will have someone at your side to help you."

She did. Ironically, Jean, who had served as God's instrument to shepherd me back to the flock, had me at her side. Even though I did not know what to do or what I was doing when I was doing it, I had God to guide me. So, Jean, though she did not know it, could not feel it, and even at times did not believe it, had God at her side throughout her ordeal. I was clearly little more than a conduit, once more an instrument, through which God pulled Jean back from the forces of darkness that were dragging her away and deposited her back in the light.

## Katya of Tula

Why do I so frequently feel the need to question God? Before I knew that God existed, I questioned nothing. I just accepted what happened to me as the way life is. Why now do I ask where was God in my tormentd youth? Why do I ask why my children were born with birth defects? Or, why I am being sent to a Catholic church? Or, was I really supposed to become involved with Konstantin of Kaluga?

Yet, every time I have asked why, in time I have received a far better explanation than any I could have postulated. Any time I have asked "where are You?" I have found God waiting. Every time I have set into a motion a plan on my own, I have found God extending a far grander plan with a more patient hand than I deserve. Each time, the problem was within me, not with God. God has never failed to change bad to good or to use this willing soul as an instrument to bring good to others.

How weak can my faith be, having seen God's miraculous work on so many occasions, ever to question? Asking such questions is like cowering inside a box, while outside the box God is painting my universe with vibrant radiance as God does for each of us. Yet, some unreasonable fear or some need for earthly logic prevents the raising of the lid and the stepping out into sunshine to behold the vast expanse of pulchritude and love. There are, of course, days that I just tear off the lid and leap with alacrity into God's universe. Those are happy days. Those are the days that I forget to question and just respond to God with naive trust. Fortunately, they are nearly all of my days now.

These were the kinds of lessons I learned from the incident with Konstantin. I had not asked. I had assumed. I had been wrong, and now I still had the blankets, which occupied a sizable percentage of my living room, and I also had the returned money. The obvious question was what to do with them.

"Perhaps there is an orphanage in Kaluga," suggested Donnie. "They could probably use the blankets."

Now that Kaluga had captured our attention, I liked the idea of sending the blankets to someone who really needed them in the hometown of Konstantin, the spamhandler. So, I did an Internet search. Sure enough, there were three orphanages in Kaluga. All were being helped by Orphan Cry (www.orphancry.org), a church-associated organization in New York. After I had determined the legitimacy of the organization, I wrote to the director, Ken Wilcox. Then I waited for a response.

While we were waiting to hear from Orphan Cry, our part of California experienced a record cold spell. Homeless shelters ran short on blankets and appealed to the community for donations. I looked around my living room. I certainly had blankets enough to help out a shelter. Clearly, hanging onto the blankets, waiting to hear from Orphan Cry, while people were cold in local shelters was not a viable option. We gave the blankets to a very grateful shelter.

As so often happens in the land of **splat!**, the morning after we gave the blankets away, Ken responded. Yes, he wrote, Orphan Cry could use the blankets for the orphans at the Baby Home. Oops! Now Donnie and I would have to replace the blankets we had given away. Unsure of how many we could replace, I took out as much money from the ATM as I thought we could afford and set out for Target. We walked to the home furnishings section and found scores of blankets of all types. Given such a plethora, the store had put all of the blankets on sale for 20% of their original cost. As a result, we were able to purchase the same number of blankets that we had given away to the shelter. I would add the word *surprisingly* but nothing surprises me anymore where God is involved.

The money for Konstantin that had been returned by Western Union could be used for the invalid hospital, Ken told us. The administration was desperately in need of money to purchase diapers for the older disabled orphans. How well I understood that! When the blanket donors heard what had happened, they wanted to help, too. They offered cash donations.

In these ways, Konstantin's bad deed was turned to good. Moreover, the good continues to grow. For some reason, Ken subsequently googled me on the Internet and found Shura's story. How he managed to find it was remarkable because my name typically calls up 10-20 screens with my publications and consulting work. Shura's story is generally deeply buried.

That is how I heard about Ekaterina (nicknamed Katya), a 19-year-old orphan in Tula, dying from multiple brain tumors. Ken asked me to help her come to the United States. "You were used as an instrument once," Ken wrote, referring to the story about Shura. "Now it appears that you will be used as an instrument again."

Once again, as with Shura, the tenuous chain spoke of God's incredible vision and planning. Had I not encountered Konstantin and been misled by him, I would never have searched out and contacted Orphan Cry. Had I not been in touch with Orphan Cry, Ken would not have googled me on the Internet. Had Ken not googled me on the Internet (and had not the story of Shura, written by the University of Virginia PR staff years ago and generally buried on the 40th page of Google articles about me, been readily accessible to him), he would not have known about Shura. Had Ken not found out about Shura, he would not have told me about Katya. And, most important, had the tenuous chain of events that led to bringing Shura to the United States not occurred, I would not have the experience I need to help Katya and there would have been no story for Ken to read. All these pieces, all these people, all these places—only a divine hand could possibly have put all the jigsaw puzzle pieces together in just the right order at just the right time to cause so many people to join together to help just one person. One flock, one wounded sheep. Both equally important to a God of infinite love.

Katya's two younger brothers, Valery and Sasha, were adopted years ago. Ken found them in the United States, living with their adoptive mother, Erin, in New Hampshire. The boys now call and talk to Katya regularly. They also suffer from a similar medical problem and are followed by a doctor who so far has been able to keep the tumors at bay.

As we moved toward the possibility of bringing Katya to the US for palliative care, the need for an American home for Katya became clear. Ken talked to Erin, and then so did I. She not only agreed to open her home to Katya, she was eager to do so.

We hoped that the doctors who treated Valery and Sasha would agree to take care of Katya. We would not approach them, however, until we were farther down the trail to getting Katya here. This step traversed familiar territory, requiring familiar actions. Just as Noelle's medical history prepared me for Shura, Shura's immigration history prepared me for Katya.

Equally familiar was the step beyond doctors and guardian: a visa for Katya. The disquieting memories of prying Shura from Siberia through the American Embassy to the United States began to be relived. A friend at State Department, a former consul general, told me that getting Katya would be a nearly impossible task. (That was the same thing that friends at the State Department in the 1990s told me about Shura.) Specifically, he wrote, "I believe the task you have set for yourself is simply impossible at this moment in time." You mean an unreachable star, I thought silently as I read his letter. My friend, wait and see! Just watch God at work! There is no such thing as impossible! God makes the impossible possible in both small matters and large ones.

The deterioration in Katya's health continued while how to proceed through the American Embassy remained unclear. The tumors took away sight first in her right eye, then in her left. Doctors in Russian declared her tumors incurable and gave her five years to live. She knows that. We all know that. Still, to receive good palliative care and die with family is preferable to dying as an orphan in the cold snow of Tula.

As much as Dr. Omar wanted me to continue down the path he had set me upon, as much as he wanted me to find God and walk with God, he was afraid that my head would take over my heart and lead me in wrong directions. He was even more afraid that I might fall into commercialized religion and those who proselytize in the Lord's name but have never truly met God nor ever ask God's advice about their own lives. Dr. Omar calls this group by the formal title of "religious goofies" and threatened me that if I were to fall into their clutches he would pray, "Lord, this was a big mistake. Make her an atheist again!"

Dr. Omar was right in one way. Trying to help Katya has been more difficult than was helping Shura. With Shura, I worked with unconscious intuition. I was easily led by God because I was unaware of the leading. Now that I am aware, I am more likely to misstep. To avoid taking wrong steps, I ask for guidance. Nonetheless, I am more of a Martha than a Mary. In fact, nearly completely a Martha. So, once Katya was put in my path, I immediately wanted to take her by the hand, bring her here, and solve all her problems. Apparently, God had different ideas. Nothing happened.

This frustrated me deeply, and I expressed my frustration to a spiritual director. "Well," he asked, "if God were to talk to you about this, what do you think God might say?"

I did not even have to think about the answer to that question. Words that had the ring of truth about them immediately popped into my head: "Cool it, and let Me do My part."

So I cooled it. I cooled it all spring, and I cooled it all summer.

Then it happened. All the pieces that God had been working on came together at once. I was asked by one of my institute's clients to go to Russia. While there, I would have to register my passport at the American Embassy. Igor, who worked for the client and had contacts at the embassy would be coming, too, for a couple of days, August 6 and August 7, and he was willing to try to help Katya.

I wrote to Ken to tell him that the next step seemed to be in the making. He informed me that he was traveling to Tula and Moscow and would be in Moscow the same day I would be there, in fact, just a few blocks from where I would be. Also, he informed me that Tatyana, Katya's caretaker in Tula, had family in Moscow and would be there that weekend, too. August 6, 2008 became a red-letter day, then, without any of us having previously consulted one with another.

I recalled how everything had seemed so tenuous with Shura. Responses were negative, then nil, then suddenly all the pieces fell into place. The same thing was happening again. God works best, it seems, when we are not looking and hope is ebbing.

Oddly, given the surprise and excitement of learning that we were all going to be in the same place at the same time, we never met on August 6. What a great group meeting it might have been! That is the way humans think. I never would have dreamt that an actual meeting would not be necessary.

Great, I thought, when I realized that all the key players in Katya's drama would all be in the same city at the same time. God is back in action! What I missed was the understanding that God had always been in action and that we did not have to be a cohesive group of action figures in order for God to use all of us, each in our own way, to continue the story.

This was a new understanding for me. With Shura, I was unaware of God's hand in the matter. Nonetheless, I never took personal credit for all the remarkable events in Shura's life and in that part of my life which intersected with his. Rather, I gave credit to serendipity and the people involved. Unfortunately, I did not give credit to the Architect of the plan who put stairs in front us when we needed to ascend, bridges in front of us where there were rivers to cross, and open roads when we needed to travel fast and far. I did not give Serendipity the proper name, the proper credit, or the proper gratitude.

With Katya, I am aware. I know that there is Someone to whom I can turn for help when I reach dead-ends in searching for the road West. I had never prayed for help with Shura. I was, after all, an atheist at that time. What God did, God did through me by divine volition. Certainly, others were praying for Shura, but my relationship to God in the matter was not as aware supplicant but as unknowing vessel. Clearly, the experience with Katya has been different. Once one knows, everything is different

Interestingly, with Shura I may have been a better instrument than I was with Katya. Because I was unaware of God's presence, I simply followed "instinct," which really was a matter of being guided by God very simply without thinking about what it was I was supposed to do. With Katya, the "I" gets into the process from time to time. It is not for bad reasons. "I" anticipate what it is that God wants me to do next. "I" rush off to help where "I" think God wants me to help and in ways that "I" think God wants me to help. And "I" have moments of getting it all wrong. "I" constantly need to ask God what it is, indeed, that God wants. As an atheist, I was purely manipulated by God, and since there was no "I" to anticipate what God wanted, I simply responded to the flow of the moment, took advantage of the possibilities that appeared before me, and depended upon the people who showed up to help. That is what I mean when I say I was a "blest atheist." Unknowing, with no reason either to ask or to anticipate, but simply having within me the God-given desire to be of service to people, any people, as a way of considering my life to have any value at all,

I became a tool that God could use for any desired purpose. Now that I know, "I" get in the way of God's purposes, and I constantly ask God to help me step out of the way, so that I can become as much of a blest believer as I have been a blest atheist. Truly, it was easier when everything was done subconsciously, i.e. God's message received by the heart and followed. Now, the mind interferes. My beloved Dr. Omar is right to worry. I sincerely hope that I can control the mind, with God's help, so that Dr. Omar does not have to carry out his promise to pray, "Dear God, this was a big mistake. Make her an atheist again!"

August 6 reminded me that God was in charge and had not forgotten Katya. The fact that we had all focused on the same day brought that understanding. It also brought hope that the mission would now go forward, and it brought action. Although we did not meet, being in the same city did facilitate our speaking to each other telephonically. It was the first time I had heard Ken's voice and the first time I had "met" Tatyana, whom I was able to question in great detail about Katya's health. Katya, it seemed, was being cared for by local doctors, not regional experts, and a seed of doubt was planted in my mind as to how accurate the local prognosis might be. More important, being able to make multiple local (i.e. inexpensive) phone calls facilitated planning the next steps. We had several courses of action, depending on what the American Embassy response would be.

Igor and I and another friend, Vera, who was with us, went to the US Embassy to register our passports. There we spoke with a young man, who was Igor's contact, and we left our passports for registration before heading to work.

A week passed, and we heard nothing. Igor had left for Germany and Vera and I returned to the Embassy to pick up our registered passports so that we would be able to leave the following week. Our contact was not there, but his friend, whom I will call Joe, was. We repeated our request. He promised to help, and we returned to work, continuing a little nervously with our plans to leave Russia the following Friday.

The nervousness came from the fact that the day after we arrived in Russia, the Russian-Georgian war began. Everywhere on the news were anti-American reports. Of course, the Russian airwaves quickly filled with negative, hate-filled reports of the atrocities that Georgians had committed against the Russian population in South Osetia. A few days later, a friend from days of working together in Tbilisi, visited me. She told me that she was hearing from mutual friends now in high government positions that the same kinds of reports were being made in Georgia about the Russians. In both cases, Americans were blamed for the current situation although I failed—and still fail—to see what America had to do with any of the fighting, stemming from age-old animosities between the local ethnic groups, well contained by fear of Soviet authorities and unleashed when the Soviet Union was dissolved and Georgia became an independent nation. As the anti-American rhetoric built, I laid low. Few passing strangers could tell that I was an American, and I wanted to keep it that way. Nonetheless, we were in the country via American Embassy request, and at any moment, the Russian government could PNG us (i.e. label us *persona non grata* and evict us) in retaliation for perceived injuries from the US. We were in daily communication with Washington, just in case. (This was an incredible change, in just 20 years, thanks to Blackberries and modern technology, from the days Lizzie and I spent in Siberia, effectively totally incommunicado from the West, with the nearest American contact 3000 kilometers away in Moscow.)

Friday arrived without event, and we left Russian soil. Per earlier urgent request, I blackberried that information to my American office as soon as I was on the plane. By the end of the day on Friday, I was back in California.

Once again, a week passed, and then I received a note from Joe at the embassy. "I am so sorry," he wrote. "I remember that you made a request, but I don't remember what it was. Would you send me the details?"

Thank you, Joe! It did not matter that he had forgotten the details. He had remembered the request!

I carefully and honestly gave all the information I could about Katya, her medical situation, her adopted brothers, her lack of family, the kinds of details that deep down I knew might close the door. As my friend, the former consul general in St. Petersburg had said, we were taking on a nearly impossible task.

Joe contacted the deputy consul general in Moscow, someone he knew well, and asked for guidance. That person, whose name I never did learn, responded with one question: "What is Beth's role in this? How is she related to Katya?"

I had an easy answer to that. "I am a Good Samaritan, trying to help a stranger in trouble."

Another week passed, and then the deputy consul general sent advice. It was a list of instructions and steps for a visa application. I could not believe what I was reading.

"Oh, my God," I wrote to Ken, Erin, Tatyana, Vera, Igor, the blanket donors, and a dozen other people in the USA who had become interested in the case, "They are going to let Katya come!"

Everyone was in shock. Erin wrote an excited note in response, signing it "Erin (stunned)." Ken thanked me profusely for my help. Hah! What help? Two conversations and two e-notes? It was not my doing, I told him. It was God working through others. I was simply God's Tom Sawyer, handing out paint brushes to all who would stop long enough for me to attract them into helping paint the fence.

The next steps are being taken now, and they are good. More divine intervention, it seems. The embassy has allowed Tatyana to pick up the paperwork on behalf of Katya, an incredible help since Tula-to-Moscow would have been a difficult trip for Katya. Tatyana, Ken, and friends of Orphan Cry in Russia are working on the visa papers in order for Katya to enter the United States.

One of the requirements, as with Shura, is to identify a sponsor, a home, and a doctor, and to have all of that in writing. Obviously, Orphan Cry stepped forward as sponsor, and Erin, as planned, offered her home. Ken then contacted the doctors at Tufts who were caring for Katya's brothers. We expected them to agree to donate their services, and they did. We did not expect them to make a tentative prognosis based on the slightly outdated medical records we have in hand, but they did.

"Why do the Russian doctors think Katya's condition is fatal?" they asked. "We believe it is treatable." Once again, a shock wave passed through the community of Katya's supporters. The doctors' words changed everything. Katya might not be coming to the US in order to die surrounded by her brothers, the only family she has. She might be coming to live!

The sponsor is usually seen as a bill payer, but in the case of both Shura and Katya, neither supporting organization (Global Studies Institute or Orphan Cry) had the funds to be a true bill payer. Shura's costs eventually exceeded a million dollars. Very likely, Katya's will, too. Thank God, we found John Kluge for Shura—and, as it turned out, it was principally through unexplained means (or, more likely, divine intervention) that a misaddressed package made it 800 miles north to its intended recipient. Similarly, the bill payer for Katya fell into our laps. Although Orphan Cry was willing to step up to the plate and try to raise the money, that commitment, which would have been difficult to fulfill, turned out not to be necessary. The doctors at Tufts made a few inquiries of their own and then informed Ken that they had found a charitable organization that has often supported indigent Tufts patients to pay Katya's medical bills.

Of course, this kind of endeavor never chugs along a smooth track without hills and other sorts of obstacles. Thus, it has been with Katya. The first obstacle was the expiration of her external Russian passport. (All Russian citizens carry an internal passport that allows the government to track where they are living at any given time. Those who travel or wish to travel also carry an external Russian passport, which allows them to leave the country. Katya needed this latter passport. In September she applied for it, and just days before Christmas she received it. During this period, she asked her doctor for the required *spravka* (medical certificate) that both the Russian and American governments require for exit and entry of ill or disabled individuals. Her doctor refused to provide it. While those who knew about this impediment worried about what to do next, I would not have. These are the kinds of impediements that God takes care of for us, and had I known about the doctor's tactics, I would simply have said, "Wait. Don't worry. God will handle it." God did. No one knows where she went or why, but about the time that the passport appeared, the doctor disappeared.

Now we wait. We wait for the *spravka*, which should arrive any day from Katya's new doctor. We wait for the American visa, which should arrive a week after the all the application and accompanying documents are turned in. We wait for the results of Katya's first visit to her American doctors. We wait with confident trust that God will take care of Katya because we have seen what God has already done for Katya, and we have been blessed in having the opportunity to paint a slat or two of God's fence in Tula.

God touches hearts to make good things happen. That we know. To do that, we also know that God must often use the Good Samaritans, the Tom Sawyers, and the painters who willingly or unwittingly make themselves available.

Shura's visa ultimately became attainable because many of the diplomats at the American Embassy in the Soviet Union had been my students. They trusted my motivations, and they vouched for me to the consular officer in charge of his case, who did not know me.

Katya's visa became attainable because I had travelled to Russia with someone from Washington who was in a similar position today as I was back then. That advantage was reinforced by the fact that I was working in a position generally trusted by embassy employees.

In that connection lies a great irony. Earlier in the year, I had decided to leave my current position. I began to look for jobs and in late June had an interview for a very nice position. Things were looking up for my moving on, but while that was my intention, it was clearly not God's plan. I was supposed to be exactly where I am.

That I was supposed to come to this position had been made clear three years earlier when all the doors I opened in Jordan with the help of friends there instantly slammed shut, as did doors elsewhere. That I was supposed to stay here became clearer with each passing day as one person after another at work would unexpectedly drop by my office, telling me how much each of them appreciated my leadership and what good things had happened to them since I arrived. Finally, when, still being hardheaded (some attributes do not change easily), I forged ahead in my "new job" plans, Fr. Barry happened to come to my door with an article about a difficult ethical situation I was encountering at work, saying that he thought I should stay the course because even if I did not think so I probably could influence the situation in positive ways. He knew I was troubled by the situation, but he did not know that I had actually taken steps toward leaving. Even as obtuse as I can be, the message was now clear. I withdrew my applications and stopped looking for a new job. My Jonah period of trying to run away from a responsibility I had been given had ended with God fully in charge.

Thirteen years have passed since Shura arrived in the United States from Russia. There is not anything special about this year, 2008. It is not a locust cycle year. It is not the start or end of a decade. It is not a "round year" (what the Russians call years ending in the number 0: 1990, 2000, 2010, etc.)

Nonetheless, 2008 is special for it has been a year of passages. Shura has finished his American sojourn and has plans to return to Russia after Christmas to be with his aging parents, who have moved to the outskirts of Moscow. Russia has made significant advances in the means to take care of spina bifida children and adults. Antibiotics and modern medicine are now available, especially in Moscow, so it has become safe for Shura to go home. Now Shura's story is repeating itself in the form of a Russian girl, about the same age as Shura when he came to the United States, and also with a physical handicap: blindness. Ironically, it appears that Katya and Shura will swap continents the same month, perhaps even the same week, one coming to the United States in hope of medical treatment and a new lease on life and one returning to Russia with that lease on life in hand.

One ending. One beginning. A perfect circle.

## San Ignatio on Easter Morning

Shura, Katya, Beth. These stories have woven together like a novel. My first clear job as God's agent was with a Russian (Shura). Now, after circumnavigating the globe, I have come full circle back to Russia and to another Russian (Katya). This time, though, is different. This time I am aware of God's presence in all our lives. This time walking into a church on Easter morning has a different meaning for me.

Walking into the mission at any time has a different and very special meaning for me. Catholicism at its core is a beautifully simple religion, one that has survived in more or less the same form for centuries. Powerful are simple masses celebrated in a natural environment, like that of the two-hundred-year-old San Ignatio mission with its uneven tiles, singularized by the paw prints of various kinds of animals that walked across the baking tiles before they were "done." Such a humble environment, for me, brings one closer to God.

Even simpler and therefore more powerful are celebrations of the eucharist by a dozen or so faithful at a private home. Such services are reminiscent of the gatherings of the converted gentiles by the early apostles. I had the fortune to attend one such gathering, over which presided Padre Julio, the young priest to whom I taught English, not long before he returned to his home country of Colombia. Held in Salts at the home of a member of his former parish there, the mass was more emotionally moving and the presence of God more strongly felt than in any proud cathedral or large-group mass I have ever attended where often celebration equates to little more than habitualized ritual.

The mass, after all, is about gathering together in God's presence. It is about sharing God's love, returning God's love, and, through the eucharist, receiving and accepting God's love. For that, adornment is not necessary, but humility is. That is why Old Mission San Ignatio has a very special meaning for me. By its very structure, it symbolizes God's humility. By all that I have felt wtihin it, it is a place of God's love.

Easter morning 2007 arrived in San Ignatio in sunny splendor. I walked to the morning mass under blue skies, puffy white clouds, and streams of sunlight splashing down onto San Ignatio's prayer-drenched streets.

After reminding the crowd that spilled beyond the walls of Old Mission San Ignatio past the open doors and into the garden that there were 51 other Sundays with masses at which they were also welcome, Fr. Barry pronounced words that were very familiar to me. "In Moscow," he said, "on Easter morning, people greet each other with the words, *Christ is risen.*"

They do, indeed. Just as they do in Siberia. I thought back to the Easter morning a decade earlier when I had stood, as an atheist with a Good Samaritan heart, before the congregation in the wooden church on the Siberian steppe and heard those very same words.

Then my mind moved forward to the mass that had been celebrated on Easter eve at Old Mission San Ignatio. Once again I had stood before a church congregation. This time it was for confirmation. This time I was about to become a member of the congregation, not an outsider, a believer, not an atheist. This time both my heart and my head knew I belonged to God.

## Parting Words to the Reader

I don't know why God has been so kind to me. I don't know why the Good Shepherd came after the single lost sheep. My words, opening the door to the presence of God, were neither invitation nor challenge but rather an irritated attempt to get past saying grace and on to a mundane meal. God knew that but used my words to occupy my life, anyway. I have often wondered, after reading the story of Saul/St. Paul, if God intervened in my life because I needed to be stopped. I was not killing any Christians physically, but there were ones I killed spiritually by turning them away from their faith through my atheistic leadership.

At the same time, I do not know why for so many years previous to that God flowed nearly undefiled help to those needing it through the life of an atheist or why God bothered to be present in the trials of an atheist and turn those trials to good for a large group of people when I did not (could not, would not) see or affirm the Source of my strength. Indeed, I do not understand the profound kindness of God at all, but I am grateful for it. My gratitude grows daily.

That God had and has a purpose in showing such kindness is told to us in *John 15:16*: "You have not chosen Me, but I have chosen you, and I have appointed you, that you might go and bear fruit and keep on bearing and that your fruit may be lasting..." Clearly, God does decide to pluck people from their atheism. History is replete with known instances of people being so chosen. They are likely the tip of the iceberg. The majority of people transformed in this way may not become as well known as the few, and while their fruit may be long-lasting, it, too, may not be well known. This particular verse tells me that God in reality chooses all who open the door whether intentionally or inadvertently, working on a microcosmic scale with those whose fruit will feed a few very needy souls in their vicinity and on a macro scale with those whose fruit is spread over a wider area. Each of us, and our fruit, is important to God.

What I have noticed from working with people from many walks of life from all over the world is that we all have trials. Some trials we cause for ourselves through misapplication of our free will. Other trials come to us via other people's free will or the workings of the laws of nature. Some people's trials may seem more difficult to other people and some less. Some involve loss of senses (eyesight, hearing, physical sensation), others abuse (physical, emotional, sexual), and still others chemical imbalances (depression, drug dependency, rage). What is more important than the nature of the trials is how we react to them. What compensates for and even glorifies them is experiencing how God can turn even the worst trial into good if we are open to that. Our reaction to our trials is, in many cases, our "fruit."

There are people who pray to die because life is too tough. That was not me. Not believing that God existed and therefore having no higher power to which to turn for help, I nonetheless wanted to live, grow up, and set right what my parents and others had put wrong. For that reason, I rescued cats. The image that had been branded into my memory of our pet burning in the furnace pushed me to risk the bites and scratches that are inevitable with taming feral felines. For that reason also, I helped anyone who appeared in my path, remembering how almost no one had helped the 8-pack and our long-term gratitude to the few who had tried. I would agree with Shakespeare's words in *MacBeth*: life, lived only for ourselves, is like a player strutting upon a stage and fretting over insignificances. It is when we get off the stage that life begins to have meaning.

Thanks to the grace of God and the support of each other, the members of the 8-pack all developed the ability to think that made all of us more than simply reeds in the pond of abuse in which we were raised. Nouwen, in the *Life of the Beloved*, writes, "When we do not feel loved by those who gave us life, we often suffer our whole life long from a low self esteem that can lead easily to depression, despair, and suicide." Yes, that is a common outcome of the kinds of things we experienced. I have seen adult lives over which hangs an eternal gray pall of abused childhood. By way of contrast, when we turned 18 and left home, we 8-packers picked up our own Crayola boxes and began coloring our adult lives in other colors. My colors sparkle with laughter. Katrina's, Danielle's, Keith's, and Sharon's are also cheerful. Willie's and Victoria's colors are more muted, but in general pleasant to look at. Willie still suffers from the syndrome of laying down his old emotional "baggage" only to have Ma scoop it up and ask him, "Didn't you forget something?" Victoria had to extricate herself from an abusive marriage, twice. As for Rollie, his coloring at times has had swaths of red—angry slashes that reflect nightmares of Ma meeting a fiery end. Depression, despair, and thoughts of suicide, however, have not grayed our days. We have all gone on to lives that have been satisfying and that have released us from our past. Even Rollie. In spite of his vengeful nightmares, Rollie raised his children in a loving environment.

How were we able to turn the tables on our lives when so many others have not been able to survive far less life-threatening situations? Was God there with us in the burning house? Did God teach us lessons beyond those we learned at school that would stand us in good stead all the rest of our lives?

Wayne Muller wrote in *Legacy of the Heart*, "With each painful event, we renewed our efforts to explain the causes of our suffering." The 8-pack was unlike most in that respect; we knew the causes and each time we knew we were not the cause. Rather than seeking the causes of our suffering, the question that I have perpetually raised is why we survived such extreme abuse when others who experienced less abuse did not reach adulthood intact.

Danielle believes that she has the answer to that question. Her earliest memory—she insists that she was only two years old at the time—is of a prayer. "Dear God, Daddy is gone all the time, and Ma is a child. I guess *You* have to raise me. Please."

Could the explanation be that simple and that powerful, that God heard a precocious child's perspicacious prayer, took it seriously, and answered it for all of the 8-pack? And more awe-inspiring, could a loving God, acting *in loco parentis*, unseen and unbidden by most of us, have been watching over and protecting the 8-pack all of our lives, ensuring our physical, emotional, and ethical well-being?

Survival extended beyond physical continuation. It involved as well mental health. How is it, for example, that none of us learned to hate? We did not hate our parents. I admired Dad, and Katrina's compassion for Ma was legendary. While we were disgusted by their behavior, I don't believe that any of my siblings truly hates Dad or Ma. Dad, of course, has been dead for 35 years; there are few feelings left one way or another toward him. As for Ma, Keith keeps a monthly eye on her to make sure she is not in need of anything, and we all came back to New England for her 80th birthday (well, all except Rollie, who seemed relieved that he had to work but otherwise would have come despite his emotional discomfort).

That forgiveness took nearly six decades of God's rain of gentle love slowly eroding the stone in our hearts, leaving pulverized, fertile soil where tender mercies could grow, like the rain and wind over centuries reshape stony mountains into fertile valleys. As Katrina, the most compassionate of us, says, "Ma's an old lady now, and we should grant her the peace in her final years that she never had in her prime years." As for me, until I had been bathed in the powerful peace of God's forgiveness of the many anti-divine things I spoke in my days of atheism, I could not forgive Ma or allow her a final peace.

We all learned altruism, as well. Was it only because we *had* to help each other? Or did a divine parent teach us that, too?

And the most important question: Are we alone in this experience? Truly, I wonder how many others are being watched over who do not know it.

God came to us in our hours of need in various forms. For me, God often came in the form of childhood friends who would comfort me, rail at my parents in their absentia, and walk me home to make sure that I was not immediately beaten. There is a saying that friends are God's way of taking care of people on earth. It was in childhood that I learned the value of friendship that ultimately led to my finding friends all over the world.

God also gave us good teachers. While we could blame the teachers for perhaps deliberately not noticing our distress because Dad was on the school board and Ma was truly the town crier, we could not blame them for inattention to our learning. School as an alternate reality brought us peace and success, and my teachers' overt pride in my learning success certainly helped bolster my self-esteem. They let me write and present plays in elementary school. They came to my spelling bee competitions, my science fair exhibits, and music contests in junior high. They promoted my public speaking opportunities in high school. They thought I had something to share with the world, and that counteracted Ma's constant comment, "You're no gift to the world." Thanks to my teachers, I did not believe Ma.

We of the 8-pack knew we were the wronged ones, not the wrong ones. All eight of us were experiencing the same thing, so something must have been wrong with our parents. The 8-pack maintained the mental health of the group. How could that positive sense of sanity, self-worth, and aplomb not be a gift from God? Many people with much less abuse have folded to emotional distress. Without the 8-pack and God's parenting, any one of us might have done the same.

Instead, we all grew up to be moral individuals. I don't think it was the beatings that did it. The fact that we turned out good, not bad, might indicate that God was watching over us and directing us to the extent that free will allows, teaching us that while we cannot control how the wind comes at us, we can indeed adjust our sails.

The struggles, however, did not go away in adulthood. They just changed form as we moved around the various states of **splat!** Where was God when our children stopped breathing? When the doctors attempted to push us around and push us away? When the handicapped children were treated as second-class citizens in school? When the gifted ones could find no programs to let them learn? When the money kept running out to feed and clothe ourselves because post-insurance medical expenses ran into tens of thousands of dollars every year?

In retrospect, I see that God was there, keeping our children alive beyond all medical expectations and our family together against all odds, helping us all to excel in education and at work, re-shaping the strength and courage I gained from fighting childhood's battles into the confidence needed to defy the establishments and their representatives who would harm our children or ignore their needs, and at the last minute dropping onto us, like manna from heaven, just enough unexpected money to survive. From our struggles emerged a palpable familial bond that has been felt by nearly everyone who has met our family. Many, if not most, parents dread the pending teenage years and bemoan them when they arrive. Donnie and I, however, spent a dozen joyful years as our children developed independent thinking based on reason. Unlike many teenagers, our children never seemed to experience lugubrious moments or painful attempts to understand who they were or the value of their lives. They knew who they were, and they had developed an understanding of the value of their lives as young children as they watched us wrench Doah from death five times and Noelle twice. The obvious conclusion was that they had to be valuable if we fought so hard to preserve them. This early insight carried them into, through, and beyond their teenage years.

Most important, at long last I learned a very important lesson, one that finally negated the sermon of my youth in which I had pointed to the wrongdoing of the church deacons as evidence of the advantageousness of an atheistic upbringing. Thanks to God not only letting but actually forcing me to see the blessings in my life, I learned that you cannot judge God by the people who claim to be God's people. Nor, given our limited capacity to understand the divine, can we judge God at all. We can only thank God for the blessings bestowed upon us.

Why would God bless an atheist? That question has puzzled me throughout the writing of this book. One answer might be that perhaps God routinely uses atheists. The unknown author of *The Cloud of Unknowing* hypothesizes this to be the case:

> *I believe, too, that often our Lord deliberately chooses to work in those who have been habitual sinners rather than in those who, by comparison, have never grieved him at all. Yes, he seems to do this very often. For I think he wants us to realize that he is all-merciful and almighty, and that he is perfectly free to work as he pleases, where he pleases, and when he pleases.*

Abelard, in *Collationes*, suggests a second answer. His theology held that if one obeys the law—a habituation drilled into all of us by Ma—one will receive the grace of God even if one is a non-believer.

In coming to faith and examining all the contours of my life past and present, I have come to see sense in both answers. God showered the 8-pack with mercy, and God used all of us, including the two atheists, Rollie and me. Why the others turned out to be believers and we two atheists, I can only guess, but I suppose it has to do with our inborn defiant natures. Rollie railed against the abuse we experienced with words, and I fought back with fisticuffs. Perhaps our inclination to defy our earthly parents led to the same inclination first to defy the Heavenly Parent and later, not having been punished or feeling any kind of response at all—at least, no response in a way that we could measure at the time—to assume that no one was there. We did not see the hidden hand. Perhaps, too, we were afraid to look for it, afraid to think there might be a Power greater than ourselves because the power greater than ourselves that we most intimately knew—our earthly parents—hurt us frequently. Perhaps subconsciously we worried that a Heavenly Parent would do so, as well.

What I do know, though, is that any one of the 8-pack will help anyone in need without being asked. For all of us, love of neighbor is no less strong than love of family and even of self. Ironically, God used the last person imaginable to teach us how to be Good Samaritans: Ma—a case of God deliberately choosing to work in a habitual sinner.

As for omnipresence, upon examination, I have found God's presence in all the contours of my life. Wherever I have assumed God might not have been, I have found evidence that God was. The burning house has burned to the ground. We are all scorched and scarred to some extent, but we are vibrantly alive. Released from the confines of the house that trapped us, we are free to run about the fields in St. Francis-like abandon, praising the God that protected us during our ordeal and who led us out from our captivity, first from our captors and second from ourselves, from our feelings of guilt and self-recrimination. We are free to spend our days returning God's love by loving all God's creatures—the people who delight us, the people who take delight in us, the people who take delight in hurting us, even the cats and dogs, the birds of the air, the mice in the fields. The house is gone, the cycle is broken, and we are alive to build a new kind of abode.

One might examine as well the lives of the handicapped children in our family. They are now adults, contributing to the society around them. In many ways, their handicaps define their value to society, not their limitations by it.

One might ask, then, if God was there in all the contours why it took so long to find care for all of Shura's needs. As an atheist, I would have promulgated that accusation as "proof" of the non-existence of a divinity. As a believer, I think I understand why it took so long. As in so many other instances in life, the journey may have been more important than the destination. Hundreds of people were touched by Shura's story. For whole congregations, the miracles that happened were faith confirming. I was probably the only hard nut that did not give the credit to God for Shura's miracles and the only person blind enough not to see God's hand reaching out to Shura.

Now I pray that God never stops using me. For either an atheist or a believer, there is no greater destiny than to participate in God's work. Rabbi Harold Kushner in *Who Needs God?* talks about the "extraordinary things that even the most ordinary lives contain." God changed my ordinary life into an extraordinary one. I hope that my story will help other atheists and skeptics to see their blessings and to recognize the Source.

Where my story will end, no one can know. It is irrevocably tied up with that unreachable star, which keeps changing distance and shape, the star that God, not man, has dangled before me. I can now honestly say with St. Paul (*Galatians 1:10*) that the favor of men is meaningless to me; the favor of God is everything to me.

Where will my story lead before it ends? I don't know that, either. I do know, though, that even if there are difficulties ahead, there will be help and protection. There will also be rewards. There always are. With God, the rewards are unanticipated and unusual. The simplest among them are the greatest.

One evening last December, the thought came into my head that I should take my evening walk around the mission grounds early. Normally I walk there around 9:00 p.m., and it was only 6:00 when I felt the push to go outside for my walk.

No, I thought. Why would I want to go now? Even though the eventide falls around 5:30 on December nights in San Ignatio, I still prefer to go later—after dinner and dishes and before retiring for the night. It is a marvelously restful way to end the day. Walking brings out the happy endorphins, and just being at the mission provides great encouragement toward prayer.

No, I'll go later, I thought and began cleaning the kitchen in preparation for dinner. Then the impulse came again.

The "argument" went back and forth a couple of times until I approached Donnie, who usually accompanies me on these walks, still, to this day, reeling from the knowledge that his atheist wife has done a 180-degree about-face. ("I just can't get my head around it," he would repeat over and over for the first month or so after he returned from Jordan and learned what had happened.)

"Donnie, how do you feel about taking our evening walk early tonight?" I asked.

"Why?" he asked.

"I don't know why," I answered. "I just feel like we should go early."

Donnie acquiesced and quickly assembled his pipe tools. (He likes to sit and smoke while I walk.) We opened the door and stepped out under the night sky. And there it was, spread across the heavens: a breathtaking lunar ice halo.

Ice halos are rings of light that surround the sun, moon, or other sources of light, such as street lamps. The ones in the heavens are caused by millions of ice crystals in thin, cold, cirrus clouds floating in the troposphere reflecting and refracting light. This particular ice halo was circumhorizonal, a rare phenomenon for which adequately descriptive words, other than scientific ones, are even rarer. Refracted light from the moon spread in a 360-degree circle all around the sky on the same level as the moon yet at the same time touching the horizon wherever we turned—or so it seemed although in actuality the circle of light was parallel to the horizon and not lying upon it. The halo filled the whole sky, with the full moon in its zenith filtering a stream of light through a gossamer foramen in the firmament onto the mission grounds below.

I could almost hear the proud words, "Look what I did!" The hymn of Isaac Waats came to mind instantly: "The moon shines full at His command, and all the stars obey."

On the mission grounds canopied by the horizon-to-horizon crystal glow, I walked, my arms extended. Irrepressible joy spread past my fingertips, riding on the splendor of light toward the horizon.

Then it was gone. Had I come at my usual time, I would have missed it.

These then are the things that have been seen and experienced by the blest atheist. All the events reported herein have enriched my life, but the greatest of these was God sharing with me the lunar ice halo: "Look what I have done!" The hound of Heaven had finally caught me and then had shown me what I had been missing: "Look what I have done!" Indeed, I could almost hear those words and a few more: "Look at what I have done—for you, for all people, because I love you whether or not you even believe that I exist."

All the miracles that God has done in my life have been wondrous, but pulling me outside to view the ice halo stands out above them all as the most affirming act of God's love. The miracles were about actions: healing and turning bad into good. They have been important, of course. Viewing the ice halo, however, was about relationship: God's relationship with me, God's relationship with all of us. When God called me from my house onto the street and into the field at the mission, I understood that I was special—not special out of many, but special among many, special like all people are special to God.

On an individual level, I was and am at best only a Good Samaritan, and still God wanted a relationship with me. In so many ways, I was and am but a child who finds the adults who can help a sick child artist, a crying lady, a boy in white, or an orphan dying from brain tumors. Like a child, I have no burning desire for financial gain, material possessions, or fame and power. Those desires were beaten out of me in my youth. Although many of these things have appeared unbidden in my life, my true treasure is the people who have come into my life from all continents of the world. There is where my heart is. I want to "pass on" the good that God has brought into my life by using my linguistic proficiency, cultural acumen, and multi-domain knowledge gained from living in the land of **splat!** to connect people who need help with people who have the ability to give help, no matter where they live or what language they speak.

For what good is money if it cannot be used to help those in need? What good are material things unless they make this world a friendlier place: a blanket to warm a homeless man, food for a hungry family, clothes for those burned out of a home? What good is power if not used to empower the powerless to be free to flourish? What good, too, is dreaming an impossible dream if it does not kindle the dreams of others? What good is reaching an unreachable star if it does not sprinkle light onto a dark existence? What good is happiness if it does not splash joy onto dispirited ground, inspiriting the life within to sprout and reach for the heavens? If, indeed, as I have found, helping those in need, making the world a friendlier place, empowering the powerless, kindling dreams, lighting the dark, and splashing joy across the land is what a Good Samaritan does, then I want to be a Good Samaritan for life. To my delight, God seems willing to use me in that capacity. For certain, God knows my heart and what I treasure.

God has many Good Samaritans. Some, like me, are blessed to help a few wounded souls in intensive ways. Others are blessed to help many people in more extensive, but less intensive, ways. Some God leads with their full knowledge. Others, like me for so many years, God leads through their hearts alone. In return, God gives them a treasure far greater than money, honor, power, or prestige: they know a perfect joy that nothing else can give.

I am sure that others saw the ice halo that night for God encourages all people to step bravely out of the grey boxes in which they are cowering and stride buoyantly forth into a divine world resplendent with color, love, and joy. In our tiny town, though, I was the only one who showed up at the mission to see the splendor on that particular winter evening. Others may have showed up elsewhere for the ice halo could be seen for miles. Perhaps even more were called to behold it but were not listening. Those who did listen experienced an unrelenting tug to come outside and witness an awe-inspiring manifestation of God's loving caress ephemerally spread against the heavens and permanently imprinted in the mind and on the heart.

**Thank You, God, for all of it!**

*- your blest atheist*

## Other Books by MSI Press

*Achieving Native-Like Second-Language Proficiency: Speaking*

*Achieving Native-Like Second-Language Proficiency: Writing*

*Communicate Focus: Teaching Foreign Language on the Basis of the Native Speaker's Communicative Focus*

*Diagnostic Assessment at the Distinguished-Superior Threshold*

*How to Improve Your Foreign Language Proficiency Immediately*

*Individualized Study Plans for Very Advanced Students of Foreign Language*

*Mommy Poisoned Our House Guest*

*Puertas a la Eternidad*

*Road to Damascus*

*Teaching and Learning to Near-Native Levels of Language Proficiency*

*Teaching the Whole Class*

*The Rise and Fall of Muslim Civil Society*

*Thoughts without a Title*

*Understanding the People Around You: An Introduction to Socionics*

*What Works: Helping Students Reach Native-like Second-Language Competence*

*When You're Shoved from the Right, Look to the Left: Metaphors of Islamic Humanism*

*Working with Advanced Foreign Language Students*

*Journal for Distinguished Language Studies* (annual issue)

CPSIA information can be obtained at www.ICGtesting.com
Printed in the USA
LVOW100837200113

316393LV00004B/427/P